BIG GOVERNMENT
and Affirmative Action

"Won't all these new rules impact adversely on the viability of small businesses with fewer than fifty employees?"

BIG
GOVERNMENT
and Affirmative Action

The SCANDALOUS HISTORY of the

Small Business Administration

Jonathan J. Bean

THE UNIVERSITY PRESS OF KENTUCKY

Copyright © 2001 by The University Press of Kentucky

Scholarly publisher for the Commonwealth,
serving Bellarmine University, Berea College, Centre
College of Kentucky, Eastern Kentucky University,
The Filson Historical Society, Georgetown College,
Kentucky Historical Society, Kentucky State University,
Morehead State University, Murray State University,
Northern Kentucky University, Transylvania University,
University of Kentucky, University of Louisville,
and Western Kentucky University.
All rights reserved.

Editorial and Sales Offices: The University Press of Kentucky
663 South Limestone Street, Lexington, Kentucky 40508–4008

05 04 03 02 01   5 4 3 2 1

Frontispiece: © The New Yorker Collection. 1993. Ed Fisher. From cartoonbank.com.
All Rights Reserved.

Library of Congress Cataloging-in-Publication Data

Bean, Jonathan, J.
   Big government and affirmative action: the scandalous history of the Small Business
Administration / Jonathan J. Bean.
      p. cm.
Includes bibliographical references and index
   ISBN 0-8131-2187-6 (cloth : alk. paper)
   1. United States. Small Business Administration—History. 2. Small business—Gov-
ernment policy—United States. 3. Affirmative action programs—United States—History.
I. Title.
   HD2346.U5 B344 20001
   354.2'799'0973—dc21
                              00-012040

This book is printed on acid-free recycled paper meeting
the requirements of the American National Standard
for Permanence in Paper for Printed Library Materials.

♾ ⊛

Manufactured in the United States of America.

To my parents,
with love and appreciation

CONTENTS

ACKNOWLEDGMENTS

The research and writing of this book were made possible through the generous support of the Earhart Foundation, the Institute for Humane Studies, the Economic History Association, Southern Illinois University Carbondale, the Lyndon B. Johnson Presidential Library, and the Social Philosophy and Policy Center.

Students of modern American government are blessed with an abundance of documents. The archivists at the presidential libraries and the National Archives helped me mine this material. The Small Business Administration made available records not yet released to the National Archives. I am indebted to Helga Taylor and Margaret Hickey for fielding queries from an inquisitive historian. I am also grateful for the industrious research assistance of David Hurley, Rachelle Stivers, Andrew Volpert, and Mahesh Ananth. The constructive criticism offered by Melvin Holli, K. Austin Kerr, Robbie Lieberman, Paul Moreno, and Fred Siegel was extremely beneficial. Mansel Blackford, David Wilson, and David Werlich read the entire manuscript and provided useful advice on improving it for publication. A special thanks to the many individuals who shared their memories of the past. Their oral histories offered valuable insight into the politics of small business. Last, but never least, I express the deepest gratitude to my wife for understanding the everyday trials of a writer.

ABBREVIATIONS USED IN TEXT AND NOTES

ABA	American Bankers Association
AGCA	Associated General Contractors of America
BAC	Business Advisory Council
CCSB	Cabinet Committee on Small Business
CASBO	Congress of American Small Business Organizations
DNC	Democratic National Committee
DOD	Department of Defense
EDA	Economic Development Administration
EEOC	Equal Employment Opportunity Commission
EOL	Economic Opportunity Loan
EPL	(Dwight D.) Eisenhower Presidential Library
GAO	General Accounting Office
GFL	Gerald Ford Library
HSBC	[U.S. Congress] House Small Business Committee
HSTPL	Harry S. Truman Presidential Library
JCL	Jimmy Carter Library
JFKPL	John F. Kennedy Presidential Library
LBJPL	Lyndon Baines Johnson Presidential Library
MESBIC	Minority Enterprise Small Business Investment Company
NAM	National Association of Manufacturers
NASBIC	National Association of Small Business Investment Companies
NBL	National Business League (formerly National Negro Business League)
NFIB	National Federation of Independent Business

NPM	Nixon Presidential Materials
NSBMA	National Small Business Men's Association
OEO	Office of Economic Opportunity
OMB	Office of Management and Budget
OMBE	Office of Minority Business Enterprise
OSHA	Occupational Safety and Health Administration
PCGC	President's Committee on Government Contracts
RFC	Reconstruction Finance Corporation
RNC	Republican National Committee
RRL	Ronald Reagan Library
SBA	(U.S.) Small Business Administration
SBIC	Small Business Investment Company
SBDC	Small Business Development Center
SCORE	Service Corps of Retired Executives
SDPA	Small Defense Plants Administration
SSBC	[U.S. Congress] Senate Small Business Committee
WHCSB	White House Committee on Small Business (1962); White House Conference on Small Business (1980)

INTRODUCTION

On 14 January 1999, members of the U.S. Senate gathered for one of the remarkable political events of the twentieth century: the trial of President William Jefferson Clinton on charges of "high crimes and misdemeanors." Although a presidential sex scandal provided the immediate backdrop, the allegation of corrupt business dealings had prompted the original investigation. A Small Business Administration loan intended for "disadvantaged" minorities was at the heart of the initial probe. David Hale, head of a small-business investment company, had granted a fraudulent loan to Susan McDougal in 1986. Money from the SBA-backed loan ended up in the Whitewater Development Corporation, a firm owned by Mrs. McDougal, her husband, and the Clintons. Hale testified that then-governor Clinton had asked him to make the illegal loan, a charge Clinton denied. In 1996, an Arkansas jury convicted the McDougals and Governor Jim Guy Tucker of defrauding the SBA. The continued Whitewater investigation by Independent Counsel Kenneth Starr eventually uncovered evidence of unrelated misconduct that led to Bill Clinton's impeachment; although the Senate acquitted him, the episode left a black mark on his presidency.[1]

Whitewater was only the latest in a series of scandals involving the Small Business Administration. Long before Bill Clinton entered the White House, the SBA earned the title of "Small Scandal Administration," as corruption, fraud, and incompetence marred its minority enterprise programs. For example, President Ronald Reagan's administration was embroiled in a sensational scandal involving the incomprehensibly corrupt Wedtech, another minority firm benefitting from SBA largesse. The Wedtech scandal implicated White House aides, SBA officials, and several congressmen in what one reporter called "an elaborate soap opera of crime." It also reportedly resulted in Attorney General Edwin Meese III's resignation.[2] In the cases of Whitewater and Wedtech, the stated aim of helping disadvantaged business owners provided a cover for corruption reminiscent of the Gilded Age.

Despite the media attention given to these high-profile scandals, few Americans realize the important role of the Small Business Administration in promoting affirmative action. Historians have likewise ignored the pioneering efforts of the SBA in developing racial preferences.[3] Led by Eugene Foley, a young administrator who took office the month Martin Luther King Jr. marched on Washington, the agency targeted African American entrepreneurs for aid even before passage of the Civil Rights Act of 1964. The new policy was technically color-blind, but the riots of the mid-1960s transformed the program into an emergency remedy to mollify racial discontent. The election of Republican presidential candidate Richard M. Nixon, who ran on a "black capitalism" plank, solidified the agency's commitment to racial preferences. Nixon and his Republican supporters in Congress defended affirmative action at a time when it faced a strong challenge from Democrats. Later, the Reagan administration's self-contradictory stance on the issue—denouncing "quotas" while establishing them within the SBA—further demonstrated that the politics of affirmative action made for strange bedfellows.

Researching the history of affirmative action is difficult because documentation is often lacking and civil rights agencies have resisted opening their sensitive archives to outside scholars. Nonetheless, this history provides valuable insight into the SBA's development of racial preferences by drawing upon substantial archival research and interviews with officials who created and administered minority enterprise programs before affirmative action rose to the heights of controversy. The ensuing history makes for a lively story of racial and ethnic conflict and fierce debates among policymakers over the merits of the SBA's inherently divisive policy.

It is important to stress that the SBA was an affirmative action agency even before becoming involved in racial policymaking. In 1953, Congress created the SBA to take affirmative action on behalf of small business. By awarding loans and government contracts to a select group of small firms, the agency gave them a competitive advantage over other companies. As critics noted in the early 1960s, the practice of "setting aside" contracts for "small" firms constituted reverse discrimination against "large" companies. The SBA responded with arguments that will sound familiar to students of affirmative action: As a matter of justice, small firms deserved special consideration because they suffered "institutionalized discrimination" by banks and procurement agencies. SBA officials also argued that statistical disparity in the awarding of contracts was prima facie evidence of such discrimination. Since then, few have raised objections to affirmative action for small business.

While nearly everyone in Congress agreed that small business deserved special treatment, questions remained: What is "small" business? Is it really a group with interests separate from "big" business? The latter question is of great importance, as political scientists usually assume that our modern federal bureaucracy embodies the influence—past and present—of organized interest groups. Policy historians trace the emergence of interest-group democracy to the New Deal era when Franklin D. Roosevelt's recognition of various interests—labor unions, trade associations, senior citizens, and others—created a "broker state" with the federal government mediating between conflicting interests. The proliferation of interest groups accompanying the subsequent growth of the American government resulted in the term "hyperpluralism," which political scientists use to describe the dizzying array of interests seeking governmental attention.[4]

Created by Congress in an interest-group vacuum, the Small Business Administration is one of the most important government agencies to challenge the assumptions of interest-group democracy. Support for the agency came from members of Congress rather than small business owners, who were unorganized and considered classical liberals opposed to the New Deal welfare state. Congressional sponsorship reflected the vitality of a small business ideology associated with the widely held "American Creed"—a belief in individualism, equal opportunity, and democracy. Political scientist Sandra Mary Anglund notes that "when small business, viewed as an institution, is judged with these values, it passes with flying colors."[5] The SBA embodies this popular sentiment.

Defining interests is simple in theory, but often problematic in practice. "Interest-group liberalism," notes political scientist Theodore Lowi, is based on the questionable assumption that "organized interests are homogeneous and easy to define, sometimes monolithic." Broker state theory promoted a crude "myth of the group and the group will." In practice, however, organized interests conceal splits within their own membership. Furthermore, organizing large groups is difficult. In *The Logic of Collective Action* (1965), Mancur Olson Jr. theorized that small interest groups are easier to organize than large, heterogeneous ones. Thus, narrow interests seeking special advantages from the government are better-represented than large groups with diffuse interests (e.g., taxpayers, consumers).[6]

The small business community fell into the category of a large group with conflicting internal interests. What did a "Mom-and-Pop" grocery have in common with a "small" manufacturer employing hundreds of people in a high-tech industry? At what point did a "small" business become a "big" business? Was it possible to organize the entire small business community? Small business owners were notoriously independent and often too busy to monitor political developments. And the one thing that many small business owners had in common was a resentment of government interference. For a minority of business owners—those who joined national associations—this ideological animus overcame the "free rider" problem inherent in the "logic of collective action." The New Deal broker state was anathema to these small companies, especially since it legitimized the interests of the labor unions.[7] Here we confront a fundamental paradox: could a federal agency represent the interests of a group that rejected the underlying premise of the broker state?

By establishing the SBA, Congress declared that a federal agency could indeed represent small business. But what was a "small" business? The public definition of small business encompassed "Mom-and-Pop" firms with fewer than ten employees, yet SBA size standards included companies with hundreds or even thousands of employees because they were "small" within their industry.[8] Congressional pressure to raise size standards eventually allowed larger companies to benefit from agency resources. Furthermore, the inherent economies of scale in some programs, including procurement and venture-capital investment, forced the agency to lift size standards even higher. Critics charged that the SBA was biased toward these "not-so-smalls." This theme of the smalls versus the "not-so-smalls" runs throughout the agency's history.

Finally, this book examines an important trend in modern United States history: the growth of government. In 1913, total government spending accounted for 8 percent of the Gross National Product (GNP). By 1990, this share had quintupled to 40 percent. Since the 1970s, budgetary growth has slowed but regulatory mandates have extended governmental authority over areas once considered private. This enduring phenomenon has led many observers to conclude that "big government" is inevitable.[9]

Scholars attribute government growth to many factors, including interest-group pressure; bureaucratic aggrandizement; economic and military crises; statist ideology; the breakdown of fraternal organizations; and the establishment of countervailing powers to deal with big business.[10] With the passage of time, American attitudes toward government have softened. Voters increasingly expect more from the state. And although they are not always happy with the results, most Americans have grown accustomed to a large state role in their lives. Consequently, eliminating government programs has become nearly impossible; they are approaching immortality.[11]

Despite the vast literature on government growth, there are few administrative studies exploring this important topic. As Hugh Davis Graham notes, historians have neglected a fertile field of research, leaving it to political scientists specializing in public administration.[12] Agency insiders have written most administrative histories. These federal historians have made outstanding contributions to our understanding of American government, yet they are not free to explore controversial topics that may have political consequences.[13]

The present study of the SBA thus offers a rare, in-depth, and comprehensive analysis of a federal agency over a considerable span of time.

During the past half-century, the SBA has experienced remarkable growth. Established as a tiny lending agency in 1953, the SBA eventually mushroomed into a multibillion-dollar financial institution with a significant presence in credit markets. New programs were later established to provide venture capital to growth-oriented companies, assist minority entrepreneurs, and lend management assistance to firms struggling to compete. By the 1990s, the SBA had become a conglomerate agency pursuing multiple policy objectives.

The piecemeal construction of the American state suggests that no one theory can explain all incidences of government growth.[14] In fact, the SBA's history reflects a complexity of causes. In an earlier work, I demonstrated how political entrepreneurs in Congress used crisis rhetoric to secure government assistance for small business during the Great Depression, World War II, and the Korean conflict. Congress responded by enacting anti-chain store legislation and creating two temporary agencies for small manufacturers, the Smaller War Plants Corporation (1942–1946) and the Small Defense Plants Administration (1952–1953).[15] However, with the establishment of the SBA in 1953, the crisis rhetoric faded and other factors became prominent. As an outgrowth of the antitrust tradition, the SBA fit the countervailing theory of government. The bureaucratic imperative became evident during the tenure of activist administrators who exploited the "urban crisis" of the 1960s to promote a minority enterprise agenda. Partisan, presidential politics also contributed to the agency's growth, though the stalwart support of the congressional Small Business Committees is probably the most important factor explaining the SBA's development during the past half-century.

The agency's political support derived from an ideology that has always been contested. Conservatives held to the original Jeffersonian conception of small business as the embodiment of self-reliance; a thriving small business sector was a bulwark against an overreaching state. For these ideologues, government assistance to "free enterprise" was a contradiction in terms. Officials in the Eisenhower and Reagan administrations embraced this view yet were unsuccessful in eliminating the SBA. In fact, when President Ronald Reagan tried to abolish the SBA in the mid-1980s, Congress defeated him resoundingly. This life-or-death struggle highlighted the failure of the Reagan Revolution, proving how difficult it is for a determined president to cut spending, even when the presumed beneficiaries support his small government policies. Reagan's failed attempt at reversing the growth of the SBA provides an object lesson in the futility of the conservative crusade to roll back government.

The dominant strain of the ideology supported government assistance to level the playing field between big and small business. According to this idea, small business owners deserved assistance because they were morally worthy and faced what some considered to be unfair competition from big business. Over time, this statist ideology evolved as small business advocates offered new rationales for government aid. During the civil rights era of the 1960s, SBA administrators pointed to racial disparities as justification for assistance to disadvantaged businesses. The economic crisis of the 1970s gave rise to a "small is beautiful" ideology depicting small firms as dynamic job creators, an image that indirectly benefited the SBA in the long term. This belief in small business as the engine of economic growth continues to captivate policymakers.

The following chapters trace the growth and evolution of the Small Business Administration from birth to a near-death experience in the late-1980s. As the agency grew, it took on new missions to wage war on poverty and promote affirmative action. Yet the SBA remained controversial with opponents of big government, including Ronald Reagan and David Stockman, who tried unsuccessfully to eliminate the agency. Controversy continues to surround the existence and nature of the small business interest. Do small business owners want more or less government, and what role, if any, should the Small Business Administration play in fostering their interests? These issues were still unresolved as the agency entered the new millennium.

In sum, the SBA was and is an affirmative action agency for small and minority enterprise. By affirmatively discriminating in favor of ill-defined interest groups, the SBA has become embroiled in constant controversy. Preferences designed to overcome disadvantage have flowed disproportionately to the not-so-small businesses and affluent minorities. Yet, these programs continue to grow and have become entrenched in government. Critics have failed to overcome the presumed moral worthiness of the groups these preferences serve. To attack the SBA is to malign minorities and "Mom-and-Pop" businesses. Nonetheless, periodic scandals and policy failures will likely fuel the continued controversy surrounding this troubled agency.

POLITICS AND PATRONAGE

The Small Business Administration was born as the unwanted offspring of the Reconstruction Finance Corporation, an agency eliminated in 1953 by President Dwight D. Eisenhower and a Republican Congress. In principle, Eisenhower rejected this government interference in the credit markets and questioned the existence of a separate interest group of small business owners. Nonetheless, he subsequently approved substantial increases in the SBA budget. Partisan politics explain this apparent contradiction. First of all, Eisenhower used the SBA to deflect criticism that Republicans were "the party of big business." The agency also served as a "safety valve" for small business as the administration pursued a "tight money" policy. Finally, the Republicans used the SBA to distribute patronage. In short, President Eisenhower reluctantly accepted the agency's rapid growth because SBA served his political purposes.

The issue of interest-group representation dogged the SBA in its early years. Most leading business organizations rejected the notion of a small business interest, as did the U.S. Commerce Department, which repeatedly tried to acquire the upstart agency. Political observers considered small business owners classical liberals opposed to big government; consequently, the Congressional Small Business Committees filled the interest-group void by becoming the prime backers of the SBA. Their support was crucial to the survival and growth of the agency.

Birth of the SBA

In November 1952, American voters elected Dwight D. Eisenhower president and gave his Republican Party control of Congress for the first time in twenty years. The Republicans were dedicated to balancing the budget and eliminating unessential federal programs, including the Small Defense Plants Administration (SDPA), an agency created during the Korean War to help small manufacturers secure defense contracts. The resulting debate exposed sharply differing interpretations of the small business ideology. The Democrats challenged Eisenhower to maintain an independent SDPA, while he favored transferring the agency to "its proper place in the Department of Commerce." Conservative Republicans likewise opposed creating a small business agency. The chair of the House Appropriations Committee, Glenn Davis (R-Wis.), noted that "one group of people [in Congress] support the theory that the only way you can help small business is to create a Government agency . . . and the other . . . believes the way to help small business is to cut the Government expenditures." The conservatives were determined to "take Government off the back of small business," even if this meant eliminating the SDPA.[1]

The Republicans' main target was not the SDPA, but the Reconstruction Finance Corporation (RFC), a billion-dollar lending agency created during the Great Depression. In 1932, Congress established the RFC to make loans to financially distressed banks and large corporations. During World War II, the agency lent to defense contractors but lost its emergency rationale once the war ended. Subsequently, the Republican Congress of 1947–1948 curtailed RFC operations but enacted an amendment authorizing loans to small business. Nevertheless, with the outbreak of the Korean War, the RFC returned to its original mission of lending to large corporations.[2]

Allegations of influence peddling by top aides of President Harry S. Truman tarnished the RFC's reputation, making it especially unpopular with Republican voters. In 1949, the Hoover Commission on government reorganization advocated an end to direct lending by government, because it "invites political and private pressure or even corruption." Congressional investigations confirmed the critics' suspicions that the RFC was guilty of "favoritism." Republican politicians capitalized on the issue in the 1952 elections, blaming the corruption on the Democrats' one-party rule.[3]

Eliminating the RFC would help the Republicans balance the budget and fulfill their campaign promise to "clean up the mess in Washington." However, because the GOP held only a slim congressional majority, the Eisenhower administration considered it "politically essential" to continue making loans to small business. Although the president believed that a small business agency should reside in the Commerce Department, he conceded that there was bipartisan support for an independent Small Business Administration (SBA).[4]

Was there indeed an interest group of small business owners deserving of governmental recognition? Congressional testimony revealed disagreement over this fundamental issue. The largest small business association, the National Federation of Independent Business (NFIB), supported establishment of the SBA but took little interest in the details. NFIB seemed primarily concerned with the symbolic importance of having a small business agency. On the other hand, the Conference of American Small Business Organizations (CASBO) and the National Small Business Men's Association (NSBMA) wanted to "get the government out of business," including banking. These two groups echoed the Republican platform plank advocating "limitation of competition by governmental organizations." The American Bankers Association (ABA), the National Association of Manufacturers (NAM), and the U.S. Chamber of Commerce also testified against the creation of a lending agency that competed with private banks. The SBA, they argued, would simply duplicate the work of the Commerce Department and waste the taxpayers' money. Moreover, granting preference to one class of business owners was unfair; the government should not affirmatively discriminate on the basis of size.[5]

President Eisenhower, while sharing this perspective, accepted political reality by approving the establishment of a Small Business Administration, yet his support was equivocal. Thus, Treasury Secretary George M. Humphrey reacted uneasily when called before a Senate committee to explain the president's position. Conservatives demanded to know why Eisenhower backed a measure that contradicted his self-proclaimed opposition to big government. "In theory," Humphrey admitted, "you ought not to make any loans at all," but the SBA could temporarily counter the high taxes that drained investment capital away from small firms. He agreed, however, that the president's ultimate goal was to "get out of the Government loaning business entirely."[6]

Eisenhower made his support of the SBA contingent upon the RFC's elimination. In April 1953, Senator Edward Thye (R-Minn.) and Representative William Hill (R-Colo.) introduced legislation to create a Small Business Administration. A separate bill ended the RFC. Responding to opposition from the Commerce and Treasury departments, Thye and Hill granted them each a seat on the SBA's Loan Policy Board. The Republicans aimed to please their conservative constituents by eliminating the RFC, and by creating the SBA, "refute the canard of the opposition" that the GOP was the party of big business. The Democrats' general opinion was that the SBA was "no more than a sop . . . the administration wanted only to get rid of the RFC."[7]

The final Small Business Act, signed on 30 July 1953 by President Eisenhower, abolished the RFC and created a temporary Small Business Administration. Congress approved a spending authority of $275 million, including $150 million for business loans; $100 million to help small firms secure government contracts; and $25 million for disaster assistance, a function carried over from the RFC. Unless Congress took action to extend the SBA, it would expire on 30 June 1955.[8]

What did Congress hope to achieve by creating the SBA? The primary legislative intent was to retain a governmental source of credit for small business. Disappointed with the results of earlier antitrust laws, Congress increasingly adopted affirmative measures favoring small business. According to Senator Thye, the "only purpose" in creating the SBA was to "equalize the scales." Others hoped to make a statement about the symbolic importance of small business. By establishing the SBA, Congress proclaimed that small business was still "the economic backbone of the nation." Anticommunist ideologues supported the creation of a small business agency to defend independent enterprise from "the Pinkos and the Marxist Reds" who threatened the American Way of Life.[9] Clearly, the shades of meaning invested in the SBA were as varied as the small business ideology itself. The only losers were the laissez-faire conservatives who viewed the small businessperson as the epitome of independence.

Interest-group Representation

Whom did the Small Business Administration represent? Unlike other government agencies, the SBA did not represent an organized interest group seeking government favors. In fact, the SBA garnered little support from business organizations. The Chamber of Commerce, NAM, and the ABA rejected any division of the business community into "small" and "large" companies; according to these groups, there was no small business interest. Two of the three national small business associations also opposed the creation of SBA. The sociologist Richard Hamilton states that these associations were remarkable because they were primarily concerned "that the agencies of government *not* give their clientele special consideration."[10]

Were small business owners really so conservative? If so, how could the SBA represent their interests? Or did these groups represent an ideological minority? Democratic critics noted that the associations represented only a tiny fraction of the nation's five million business owners. The autocratic founders of these associations ran them as for-profit enterprises and took contributions from large corporate interests. In addition, they inflated their membership totals and issued biased questionnaires to their constituents. For example, in 1940, the founder of the NSBMA, DeWitt Emery, claimed that 98 percent of small business owners supported Republican presidential candidate Wendell Willkie![11]

Notwithstanding these questionable claims, most political commentators believed that small business owners were "conservatives" or "classical liberals" opposed to big government. Surveys taken by the Opinion Research Corporation (ORC) confirmed the "strongly free market" views of "small businessmen," a category not defined by the ORC.[12] On the other hand, Richard Hamilton has tried to debunk what he calls the "myth of [small] business conservatism." Hamilton cites surveys showing that independent business owners were no more conservative than other segments of the middle class. Hamilton's research revealed a split in the small business community between very small businesses and the "upper middle-class" independents. The smallest firms operated on the margin of the economy. Their working-class owners lived in blue-collar neighborhoods. These companies were so small that they were exempt from government regulation. They had no paid employees and faced no threat from the unions. Consequently, these working-class business owners retained their allegiance to the Democratic Party. Conversely, the "upper middle-class" independents felt threatened by labor unions and government regulation. They were active in political affairs and identified strongly with the Republican Party. In short, the conservative business associations did not represent the entire small business community, but did speak for those business owners most affected by government.[13]

Members of the Congressional Small Business Committees sensed that they were out of step with this segment of the small business population. One congressional aide stated that "if many small businessmen knew about the various small business programs [of the SBA], they would be opposed" to them. After conducting interviews with committee members, C. Dale Vinyard concluded that "often the Committees rather than acting in partnership with interest groups appear to be acting as self-appointed spokesmen for small business." The committees did not take the small business associations seriously, because they represented businesspeople who were hostile or indifferent to government assistance. Thus, the committees represented the true constituency of the SBA. Over the opposition of business groups, Congress created the SBA, and the agency became a "creature of Congress." The Small Business Committees maintained this political monopoly until the 1970s, when a powerful small business lobby emerged from a populist backlash against big government (see chapter 7).[14]

The Administration of William D. Mitchell

Eisenhower's attitude toward the SBA was less favorable than that of Congress. While accepting a minimal welfare state, Eisenhower was a fiscal conservative whose "underlying ideology was strongly antigovernment." He was committed to "holding the line" against government growth, unless the benefits clearly justified the costs. Eisenhower sought to reduce taxes by maintaining a balanced budget, his top priority in domestic policymaking. Eisenhower's fiscal conservatism thus subordinated the SBA's needs to the larger goal of achieving a balanced budget.[15]

The president appointed an administrator on whom he could rely to limit the demands for funding. Eisenhower selected William D. Mitchell, a lawyer for a small Colorado firm and a conservative Republican. Declaring that the SBA must "work with and not against the spirit of self-reliance," Mitchell refused to make direct loans; instead, under its "participation loan" program, the SBA took part of each loan and backed the rest with a government guarantee. Even so, by November the regional offices had endorsed several dozen loans, but the Central Office had approved none. Rather than spend money, Mitchell emphasized management assistance, which amounted to the publication of pamphlets and the sponsoring of management courses in business schools.[16]

The fallacy of assuming a unified interest group of small business owners became evident when Mitchell tried to define "small" business. The agency's enabling legislation defined a small business as "one which is independently owned and operated and which is not dominant in its field of operations." Within these guidelines, the SBA administrator could devise other criteria. The Congressional Small Business Committees urged Mitchell to adopt a relative definition, because they hoped to counter big business by helping firms far larger than "Mom and Pop," especially in concentrated industries. Consequently, the SBA varied its size standards by industry or trade. A "small" manufacturer could have as many as one thousand employees; a small retailer could report annual sales as high as $1 million.[17] But despite the SBA's attempts to fairly define "small," very small businesses complained that the agency neglected their needs. Paradoxically, the SBA gained public support by claiming to represent the "little guy," while its real constituency consisted of the "not-so-small" independents. Furthermore, the Small Business Act made it difficult to aid "Mom-and-Pop" enterprises, because "all loans shall be of such sound value or so secured as reasonably to assure repayment."[18] By adopting an expansive definition of small business and maintaining strict credit criteria, Congress and the SBA caused an unavoidable split between the very smalls and the "not-so-smalls."

Wendell Barnes Takes Over

In early November, without warning, the president replaced Mitchell with Wendell B. Barnes, a former small business owner, lawyer, and state representative from Oklahoma, who was agency general counsel. According to the press, the White House fired Mitchell because he was "a hard man on lending," but his tightfistedness was consistent with administration policy. The real reason for Mitchell's firing was more sordid. He had given a drunken speech before an audience of small business owners in Minnesota, the home state of Edward Thye, chair of the Senate Small Business Committee. Mitchell's misconduct horrified Thye, who demanded that the White House remove him.[19]

A politically savvy administrator, Barnes mediated the conflicting demands of president and Congress. In a bid for congressional support, Barnes declared that he was the sole "proprietor" of SBA and that the Loan Policy Board would not control him. He also authorized regional offices to make participation loans without waiting for Washington's approval. Yet Barnes maintained a conservative lending policy. As the administrator of "a public agency using the taxpayers' funds," he kept an ever-watchful eye on expenditures. Like Mitchell, Barnes stressed the importance of "local self-help" and emphasized that a balanced budget took precedence over the immediate interests of small business.[20]

The agency's organizational structure reinforced the Eisenhower administration's strategy of restraining the SBA. As head of an independent agency, the SBA Administrator reported directly to the president. The Loan Policy Board added another check on the potential policy ambitions of top SBA officials. Also, by concentrating agency personnel and decision making in Washington, D.C., Barnes kept a tight rein on the field offices.[21]

Agency staffing strengthened these internal restraints. The SBA hired lending officers from the RFC and procurement specialists from the SDPA, who carried over the conservative tendencies of their prior agencies. The loan officers reflected a "banker's culture"; one official recalls that "they could have left the agency and gone to a bank and fit in very well." Accustomed to working with larger corporations, these SBA "bankers" held loan applicants to high standards. Many procurement specialists were also retired military officers who tried not to antagonize the Department of Defense.[22]

While Eisenhower administration officials were pleased with the SBA's parsimony, the Congressional Small Business Committees criticized the agency's tightfisted approach. As the Federal Reserve restricted the money supply to dampen inflation, banks made fewer loans and the committees charged that small firms could no longer secure credit. According to congressional critics, the SBA failed to serve as an adequate "safety valve" during this period of "tight money." After one year of operation, the agency had lent only $35 million to small business.[23]

Partisan political considerations made Eisenhower more amenable to these congressional demands. The Republicans were rapidly turning the SBA into a patronage machine. Barnes reported proudly that his agency "employed 197 persons who have been recommended by the [Republican Party]. These people constitute approximately 32% [of the agency workforce] . . . there is no other Federal agency which can approach this percentage of Republicans employed." The agency's advisory boards served as an "effective political tool," because "Republican Senators and Congressmen . . . may have as many appointments . . . as will serve their particular needs." The SBA also hired nearly two hundred Republican attorneys as outside consultants. The chair of the Republican National Committee, Leonard Hall, praised Barnes for circumventing the civil service regulations, "which are presently such a handicap in employing Republicans." Hall complimented Barnes by stating that "no Federal agency has worked as closely and as cooperatively with the Republican National Committee as has the SBA."[24]

During the 1954 election year, Barnes convinced Eisenhower that the political gain from boosting the SBA budget outweighed the cost. In March, Barnes notified Eisenhower that the agency needed additional money and personnel to handle a surge in loan applications. The SBA had taken on the combined responsibilities of the SDPA and RFC yet had only 550 employees, far fewer than the 2,300 employed by the two prior agencies. By stressing the "political aspects of this situation," Barnes secured Eisenhower's endorsement of legislation giving the agency an additional $50 million.[25]

The debate over extending the SBA beyond its 1955 expiration date highlighted the agency's political importance and renewed the controversy surrounding the existence of a small business interest. Commerce Secretary Sinclair Weeks advised the president to allow the SBA to expire. Weeks wrote that "no need has ever been expressed for a Department of *Small* Farmers" or "Department of *Small* Labor." Although Barnes agreed "in principle . . . to the eventual assignment . . . of the [SBA] to the Department of Commerce," he cited "Congressional opposition" and the "realities of the political situation." He noted that the Democrats had just regained control of Congress, and Eisenhower did not have the votes needed to eliminate the SBA. Meanwhile, several business groups—including the NAM, ABA, and Chamber of Commerce—lobbied to abolish the SBA in the interest of governmental economy. The Chamber denounced what it called a government "invasion" of banking. Uncreditworthy firms should not receive "preferential treatment." A Hoover Commission Task Force also recommended ending the SBA, because its "object is to help individual people and businesses gain competitive advantages" over those not so favored. However, the full Commission supported continuing the agency because it did not want to "take action adverse to a program which *appears* to help small business and hence is politically unassailable" (italics in original). In August 1955, motivated by this political concern, Eisenhower signed a bill extending the SBA for two years and doubling its business loan fund to $300 million.[26]

During the agency's first two years, congressional criticism and the prospect of short-term electoral gain moved the Eisenhower administration to increase SBA spending. With the return of a Democratic Congress in 1954, the administration could no longer consider eliminating the SBA. From then on, the Democrats put Eisenhower on the defensive by depicting him as a "big business" president. In the 1956 election, this partisan debate contributed to even greater agency growth.

Election-Year Politics

The chair of the Democratic National Committee (DNC), Paul Butler, thought that his party could exploit the small business theme in the upcoming election. DNC surveys of party officials reported strong interest in attacking Eisenhower's alleged favoritism toward big business. Moreover, the popular appeal of small business fit well with Butler's overall strategy to "organize the unorganized" and build "new sources of power" around the Democratic Party. Therefore, he created a special small business division within the DNC. Small business issues took up three of the "Top Ten Issues of 1956," as outlined in Democratic campaign material. Butler's approach reflected the continued vitality of broker state theory. By organizing small business, Butler's DNC hoped to complete what Franklin Roosevelt began in the 1930s.[27]

Throughout 1956, Congressional Democrats blasted the small business policy of Dwight D. Eisenhower. The House Small Business Committee chair, Wright Patman (D-Tex.), condemned "a big business Administration" for its refusal to do more for the "forgotten man," the small business owner. The chair of the Senate Small Business Committee, John Sparkman (D-Ala.), joined Patman in denouncing Eisenhower's "tax favoritism" toward big business. Other Democrats demanded the elimination of the Loan Policy Board and an end to "tight money."[28]

In the presidential campaign, Democratic candidate Adlai Stevenson and running mate Estes Kefauver promised to make the SBA a more powerful voice for small business. Stevenson gathered support from the "Independent Businessmen for Stevenson-Kefauver," a group set up to counter "Small Businessmen for Ike." On the eve of the election, the Democratic organization exploited the timely release of a study by the Public Affairs Institute (PAI) characterizing the SBA as "only one-tenth as effective as [the] R.F.C." (as measured by total business loans). The pro-Stevenson business owners cited the PAI study and dismissed Eisenhower's business rhetoric as "nothing more than political drivel."[29]

The high visibility of the small business issue placed Eisenhower on the defensive. In June, he sought political cover by establishing a Cabinet Committee on Small Business (CCSB) headed by Arthur F. Burns, chair of the Council of Economic Advisers. The CCSB recommended tax relief for small business, yet the proposed cuts saved a small corporation a maximum of only $2,500—hardly enough to stimulate investment. Consequently, the business press considered the proposal "politically motivated," and a committee member admitted privately that "the chief motive was a political one." The political significance was not lost on President Eisenhower. Twenty years later, Arthur Burns recalled that "Eisenhower was anxious to have that Committee's report . . . because he thought very explicitly that it would help him in the election."[30]

Eisenhower also countered Democratic criticism by noting that "we—not they—created the Small Business Administration." The Republicans emphasized this point throughout the campaign; their party platform praised the president for creating "the very successful Small Business Administration." The Republican National Committee (RNC) produced a campaign film entitled "The Republican Small Business Program" used by dozens of GOP congressional candidates. The movie showed a small business owner grateful for his SBA loan. A narrator intoned, "The film that you are going to see is a film about small business since 1953 . . . since Ike was elected president. In it you will meet one small businessman . . . typical of many . . . who has been helped by the S.B.A."[31]

The Republican Party relied upon the SBA, which, according to RNC workers, "had quietly been performing a task that proved that our administration is not Big Business minded." Barnes presented the administration case before groups of small business owners, leading Democrats to complain about his "political barnstorming." He conceded privately that the relative position of small business was still "not so good" and blamed the situation on monetary restrictions. Therefore, Barnes persuaded the Loan Policy Board to liberalize lending and introduced a new small-loan program ($15,000 maximum) with relaxed credit requirements. As a result, the SBA doubled its loans to small business during the last half of 1956.[32]

Following the election, the Department of Commerce tried once again to acquire the Small Business Administration. Assistant Secretary of Commerce Frederick H. Mueller complained to the White House that the SBA drained clients away, so that the public now considered his agency "the Department of 'Big Business.'" By abolishing the SBA, the administration could remove this negative label and eliminate the false impression that "big" and "small" business were antagonistic interests. Mueller failed, however, to convince the president that the political benefits outweighed the criticism that would result from the SBA's demise.[33]

Meanwhile, congressional small business advocates favored extending the SBA. In June 1957, the House Banking and Currency Committee submitted a bill to make the agency permanent. The legislative debate centered on the proposal to eliminate the Loan Policy Board. Democrats argued that the Board placed the agency "under the control of people who do not want to see the program succeed." The House voted 393–2 to eliminate the Board and make the SBA a permanent agency. The Senate did not have time to consider the bill before the agency's expiration date and agreed to a one-year extension, postponing further action until the following year.[34]

The White House debated whether to support a bill to increase the SBA's total lending authority to $650 million and to raise the loan ceiling to $350,000. Barnes argued that with participation loans the SBA could limit its expenditures; at any rate, agency spending amounted to less than one percent of the federal budget. The president ultimately supported the legislation because, as one official noted, "It is good politics to be on the side of the numerous little fellows against the large fellows." However, the administration insisted on retaining the Loan Policy Board; Congress acquiesced, and on 18 July 1958, President Eisenhower signed an act creating the nation's first permanent small business agency.[35]

The Fourth Banking System

Small business advocates had finally attained a permanent SBA, but failed to wrest control away from the Loan Policy Board; therefore, they sought the establishment of a separate body to provide for the long-term credit needs of small business. Again, presidential opposition forced a compromise that left the Small Business Administration in full control of the new program.

Since the 1930s, supporters of small business had expressed concern over the "MacMillan Gap," named after a British politician who noted the credit gap created when a small firm has grown beyond its own resources but was still not large enough to issue stock at reasonable cost. Experts debated whether a "MacMillan Gap" existed in the United States. Studies by a Congressional Subcommittee on Investment and the Federal Reserve found that many small firms could not secure long-term financing.[36] Others disputed the notion of a shortfall in the supply of long-term credit. Surveys conducted by the Commerce Department and Dun & Bradstreet revealed no MacMillan Gap. The problem lay not with an inadequate supply of investment capital, but with the reluctance of small business owners to give up control by issuing stock to outsiders.[37]

Did small business suffer from a venture capital "drought?" The truth is that no one knew. The above studies were based on limited economic data, which included only institutional sources of venture capital. Yet small firms received most of their venture capital from "angels," wealthy individuals who invested small amounts in promising new ventures. The Federal Reserve conceded that "angels" formed the "backbone of this market," but these individuals kept a low profile, fearing that other investors would move in on their ventures. A congressional staffer recalls that "we knew they were there but they were really hidden."[38]

Whatever the economic reality, many members of Congress believed that small business needed government investment. In April 1958, Wright Patman and Senate Majority Leader Lyndon B. Johnson (D-Tex.) introduced legislation to create an independent agency with a $250 million investment fund. This new agency could lend money or purchase debentures from privately owned small business investment companies (SBICs). In turn, these SBICs would invest public and private funds in small firms with growth potential. By requiring a minimum capitalization of just $300,000, the bill's sponsors sought to encourage small investment companies to work with small clients. They predicted that private capital would eventually take over the SBICs and that there would then be no need for government investment. Patman viewed it as "a way to help free enterprise help itself." Johnson stated that the goal was "eventual private ownership." Senator J. William Fulbright (D-Ark.) went further; he foresaw an end to all government financing of business—including the SBA's loan programs—and anticipated that "the Government may be able to work itself out of this [financial assistance] field."[39]

Conservative small business advocates were skeptical of the claim that this intervention would be temporary. Republican members of the Senate Small Business Committee described the bill as "the first step toward the socialization of an important segment of our free enterprise system." Small business owners did not want to relinquish control of their companies, they argued, hence there had been no grassroots demands for additional equity capital. Likewise, the American Bankers Association and the Chamber of Commerce feared that these federally subsidized SBICs would outlast their usefulness. They adamantly opposed "direct equity ownership" by the government of shares in small businesses.[40]

President Eisenhower realized it was futile to oppose a measure that had strong congressional support; however, he demanded that the new organization be placed within the SBA, and Congress agreed. On 21 August 1958, the president signed the Small Business Investment Act. The SBA could license SBICs and finance them with long-term loans or match private investment with the purchase of convertible debentures. The goal was to attract speculative investors with low-interest loans and preferential tax treatment. Small business advocates had great hopes for what Neil Jacoby, a member of the Council of Economic Advisers, called the "fourth banking system" (after commercial, investment, and mortgage banking). Thus, the SBA was "born a second time," with an even bigger role to play in the financing of small business.[41]

In the midst of this euphoria, the bill's sponsors overlooked serious problems with this new approach to financing small businesses. Small firms with growth potential needed equity investment, not more debt, but Congress could not accept government ownership of business, because it smacked of socialism. It was also questionable whether small investment companies had adequate resources to investigate prospects. For the time being, however, Congress prided itself it on having passed this landmark legislation.[42]

The Democrats claimed credit for passing this small business legislation and believed that the bill contributed to their victories in the 1958 midterm elections.[43] Faced with large Democratic majorities in Congress, Eisenhower redoubled his commitment to a balanced budget. In December 1958, the Budget Bureau declared that the SBA was "an uncontrollable program" and asked Barnes to tighten the agency's loan requirements. The SBA directed its loan officers to "moderate demands for credit." By the end of 1960, business loan approvals had declined to $207 million, down from the 1958 high of $250 million.[44]

Conclusion

Despite these late-term cutbacks, the Small Business Administration grew considerably during the Eisenhower years. Between 1954 and 1960, SBA financial assistance quadrupled, and agency personnel expanded from 550 employees to 2,200 employees.[45] The addition of the Small Business Investment Division laid the foundation for further agency growth in the venture capital markets.

Partisan politics was largely responsible for the SBA's early expansion. Both parties appealed to small business owners, a large bloc of voters. More significantly, small business symbolized public concern for the individualistic values associated with the "American Creed." The historian Ellis Hawley notes that large corporations were the economic wonder of the world, yet "deep in their hearts," Americans "retained a soft spot for the 'little fellow.'" The Small Business Administration embodied this public sentiment. Thus, rather than representing a coherent interest group, the SBA reflected "majoritarian" values.[46] Because the benefits and costs of SBA programs were widely diffused, politicians had little to lose by supporting increases in the agency's budget. Conversely, voting against the SBA left a politician vulnerable to the charge that he or she was anti–small business.

President Eisenhower's reluctant backing of the SBA reflected the symbolic appeal of small business. The election-year timing of his support for increases in the agency's budget showed his political opportunism. Eisenhower compromised his conservative principles both for immediate political gain and to dispel the public impression that he represented big business. By lending his support to the SBA, Eisenhower promoted an image of the Republican Party as speaking for "all Americans everywhere."[47] Nonetheless, the president imposed restraints on the SBA. By controlling the Loan Policy Board and the newly created Small Business Investment Division, Eisenhower kept the agency from becoming entirely beholden to Congress.

Nevertheless, from the beginning, the SBA was a "creature of Congress." Lacking the support of an organized interest group, the Small Business Committees took upon themselves the role of a small business lobby in Washington. What did they gain from their support of the SBA? First, the agency embodied a sincere congressional effort to "do something" for small business. Second, the committees acted as "complaint bureaus" for small businesspeople with grievances against the government; committee members frequently referred disgruntled business owners to the SBA. Finally, members of Congress used the SBA to distribute "pork" to their constituents. Representatives sometimes pressured the agency to "have an individual business declared small; others, to have a constituent's competitor declared not small." The counsel for the Senate Small Business Committee recalls that "everything was political."[48]

Neither Congress nor the SBA tackled the hard questions of interest-group representation. The definition of group status had practical consequences—firms declared "small" were eligible for SBA benefits. Yet the smallest firms complained that the agency was biased toward the "not-so-smalls." SBA loan officers favored larger firms with well-established credit histories. Congressional pressure to raise size standards reinforced this upward bias. For the most part, however, the issue of the smalls versus the "not-so-smalls" was lost in the partisan politicking of the 1950s.

Policymakers were oblivious to other important developments within the small business population. Controversial issues involving race and gender lurked beneath the surface calm of the 1950s. In subsequent decades, the SBA would act as an advocate for an ethnically diverse community of business owners. During the 1950s, however, the agency was little more than a government-financed bank. Nonetheless, the political tide was turning toward politicians who promised greater activism in domestic policy. In 1960, the voters elected John F. Kennedy, a president who pledged to "get America moving again." This change in attitude fueled the SBA's rapid growth in the early 1960s and led the agency to extend affirmative action to minority businesses.

SMALL BUSINESS ON THE NEW FRONTIER

During his presidential campaign, John F. Kennedy declared, "We stand to-day on the edge of a New Frontier: the frontier of the 1960s, a frontier of unknown opportunities and paths, a frontier of unfulfilled hopes and threats."[1] Such grandiose rhetoric placed the president in conflict with business leaders who feared a return of New Deal-style regulation and spending. Kennedy scholars have explored the resulting conflict between big business and the White House but have ignored the role played by the Small Business Administration. Kennedy's strong support for the SBA shielded him from criticism that he was "antibusiness." The agency also served as an outlet for domestic spending that proved popular with members of both parties in Congress.

These two factors—strong congressional support and presidential image building—contributed to the rapid growth of the SBA in the Kennedy years. Yet a bitter dispute over procurement preferences underscored the difficulty in defining small business as an interest group. The controversy also foreshadowed arguments later made to justify race-based affirmative action.

John F. Kennedy and the Politics of Small Business

As a member of Congress, John F. Kennedy showed little interest in economic issues. Although he sat on the Senate Small Business Committee in the late 1950s, Kennedy did not seem to take his assignment seriously. The committee's staff director recalls that Kennedy was "bored with the whole bit of being a senator." He went along with his Democratic colleagues in supporting tax incentives for small firms and stronger antitrust measures, but small business was not one of his top priorities.[2]

However, during his presidential campaign, Kennedy developed a no-ticeably heightened interest in small business. Once again, the SBA became the focal point for the partisan debate over small business. Republicans cited the SBA as an example of their "outstanding" record on small business, while Democrats characterized the agency as "a microscopic dot on the map of American business." The Democratic Party platform called for a dramatic increase in SBA loans. This emphasis on small business dovetailed with Kennedy's desire to portray himself as a New Democrat who would overcome the traditional hostility that marked relations between business and government when his party held the White House. His support for the SBA indicated that he was "anti-administration and pro-business at the same time."[3]

After the election, Kennedy courted the Congressional Small Business Committees by nominating John E. Horne to become SBA administrator. Horne was the former head of the Small Defense Plants Administration, who later became administrative assistant to Senator John Sparkman (D-Ala.), chair of the Senate Small Business Committee. Horne had easy access to the president and was on good terms with influential members of Congress. His nomination signaled Kennedy's wish to increase federal spending on small business.[4]

Congress followed suit by hiking the SBA's budget. In 1961, the total volume of business loans doubled to a record high of $400 million before settling back to roughly $315 million in each of the following two years. To increase spending, Horne relaxed loan requirements by emphasizing "ability to repay" rather than "the liquidating value of collateral." Consequently, the agency soon faced an avalanche of loan applications, which strained the ability of SBA personnel to meet the demand. Horne therefore offered banks a chance to participate in a new program guaranteeing up to 90 percent of a business loan if they processed some of the paperwork. This loan guarantee program received the endorsement of the American Bankers Association (ABA), which was slowly warming up to the idea of government backing for small business loans.[5]

Other SBA programs enjoyed substantial growth during the Kennedy era. Attendance at management training seminars quadrupled, and SBIC financing skyrocketed as these venture capital firms gained favor with speculative investors. Disaster lending increased approximately fifty percent, as did loans to local and state development companies. Although the SBA's lending still amounted to only a tiny percentage of small business loans outstanding, it was becoming a more significant player in the finance markets, especially in long-term lending.[6]

The SBA also took part in the Kennedy administration's efforts to stimulate the economies of poverty-struck regions such as West Virginia. The agency processed loans made by the Area Redevelopment Administration (ARA), a newly created agency lending financial assistance to businesses willing to relocate in economically distressed areas. The president further directed the SBA to target "labor-surplus" regions and sick industries, including textiles and lumber. Thus, the SBA became an instrument of U.S. industrial policy as well as an agent in the early War on Poverty.[7]

To reflect the new growth strategy, Horne altered the agency's structure. He initiated a long-term trend of decentralization by giving regional directors greater loan approval authority. In addition, to publicize agency services, Horne appointed an Assistant Administrator for Public Relations and established Small Business Advisory Councils at the regional, state, and national levels.[8] Decentralization improved SBA visibility in the small business community but eventually caused problems with staffing and inadequate Central Office oversight. For the moment, however, the SBA enjoyed a reputation as a competent, customer-oriented agency.

The SBA's standing within the executive branch improved dramatically, with the agency receiving strong backing from both President Kennedy and Secretary of Commerce Luther H. Hodges. Kennedy was pleased with the SBA's growth; Horne recalled that "he wanted me to keep on pushing for loans and contracts to go higher." Moreover, the Commerce Department temporarily abandoned its attempts to take over the SBA. A former small businessman, Secretary Hodges admitted that his department had historically ignored small business. He looked approvingly on the expansion of the SBA, saying, "It has now grown big, as a strapping boy gets bigger than his daddy."[9]

Congressional criticism of the SBA dissipated as a Republican presidency gave way to a Democratic administration. C. Dale Vinyard even went so far as to term the relationship between the SBA and Congress during the Kennedy years as a "love feast." John Sparkman lauded the agency's "energy and vigor," while Senator Hubert Humphrey (D-Minn.) praised its "unprecedented performance."[10] And even though the Small Business Committees grumbled about the continued existence of the Loan Policy Board, it exerted no influence over SBA policymaking (President Lyndon B. Johnson abolished the board in 1965).[11] In general, the agency's performance pleased the committees.

The Smalls Versus the "Not-So-Smalls"

This positive assessment did not go unchallenged, with criticism emanating from predictable sources. The editors of the *Wall Street Journal* repeatedly denounced the SBA as a "highly questionable venture" that kept marginal businesses alive when they should have died a natural death. The *Journal* was dismayed at the agency's growth and lamented that "small" was a "stretchable word, whether for measuring small business or its appointed shepherd." In fact, *Journal* editors advocated eliminating the SBA altogether.[12]

Yet, surprisingly, it was a Democrat, Senator William Proxmire (D-Wis.), who emerged as the SBA's chief congressional nemesis. Proxmire described himself as an "eclectic middle-of-the-roader" who favored "economy in government" and hated "special privilege." He spent a thirty-year career in the Senate waging a one-man war on government waste. The senator also chaired a Subcommittee on Small Business. In 1964, he published *Can Small Business Survive?*, warning that the littlest businesses faced a crisis.Not only did they generally lack long-term capital, but they were also excluded from suburban shopping centers and often met with stiff competition from discount stores. Proxmire advocated a national "fair trade" law to equalize the prices of chain stores and independents. His book drew attention to the difficulties of "Mom-and-Pop" firms. Although "small" businesses (defined as companies with fewer than five hundred employees) maintained their position vis-à-vis big business, the tiniest establishments (zero to three employees) were rapidly losing market share.[13]

Proxmire's fiscal conservatism and preference for "little" business led him to oppose increases in SBA spending. The maverick senator raised the issue of interest-group representation: whom did the SBA represent? He characterized the SBA as a "big-spending agency" that offered only a modicum of support to the "truly *small* businessman." In Proxmire's eyes, the SBA had "become a medium-size or even a big business administration."[14]

Congress faced the issue of the smalls versus the "not-so-smalls" when a financial crisis struck the SBIC industry in 1962. The near-collapse of the SBICs showed that the economies of scale inherent in organized venture capital investment made it impossible to aid very small firms. Congress resolved the crisis by expanding the program to include much larger firms. Hence, there was a certain irony to the idea of a "small business" program serving an interest group of "big" businesses.

Between early 1961 and mid-1962, the SBIC industry rode a spectacular "popularity bubble." SBIC stock prices increased as much as 250 percent. President Kennedy told investors that the program had "great potential as a Fourth Banking system" and directed the SBA to publicize the advantages of SBICs. Moreover, Congress increased SBA leverage and raised the ceiling on SBIC investment in a single company to $500,000. During the ensuing "stampede" for SBIC stocks, speculators convinced themselves that they were "getting in on the ground floor of the growth companies of the future."[15]

But the euphoria was short-lived. In May 1962, the stock market crashed and the bottom fell out of the SBIC sector. The bright optimism of 1961 gave way to the dark pessimism of 1962 and 1963. Angry investors blamed the SBA for overpromoting SBICs and not properly policing the industry. Many inexperienced venture capitalists established SBICs for "the wrong reasons and with the wrong abilities." One investment banker commented that "SBIC stock issues were too often sold to people who didn't know what they were by people who didn't know what they were." Rumors of "shady goings-on" circulated on Wall Street. And in July 1963, The *Wall Street Journal* reported cases of "self-dealing" by SBIC directors who invested in their own companies. Subsequent investigations brought more examples of wrongdoing to the surface (see chapter 4).[16]

The crash revealed serious structural problems in the program. It was evident that the SBA relied too heavily on low-interest loans to attract investors into the industry. Many SBICs, in turn, provided debt to small companies that needed equity investment. Although Congress had originally hoped to channel investment dollars through small SBICs to very small businesses, the diseconomies of scale made this impossible. The "minimum capital" SBICs could not afford the staff needed to evaluate prospects and advise companies. Furthermore, the costs of investigating small firms proved prohibitive. Ultimately, industry analysts urged the SBA to abandon its emphasis on smallness and concentrate on financing large SBICs serving large corporations.[17]

Senator Proxmire was virtually alone in his defense of the very smalls. He called for structural reform, including possible elimination of the program, because it offered "little or no help to the really small businesses, which the SBICs were set up to serve." Other members of Congress were reluctant to admit that the program had failed to meet its original objectives. In April 1963, the Small Business Committees submitted legislation increasing the SBA debt available to SBICs and lifting the ceiling on investment; there were no longer any limits on the amount an SBIC could invest in a single company. The authors of the legislation hoped that throwing money at the SBICs would solve the problems of the industry—a hope that proved illusory.[18]

Procurement Preferences

The Kennedy years witnessed another debate over the fundamental principles underlying SBA programs. The president's aggressive use of procurement preferences for small business sparked an intense controversy over the equity of size-based discrimination. Historians of affirmative action have cited precedents—such as veterans' preferences—that violated the merit principle to assist some "deserving" group, but they have overlooked one of the largest nonracial preferences in existence prior to the mid-1960s: the small business set-aside program.[19] The theoretical justifications for set-asides bore a striking resemblance to arguments later advanced in support of racial preferences. Proponents maintained that affirmative action was necessary to overcome past and present discrimination against small business. Opponents of set-asides maintained that this was a form of reverse discrimination that benefited the "not-so-small" independents but did not help truly small businesses. This debate offered rare insight into the reasoning behind SBA preferences for small business.

The Small Business Act authorized the SBA to "set aside" contracts for small firms and prevent larger companies from bidding. During the 1950s and early 1960s, the SBA resorted to two types of set-asides—total and partial. A total set-aside reserved an entire contract for bidding by small firms only. A partial set-aside broke procurement into two categories: competitive contracts (open to large and small firms) and set-aside contracts. The military negotiated a set-aside contract with a small company, but the firm's bid had to be within 120 percent of the highest award made in the competitive-bid category. The SBA and the procurement agencies "jointly determined" which contracts would be set-aside. The volume of small business set-asides increased steadily between 1954 and 1960, from $161 million to nearly $1 billion, but the program failed to reverse the long-term decline in the small business share of military procurement dollars, which dropped from 25 percent to 16 percent (small firms did much better in civilian procurement, securing half the dollars spent by civilian agencies).[20]

The Small Business Committees constantly complained that small firms did not receive a "fair proportion" of military contracts. They hoped the set-aside program would boost the small business share and inject greater price competition into government contracting by breaking up the cozy arrangements that allegedly existed between procurement officers and large corporations. As a U.S. Senator, Kennedy devised additional uses for set-asides. In 1957, he proposed that government contracts be placed with firms operating in poor communities. Three years later, he made a campaign pledge to significantly increase the use of set-asides, a promise he implemented in his first year in office.[21]

On 16 February 1961, Kennedy directed the Department of Defense (DOD) to increase the small business share of defense contracts by 10 percent in the coming fiscal year. Secretary of Defense Robert S. McNamara developed "goals" and "quotas" for every branch of the military, "with a further breakdown . . . going down to individual installations, activities, and bases." Furthermore, the president ordered the military to use a little-known clause in procurement regulations allowing the military to award a contract to the smallest of companies making identical bids. Kennedy also backed legislation granting preference to prime contractors who outsourced much of their work to small firms.[22]

Concerned with achieving "tangible results," Kennedy appointed a White House Committee on Small Business (WHCSB) to monitor the program's progress and publicize the administration's efforts in this area. John Horne served as the chair of the WHCSB, which also included assistant secretaries from key government agencies. The WHCSB's agenda soon expanded beyond procurement to include a range of issues related to small business. The group met monthly to develop a policy agenda and provide "sufficient grist for programs and publicity statements."[23]

Kennedy's program of quotas and set-asides produced the desired result: for the first time in seven years, the small business share of defense dollars rose from 16 percent to 17.7 percent, thus meeting the goal set by the president. The share of civilian procurement dollars awarded to small business also increased substantially. The timing of the increase was critical because Congress was becoming as quota-minded as the president. The Senate Small Business Committee threatened to mandate a 20 percent quota if the president's target was not met. Members of Congress could not agree on percentage goals; nevertheless, there was general agreement—even among archconservatives such as Barry Goldwater and Homer Capehart—that goals might be required.[24]

John Horne warned the president not to oversell the set-aside program. It was possible to achieve short-term results (hence the political popularity of the program), yet set-asides failed to address the long-term problems of small business in government contracting. Many small firms knew too little about the defense sector, lacked legal advice about contractual obligations, and were unprepared for the high volume of work often required by the military. Horne's warning was prescient—one year later, the small business share of defense dollars dropped back to 15.8 percent.[25]

The set-aside program was beset with difficulties. First, it was debatable whether small firms were "under represented." Advocates of set-asides pointed to the disparity between the small business share of the private sector and its share of military contracts. Overall, small manufacturing firms received less than their comparable share of the private sector, but in half of all industries, the smaller firms were actually overrepresented in military procurement. There was no disparity in civilian procurement. Second, the set-aside program increased the small business share in markets already dominated by small companies, but did not significantly increase small-firm participation in industries dominated by big business.[26] The nation's largest corporations suffered no loss of business; the set-aside burden fell upon firms that were large by industry standards yet small when compared to the business population as a whole. Set-asides penalized companies that had never "discriminated" against small business, unless competition is synonymous with discrimination. Third, there was the issue of "fronts"—subsidiaries of large corporations that qualified for set-asides. "Fronts" also took the form of small companies that received a set-aside and then subcontracted the work to a large corporation. The SBA lacked the personnel to investigate whether small firms were "affiliated" with large corporations; the agency relied on self-certification and policing by competitors.[27] Fourth, the set-aside program did nothing to improve the profitability of government contracting by small businesses, which one expert said was "shockingly and appallingly poor."[28] Finally, the demand for set-asides came primarily from members of Congress rather than small contractors. Two large surveys of small defense firms, taken in 1959 and 1960, found that the vast majority rejected the idea that the military was biased in favor of big business. Two out of three respondents believed that small companies could compete effectively with large defense contractors. There was strong support for less government regulation of procurement.[29]

The issue of preferences for small business turned controversial in 1961. The Council of Economic Advisers (CEA) startled the SBA in November, when it circulated a draft report highly critical of the agency and its role in the economy. The CEA argued that by providing "subsidies" and "special treatment" the SBA was "repealing the decisions of the market." For the first time, SBA officials were called upon to provide a theoretical justification for government assistance to small business.[30]

The SBA and WHCSB relied heavily upon claims of "discrimination" against small firms. First, they denied that an "ideal competitive system" existed. John Horne stated that "small business today clearly does *not* have the equality of economic opportunity" that it deserved. "It is," he wrote, "illusory to speak of the 'market' as if it were a discrete entity." The government was already so involved in the economy that it could not leave small business unassisted. Since big business received its share of "special treatment," it was only fair that the SBA counter with affirmative discrimination favoring small firms. The WHCSB echoed Horne's arguments by declaring that *"an important element of a positive policy toward small business is the elimination of discrimination against the small firm"* (italics in original). In the short term, this meant the continuation of programs discriminating against "big" business.[31]

Supporters of the SBA believed that small business suffered from a "manifold complex of discriminations," including the bias of procurement officers and bankers who refused contracts and loans to qualified firms simply because they were small. The old belief in the self-reliance of small business subsequently gave way to a new view that "small business cannot permanently survive these discriminations" without government aid. Furthermore, advocates of size-based preferences pointed to the alleged "institutional" discrimination evident in the disproportionate share of contracts awarded to big business. Horne admitted that small firms were less "efficient" than some large corporations but attributed their inefficiency to the lingering effects of past discrimination ("unfair practices, mergers which are harmful to competition, etc."). Small business advocates maintained that by favoring big business the government was the greatest discriminator of all, partly because the subsidies provided to large firms gave these corporations a "headstart" in the competitive race against small business. Military procurement, in particular, constituted a "set-aside program for big business" because only large companies could manufacture weapons systems. This "technological fact" necessitated the creation of a small business set-aside program to "balance the scales."[32]

Proponents of preferences argued that institutional discrimination was built into the American economy and government. Education and good-faith efforts at eradicating discriminatory practices were not enough, because individuals were often not aware that they were discriminating against small business. The antitrust laws dealt with overt discrimination on a case-by-case basis, but "other forms of discrimination may escape prosecution because they discriminate only indirectly among firms with regard to size." Thus, according to the WHCSB, the only way to focus attention on the problem of discrimination was to set "percentage goals." (Advocates of race-based affirmative action have made similar arguments. Barbara Bergmann, for example, states that statistical goals are "energizing devices" that awaken institutional actors to the problem of racial discrimination).[33]

Advocates of small business preferences contended that set-asides served the national interest by promoting competition and decentralizing the industrial base in case of "a red hot nuclear war." Actually, set-asides *reduced* competition in government contracting, but supporters feared oligopolies would result if small firms were not given protection—an unlikely scenario in industries dominated by small business (e.g., janitorial services, construction). But, above all, set-asides promised to preserve the "social and cultural values" associated with small-scale enterprise. The House Small Business Committee declared that preferences promoted "economic diversity." "Historically," the committee reported, "America's strength has resulted in large part from her diversity, from the fact that we are . . . a pluralistic society." Higher prices or less competition in contracting were a small price to pay for "diversity."[34]

Of course, one person's "fairness" is another person's "discrimination." Opposition to set-asides was concentrated in the construction industry, where set-asides constituted a high percentage of government business. The SBA set aside all military construction contracts under $500,000 for small business bidding. Firms with a gross income exceeding $5 million could not compete for these contracts. These "big" companies complained of reverse discrimination. In 1961 and 1962, the Associated General Contractors of America (AGCA) convinced Representative Philip Weaver (R-Nebr.) and Senator Harrison Williams Jr. (D-N.J.) to introduce legislation repealing the set-aside program in military construction. Williams criticized the SBA for subsidizing "inefficient and marginal small business contractors at the expense of solid and responsible businessmen." Weaver argued that set-asides raised prices and violated the merit principle as well as the Fifth Amendment to the Constitution, which prohibited the arbitrary taking of property. He stated that "the set-aside program . . . deprives all contractors who do not qualify as small business of the right to bid . . . and thereby limits or destroys their constitutional right to carry on a legitimate business."[35]

The AGCA lost its legislative bid to repeal the program but convinced the SBA to hold hearings to evaluate whether the current size standards in construction were "fair and equitable."[36] The hearings, held in February 1962, revealed the contradictions of the set-aside program. The so-called "big" firms complained of inflated bids and the low-quality work done by "inexperienced contractors." Although their gross income exceeded $5 million, these companies relied on many small jobs. Their wholesale exclusion from small-scale contracting had a negative impact on their bottom line. The big firms also challenged the competitiveness rationale that underlay the set-aside program. The president of Warren Brothers Company, R.F. Conard, pointed out that there was no advantage to bigness in the construction industry and no threat of oligopoly. On the contrary, small firms dominated the industry because they had lower overhead costs. More significantly, the opponents of set-asides argued that this "class distinction" violated the principles of a "competitive free enterprise system." Consequently, they urged the SBA to adopt a policy of size-blindness.[37]

The set-aside controversy exposed sharp lines of division within the small business community. The NFIB reported that its membership was split between very small businesses—which claimed the set-asides helped only the "not-so-smalls"—and the "larger independents," who felt discriminated against because they had grown beyond the size standard set for their industry. The NFIB leadership supported the set-aside program, while the U.S. Chamber of Commerce joined the AGCA in opposing "preferential treatment" based on firm size. The SBA ultimately rejected the AGCA's challenge. The agency claimed that set-asides were necessary because several hundred large construction companies formed a "monopoly" in government contracting. According to SBA statistics, ten percent of the construction firms in the nation received over half of all military construction awards.[38] This was hardly a "monopoly"; nonetheless, the agency considered this statistical disparity prima facie evidence of a bias against small firms.

The debate over procurement preferences revealed the ironies of affirmative action for small business. In the name of "competition," Congress and the SBA reduced the number of competing firms by excluding "big" business. The AGCA pointed out the contradictions of this policy, but to no avail. Politicians loved the set-aside program because it provided a tangible expression of their commitment to small business; it did not matter that most of these contracts would have gone to small firms anyway. Set-aside recipients supported the policy because it eliminated the competitive threat of larger rivals. Administrative considerations led SBA officials to rely upon set-asides rather than reform the procurement process by expanding the scope of competitive bidding. The agency's procurement specialists could not visit all of the military installations in the country, nor could they eliminate the supposed presence of discriminatory attitudes among the military's contracting officers. Indeed, the SBA admitted that the primary benefit of the set-aside program for the agency was that it saved time and effort.[39]

In his history of affirmative action, John David Skrentny writes, "The most important thing one can know about a people is what they take for granted." For example, during and after World War II, Congress approved a "comprehensive affirmative action package" for veterans, with little or no debate. After decades of controversy, policymakers agreed that veterans deserved special treatment.[40] Likewise, small business set-asides were immensely popular with members of both parties, because they took the inherent value of small business "for granted." Although racial set-asides would later become extremely controversial (see chapters 5–8), virtually no one applied the same objections to procurement preferences for small business.

Perhaps military procurement officers were prejudiced against small business, though the evidence was equivocal (why were civilian procurement officers not equally prejudiced?). Perhaps the military relied too heavily upon negotiated bidding, to the detriment of small business (though most small firms *preferred* negotiated contracts to competitive bidding).[41] Perhaps it was impossible to make the defense sector truly competitive because of the oligopolistic nature of military-related industries.[42] Still, there was something disheartening in the way the Small Business Committees treated small firms as wards of the state. The rhetoric of free enterprise remained, but the substance was gone.

Kennedy, Big Business, and the SBA

One reason the SBA grew so rapidly in the Kennedy years was that it had the strong backing of the president. Like Eisenhower, Kennedy recognized the symbolic and political usefulness of the agency. The SBA played an important role in shielding the president from charges that he was "antibusiness." John Horne defended Kennedy during and after several high-profile presidential confrontations with big business. He also lobbied for Kennedy's proposed tax cuts, a successful measure that improved relations with the business community.

John F. Kennedy's presidency was marked by extreme hostility between big business and the White House. Historians sympathetic to Kennedy have characterized the business reaction as a misunderstanding. They cite policies, such as the tax cut of 1963–1964, as evidence of his "corporate liberalism." An early chronicler of the Kennedy presidency went so far as to declare that he was "one of the best friends the business community ever had." According to this interpretation, America's corporate leaders misconstrued the president's sloganeering ("get the country moving again") as a call for greater government interference in the economy.[43] The historical reality was more complex— although Kennedy made overtures to big business, he also initiated actions that provoked legitimate fear in the business community. Consequently, as administrator of the SBA, John Horne spent much of his time defending the president from criticisms that he was "antibusiness."

During his presidential campaign, Kennedy portrayed himself as a new-style Democrat who would cooperate with corporate America, and in his first months in office, Kennedy called for a "full-fledged alliance" between business, labor, and government. Privately, he told aides, "I'm not against business. . . . I want business to do well. If they don't, we don't."[44] But the president did not really understand business. As historian Kim McQuaid puts it, businesspeople "confused him. He did not know what made them tick, or how to go about the job of reassuring them." Kennedy's top-level appointments reflected his discomfort with business. In contrast to Eisenhower, he appointed more academics and fewer businessmen to high office. Many corporate executives, in turn, considered Kennedy "an arrogant rich kid from Harvard who had never met a payroll and would never care to learn."[45]

Some of Kennedy's economic policies antagonized business. He was friendlier to labor unions than his predecessor had been, and he secured a minimum wage hike in 1961. More importantly, in the first year of his administration, the Justice Department filed over forty antitrust suits. Antitrust advocates also grew more active in Congress and on the Supreme Court. Eventually, President Kennedy decided "to let sleeping antitrust laws lie." Thus, in retrospect, historians have concluded that business's fears were unfounded, yet there was no way of knowing this at the time.[46]

The Kennedy administration's first major confrontation with corporate America involved the issue of small versus big business. In February 1961, Luther Hodges attacked the privileged position of the Business Advisory Council (BAC), a semi-official body made up of the nation's leading corporate executives. The BAC was a self-selecting body resembling a gentlemen's club of millionaire managers. The commerce secretary demanded the right to approve new members, open BAC meetings to the public, and add small business owners to the group. Hodges told the BAC that he represented "all the businesses, big and little" and that they should, too. The Council refused to go along, arguing that it was not an official government body, then went completely private and established a working relationship with other government agencies. In the end, Kennedy decided to "kiss and make up" by siding with the reconstituted Council rather than with Hodges.[47]

The "steel crisis" of 1962 proved even more damaging to Kennedy's reputation in the business community. In March 1962, the president secured a noninflationary wage agreement between labor and management in the steel industry. When several steel companies announced an increase in prices ten days later, Kennedy claimed that they had "double-crossed" him (the steel executives denied promising not to raise prices). Declaring that "this is war," Kennedy gathered a "crisis council" to face down the recalcitrant steel companies. He ordered the Defense Department to deny these firms government contracts and directed the Justice Department to investigate them for possible antitrust violations. The Federal Bureau of Investigation sent its agents on predawn raids of the steel executives' homes, while Attorney General Robert Kennedy placed wiretaps on their phones. To make matters worse, the news media reported President Kennedy's statement that the steel men were "sons of bitches." Kennedy terminated his war on the industry after the companies agreed to retract their price increases, leading some critics to note the arbitrariness of his actions.[48]

Kennedy's "war" confirmed the worst suspicions of his critics. The issue became a rallying point for opponents of Kennedy's economic policies. A poll taken in 1962 found that 88 percent of the businesspeople surveyed thought that the administration was antibusiness. Business executives began wearing "S.O.B." buttons (for "Sons of Business" or "Save Our Business"), and many blamed the subsequent stock market crash on the steel crisis. Meanwhile, Republican congressional leaders accused the president of actions that were "more characteristic of a police state than a free government."[49]

As SBA administrator, John Horne publicly defended the president against the charge that he was "antibusiness." Both Horne and Kennedy argued that there was a silent majority of small business owners who supported the president's policies. Kennedy drew a distinction between the self-appointed "business spokesmen" and the mass of businesses (mostly small) who "ask the Government for assistance." Horne likewise complained of the business press bias against the president. He commented that most small business owners did not have the time to read *Barron's*, but "are nonetheless a remarkably enlightened group on the subject of the Government's relationship with business." They knew, argued Horne, that the conflict between government and business was "imaginary."[50]

Shortly after the steel crisis, the White House Committee on Small Business issued its final report, *Small Business in the American Economy*, written largely by Horne.[51] The Kennedy administration used the report to wrap itself in the mantle of small business. Thus, Kennedy, like Eisenhower, used the political symbolism of small business to deflect the criticisms of his opponents. The WHCSB report catalogued the many virtues of small enterprise, including its ability to create jobs and spawn technological innovation. The WHCSB extolled the political benefits of small business, which "decreases the likelihood of excessive economic and political control." The committee also associated small business with America's Cold War aims, a favorite theme of President Kennedy. The report further suggested that small business was rhetorically useful "in the never-ending battle for the minds of men" and that "the great American dream" of owning a business was "a devastating concept to the promoters of Communism." The White House committee ended by recommending that the federal government redouble its efforts to promote small business.[52]

The president's relations with business improved in 1963, as the stock market recovered and media attention turned to his proposal for a massive tax cut. In January, Kennedy asked Congress to lower the income and corporate tax rates to boost consumption and increase investment in business. The president designed the corporate tax cut so that it would be "particularly beneficial" to small corporations. He admitted that there was no general credit crunch but noted that the aggregate statistics "mask the fact that thousands of small or rapidly growing businesses" needed investment capital.[53]

John Horne found it easy to sell the president's proposed tax cuts to small business groups. The president received the support of the NFIB and the National Advisory Council of the SBA. The Congressional Small Business Committees also heartily endorsed the measure. Horne believed that the support of the SBA and the Small Business Committees was crucial to the eventual passage of the legislation in February 1964. This orchestrated support swayed members of Congress by showing that the tax cuts would benefit "a great multitude of their [small business] constituents back home." Kennedy's successor, Lyndon B. Johnson, also understood the popular appeal of small business. When he signed the bill into law, Johnson stated that "business, as well as individuals, benefit by this tax cut. And small business benefits the most."[54]

Toward "The Other America"

The lingering business hostility toward the president did not reflect the prosperity of the Kennedy era. By 1963, the American economy was growing at a record pace. The Senate Small Business Committee cheerfully reported that "the brightest chapter in the annals of American business history was written in 1963. The national economy gave a dazzling performance of capitalism at full throttle." Profits were up, business failures were down, and the stock market was on the rise. The boom eventually lasted into 1969, making it then the longest period of expansion in American economic history.[55]

Liberal policymakers within the Kennedy administration looked on the prosperity as a challenge and opportunity to eliminate poverty. The last burst of welfare-state building was a response to the economic desperation of the Great Depression. By contrast, the Kennedy administration's nascent War on Poverty was born of optimism and guilt. Reformers were confident that they could eradicate poverty if the federal government devoted adequate resources to the effort. Conscience-stricken liberals argued that the world's richest nation had a moral responsibility to elevate the living standards of the poor.[56] But most Americans were not interested in the issue of poverty; they were leery of welfare spending and skeptical about the government's ability to abolish poverty. Nevertheless, the movement for a "war on poverty" gained steam in 1963, as the "elite wisdom" moved in the direction of greater social activism.[57]

As presidential aides prepared for the War on Poverty, the administration faced a rising tide of civil rights demonstrations. In 1960, black college students conducted "sit-ins" at segregated lunch counters, hotels, libraries, and swimming pools. One year later, "Freedom Riders" challenged the de facto segregation of interstate busing by traveling to the Deep South, where they met violent attacks from racist whites. In 1962 and 1963, the governors of Mississippi and Alabama resisted the court-ordered desegregation of their state universities, thus forcing the president to send in troops. In early 1963, Martin Luther King Jr. led a successful campaign to desegregate the city of Birmingham, Alabama, but only after the nation watched televised coverage of the police attacking teenage demonstrators. These demonstrations culminated in the 28 August 1963 "March on Washington." King and others organized the march to demand passage of a law guaranteeing civil rights to all Americans, regardless of race, color, or creed. This grassroots pressure forced the president and Congress to consider stronger civil rights legislation. The resulting Civil Rights Act of 1964 prohibited employment discrimination and banned segregation in public accommodations, including those owned and operated by private individuals or businesses.[58]

The events of 1963 moved the Kennedy Administration in a new direction. It was also time for a change at the SBA. In August 1963, Kennedy appointed John E. Horne to the Federal Home Loan Bank Board (FHLB) and replaced him with Eugene Foley, an idealistic protégé of Senator Hubert Humphrey. The thirty-five-year old administrator was one of the youngest persons to head a federal agency. Humphrey's influence on Foley was substantial. The young administrator described himself as a "midwestern egalitarian . . . a liberal Democrat, and a Hubert Humphreyite." He had served as Humphrey's counsel on the Senate Small Business Committee and was one of the few Irish Catholics to back Humphrey in his primary race against Kennedy in 1960. As assistant secretary of commerce (1961–1963), Foley worked with the black business community and was active in the civil rights movement. The March on Washington, which took place the month Foley took office, galvanized him.[59]

Accounts differ as to whether Foley used his influence with Humphrey to remove Horne from the SBA. A close friend of Horne claimed that "he didn't want to leave. Foley really engineered John being pushed out" (Foley denies this charge). According to this source, the move to FHLB was a "sentence to Siberia" for Horne. However, Foley insists that the president wanted someone at the SBA who would advance an agenda of social reform.[60]

In retrospect, Foley's appointment to the SBA was one of the most significant actions taken by President Kennedy in the area of small business. Three months later, Kennedy fell to an assassin's bullet, and his successor, Lyndon Johnson, carried through on his promise to wage "war on poverty" and racism. Eager to make his mark, Foley took advantage of the changed political climate to advance his own version of the War on Poverty by promoting the establishment of black businesses in the ghetto. In the next two years, he transformed the agency into a vehicle for social change. Thus, Foley's arrival marked the beginning of a new chapter in the history of the SBA.

3

THE ENTREPRENEURIAL ERA

The years 1963 to 1965 marked the high tide of American liberalism. Policy-makers were confident that they could solve problems—poverty, racism, urban renewal—that had confounded previous generations of reformers. Eugene Foley was a product of these heady times. Young, idealistic, and unconstrained in his vision of government-directed change, Foley led the SBA into new policy terrain. Under his leadership, the agency developed antipoverty programs and created a national network of volunteer counselors to provide free management assistance to small businesses. Foley demonstrated the importance of bureaucratic entrepreneurship as a cause of government growth.

During this period, the SBA pioneered race-conscious affirmative action by promoting "disadvantaged" businesses, hiring minority employees, and monitoring the hiring practices of SBA loan recipients. Agency officials hid these developments from public view as they circumvented the color-blind dictates of law and custom. By recognizing minority entrepreneurs as a separate interest group, the SBA created a potential conflict with nonminority business owners. These social programs also divided agency personnel.

Foley's Innovations

When Eugene Foley took over the SBA, he faced a propitious political environment. The new administrator enjoyed the support of several key members of Congress and the president. In 1963, Senator John Sparkman (D-Ala.) and Representative Wright Patman (D-Tex.) took over the congressional Banking and Currency Committees; both men favored spending more on small business. In November of the same year, the assassination of John F. Kennedy elevated Lyndon B. Johnson to the presidency. As Senate Majority Leader, Johnson had sponsored the SBIC program and advocated a bigger role for the SBA. Johnson's running mate in the 1964 election, Senator Hubert

Humphrey, was also a longtime champion of small business and Foley's political mentor.[1]

Eugene Foley used this external political support to transform the SBA into an innovative federal agency. First, he restructured the SBA to carry out a reform agenda and eliminate internal opposition from conservative elements. Foley was a "policy man," who disliked the day-to-day details of administration; therefore, he created an Office of the Executive Administrator to handle routine administrative duties. He placed Ross D. Davis, a career bureaucrat, at the head of this office. John Horne's efforts at decentralization had left the loan approval authority in the hands of fifteen regional directors, many of who were conservative political appointees. Foley weakened these directors by placing eight new area administrators above them and expanding the number of Regional Offices to sixty-three. He then devolved greater authority to the newly constituted regions. In public, Foley made a virtue out of political necessity by declaring, "We are taking SBA out of Washington. We are moving it to Main Street." Yet his real motive was to clear a path for a series of innovations he had planned for the agency.[2]

The young and ambitious administrator was determined to pioneer uncharted policy terrain. Upon taking office, he asked agency staffers for new ideas. Addison Parris, an economist whom Foley brought over from the Commerce Department, recommended offering financial assistance to needier applicants, including those who lacked the collateral to qualify for regular loans. Officials in the Financial Assistance Division opposed this proposal, because applicants would be risking little of their own money; the government would be the loser if such a plan failed. However, Foley thought that the agency was too conservative. He believed that the real beneficiaries of SBA lending were the banks who had the risk taken out of their loans to small businesses. He agreed with Parris that "our loans aren't reaching the risky type of business that really needs it so badly." Consequently, Foley established a Small Loan Program offering $15,000 loans based upon "character" rather than collateral. There was a huge demand for these small loans; within six months, the agency made $42 million in direct loans under the program. Fiscal conservatives feared higher loss rates, but Foley took an optimistic view, noting the low delinquency rate in the first several months of operation.[3]

The Management Assistance Division was undoubtedly the weakest unit of the SBA, with fewer than one hundred management counselors serving a population of five million small businesses. Foley revolutionized management assistance by developing the Service Corps of Retired Executives (SCORE), a network of retired managers and owners who lent their expertise to "sick companies" that could not afford a management consultant. In early 1964, the agency established the first SCORE chapters in New England and quickly expanded the program nationwide. Within three years, more than thirty-five hundred part-time volunteers were participating. Never before had the SBA been able to offer one-on-one counseling on such a large scale.[4]

The Evolution of Affirmative Action

The SBA also participated in a civil rights revolution that transformed the meaning of racial equality. During the Johnson years, federal agencies—including the SBA—abandoned color-blindness (race neutrality) for color-consciousness (race preference). The historian John David Skrentny attributes this change to "administrative pragmatism." Earlier civil rights commissions had dealt with racial discrimination on an individual basis, but officials eventually concluded that "discrimination was an injustice that was simply too difficult to prove." Consequently, in the 1960s they found it simpler to keep statistics on minority employment and cite any disparity as prima facie evidence of discrimination, thus coercing employers into hiring minorities. Herman Belz argues that this shift in emphasis was a "politically expedient response" to the urban riots of the mid-1960s. Critics of affirmative action contend that liberal bureaucrats and judges subverted the legislative intent of the Civil Rights Act by imposing de facto "quotas." Such detractors argue that there was little popular support for racial preferences, even among civil rights groups.[5]

All three factors—pragmatism, crisis management, and elitism—explain the evolution of affirmative action at the SBA. The SBA used statistics to boost minority hiring within the agency and detect racial discrimination by loan recipients. Although the civil rights agencies urged the SBA to adopt results-oriented affirmative action, Foley needed no coaxing; he was eager to promote this new conception of equality, even though there was no basis for preferences under the Civil Rights Act. The "urban crisis" of the mid-1960s reinforced the preexisting bias in favor of affirmative action.

The SBA was historically slow to take action against borrowers who practiced racial discrimination. In 1960, the General Counsel ruled that the SBA had no authority to deny loans to businesses that discriminated against minorities. In March 1961, President Kennedy issued Executive Order 10925 requiring federal contractors to take "affirmative action" to ensure that they treated minorities fairly, but the directive did not authorize the SBA to penalize companies guilty of discrimination. Two years later, the issue reemerged as the Kennedy administration confronted southern governors who resisted court-ordered desegregation. In April 1963, the U.S. Civil Rights Commission asked the president to "explore his legal authority" to cut off federal spending to Mississippi because of that state's opposition to desegregation. Kennedy criticized the commission for suggesting such a radical proposal, which he thought was unconstitutional. Concurrently, the SBA's legal counsel determined that the agency had no authority to deny financial assistance to a single state. Still, the issue refused to die. In November, Senators Philip Hart (D-Mich.) and Jacob Javits (R-N.Y.) asked Foley to withhold assistance from southern companies that discriminated against African Americans. Foley concluded that he did have this power but feared a sharp drop in lending if the agency enforced a nondiscrimination rule. He preferred a policy of constructive engagement—the SBA would continue lending to southern businesses that practiced discrimination "with an eye to compliance by borrowers in accord with [Executive Order 10925]."[6]

As the SBA considered issues of nondiscrimination, civil rights leaders debated the merits of racial preferences. Before 1964, most African American leaders sought the elimination of segregation and other legal discrimination. Martin Luther King Jr. cultivated white support by expounding upon a universalistic American Creed. Other activists, including A. Philip Randolph and Bayard Rustin, worked to create a transracial alliance of poor whites and blacks. White liberals, meanwhile, considered "the color-blindness of the Constitution as a settled thing." Yet a growing number of activists favored employment preferences as compensation for past discrimination. In 1963, the head of the National Urban League, Whitney Young, called for a "domestic Marshall Plan" to achieve economic equality for black Americans. The proposed plan would compensate for "300 years of deprivation." But Young's comments aroused a firestorm of criticism from civil rights leaders, and he soon backed away from his proposal.[7]

Other supporters of the civil rights movement recognized the historical effects of discrimination and moved cautiously to endorse racial preferences. For example, in 1962, *Fortune* writer Charles E. Silberman depicted African Americans as victims of poverty and white racism. He concluded that "these are sins for which all Americans are in some measure guilty and for which all Americans owe some act of atonement." Silberman advocated "positive discrimination" in education, job training, and outreach but skirted the issue of employment preferences. During the next two years, the mainstream press treated racial job preferences as a respectable, if not popular, position. In his influential book *Crisis in Black and White* (1964), Silberman came out in support of "reverse quotas" to counter the institutional racism that pervaded the economy. Furthermore, given centuries of discrimination, Silberman wrote, it was "unrealistic to assume that Negroes *would* be qualified. . . . The only solution, therefore, is to hire unqualified Negroes and to train them on the job." Similarly, in *Why We Can't Wait* (1964), Martin Luther King Jr. advocated "compensatory or preferential treatment," but was careful to include the "forgotten white poor" in his proposed "Bill of Rights for the Disadvantaged."[8]

Meanwhile, the Kennedy administration's civil rights bill provoked the longest-recorded debate in congressional history, with the issue of racial preferences at the center of the controversy. Title VII prohibited discrimination in private employment, but critics insisted that it required employers to hire minorities even if they were not the most highly qualified applicants. John C. Satterfield, a past president of the American Bar Association, feared the prospect of "racism in reverse." Senator Herman Talmadge (D-Ga.) maintained that the proposed Equal Employment Opportunity Commission (EEOC) could force employers to "give special preference to a particular class of people or face loss of contracts or potentially severe penalties in Federal courts." Hubert Humphrey denounced the bill's opponents for raising the "bugaboo" of quotas to "frighten well-meaning Americans." He and the other sponsors of the Civil Rights Act denied that the law required anything other than equal treatment. Nonetheless, they assuaged critics by adding section 703(j), which clearly rejected the concept of racial preferences: "Nothing contained in this title shall be interpreted to require any employer . . . to grant preferential treatment to any individual or group."[9]

John David Skrentny notes that the "acceptance of the color-blind principle of equal employment opportunity was at an all-time high in 1964." But the victory proved short-lived. Even before the Civil Rights Act went into effect (on 2 July 1965), there were renewed calls for preferences as compensation for past discrimination. In March 1965, Assistant Secretary of Labor Daniel Patrick Moynihan issued a report advocating "national action" to deal with the "tangle of pathology" associated with the black family. Moynihan argued that the color-blind approach to civil rights was bound to fail, because "equality of opportunity almost insures inequality of results." He predicted that there would be "no social peace" if the federal government failed to secure "equality of results" for black Americans. Several months later, Lyndon Johnson told a graduating class at Howard University, "You do not take a person who, for years, has been hobbled by chains and liberate him, bring him up to the starting line of a race and then say, 'You are free to compete with all the others,' and still justly believe that you have been completely fair." Johnson went on to say, "We seek . . . not just equality as a right . . . but equality as a fact and equality as a result."[10] Proponents of racial preferences now claimed that the president supported their cause.

The EEOC moved away from a color-blind model of civil rights almost immediately. The underbudgeted, understaffed agency faced a huge backlog of complaints. After only one month in operation, the EEOC considered ways to deal with broad racial disparities in employment rather than focus exclusively on individual complaints. The new approach required the use of employment surveys to measure minority representation in the workforce.

The agency used these numbers to pressure employers into hiring African Americans and other ethnic minorities. The riots of the mid-1960s intensified the pressure to achieve results. By the end of the decade, the EEOC had become focused on numbers. As for the antipreferential provisions of Title VII, they were, as one employee put it, "a big zero, a nothing, a nullity. They don't mean anything at all to us."[11]

The SBA was an enthusiastic participant in this civil rights revolution. Agency officials were deeply disappointed with the Civil Rights Act of 1964, because it "seemed to fall short of the ambitious goals for uprooting discrimination . . . which were envisioned by President Johnson." Foley believed that the act "did not go far enough." He was determined to "make a clean sweep of racial discrimination by SBA borrowers," but the Civil Rights Act exempted small businesses with fewer than twenty-five employees. Furthermore, Title VI specifically exempted insurance and guaranty programs from the nondiscrimination provisions of the law. Agency officials were horrified to learn that these loopholes "prevented the denial of an SBA loan to a Birmingham, Alabama, restaurant famous for its refusal to serve Negroes." Consequently, on 9 July 1964, Foley asked the Justice Department whether he had the authority to regulate employment practices. In response, the Justice Department ruled that section 4(d) of the Small Business Act gave the administrator broad powers to set policies "with reference to the public interest." Foley subsequently used his authority to impose nondiscrimination requirements on recipients of SBA assistance; specifically, new agency regulations prohibited discrimination in employment and other business activities. Thus, the SBA was the first federal agency to use its general administrative authority to regulate the employment practices of loan applicants. These civil rights regulations served as a model for other agencies.[12]

The SBA initially emphasized casework and voluntary compliance. Agency officials investigated complaints of racial discrimination and conducted on-site reviews to identify potential violations. Upon discovering discrimination, the SBA could accelerate the loan maturity or take the borrower to court. The agency also distributed pamphlets informing recipients that "passivity equals noncompliance." One agency publication, in a reference to the riots of 1965–1966, noted the loss of business that resulted from economic boycotts and social unrest. Voluntary compliance with the law, therefore, was good business. But, like their counterparts at the EEOC, agency officials soon came to rely upon workforce statistics to measure "discrimination." According to one official, statistics were needed, because "there is quite a bit of unconscious discrimination in all parts of our society."[13]

SBA officials used the above regulations to promote the hiring of minority workers by borrowers. The agency also used "affirmative action" to increase the percentage of loans granted to minority business owners. Here the initial pressure came from above. One week after the Civil Rights Act went into effect, Vice President Humphrey and the Civil Rights Commission directed the SBA to collect "minority group data" on loan applicants. Humphrey and the commission were "interested in the minority groups which are significant in size . . . and which are known currently to be subject to discrimination." They left no doubt as to which groups were to be included, "These minorities are: Negro, American Indian, Mexican-American, and Puerto Rican" (the SBA added a category for "Asian"). The agency needed little prodding from the White House; Foley was already thinking in terms of racial proportionalism. On 8 September 1965, he issued a directive explaining that "when qualified applicants and employees who are members of a minority group are numerically fewer than normally should be expected in a geographical area, attempts should be made to discover the cause" and come up with plans to "overcome this problem."[14]

The new racial reporting requirements placed the agency in a difficult situation. Civil rights advocates had spent decades fighting against racial classifications because they were used to discriminate against African Americans. When the EEOC argued for racial reporting in August 1965, there was an uproar among liberals and civil rights groups. Racial classification, however "benign," smacked of Jim Crow. Clarence Mitchell of the National Association for the Advancement of Colored People (NAACP), declared that "the minute you put race on a civil service form . . . you have opened the door to discrimination." He feared the use of racial categories would "put us back fifty years."[15] Consequently, SBA loan officers were told that they could not *ask* for racial data. The staff director for the Civil Rights Commission, Howard Rogerson, told members of the agency's Civil Rights Working Group that "in setting up procedures we *do not* want the following to occur:

a. The placing of a question on race or national origin on any
   application. . . .
b. Asking an applicant to state his race or national origin;
c. Marking racial or ethnic identification on any form or record
   in the presence of an applicant."

Asking such questions could result in "possible embarrassment." In order to gather the required information, loan officers would have to use "a little imagination and common sense."[16] An agency historian, writing in 1968, described the problem and solution in some detail. He wrote that "identification of minorities was a serious problem. Practices of the day were opposed to directly involving a minority member in any formal identification procedure, since such procedures in the past had been used by others as a tool of discrimination." The agency therefore came up with "a method of visual observation." Agency interviewers simply "made note of their ethnic background and later recorded the information. As a result, a precise [!] evaluation of the effectiveness of economic opportunity was made possible. . . . This system of identification is unique in government, and is still in use at SBA."[17]

Eugene Foley also made affirmative action within the agency a "top priority." In 1963, he created the position of Special Assistant for Minority Groups and selected Randall L. Tyus to fill the post. Tyus met with minority leaders and recruited on college campuses. He used internal statistical reports to goad area administrators into hiring minorities. By requiring reports, Tyus sent a message that "we really mean business." The statistics allowed Tyus to identify twenty "problem offices"—mostly in the southeast—that had few minority employees. In March 1965, he directed area administrators to set hiring "goals" and explain how they would achieve them. Tyus told the administrators that he was interested in "getting results" and finding the most "effective methods" to do so. Foley meanwhile set aside positions for "competent" minorities and women. These preferences produced the desired result: between 1963 and early 1965, the number of African American employees increased from 180 to 250 (roughly 7 percent of the agency workforce). The emphasis was clearly on African Americans; Hispanics accounted for less than 1 percent of SBA employees.[18]

African Americans were not the only beneficiaries of affirmative action. Foley sought a "break-through" in advancement for female employees and declared that a special effort would "mark us as a leader" in women's rights. He set aside top-level positions for women and created a "Women's Speaker's Bureau" made up of female employees who toured the country to discuss careers in government and business. Foley also authorized loan officers to make microloans to women-owned businesses. As a result, the number of loans to female business owners increased from 2 percent to 5 percent of the agency total.[19]

Black Enterprise and the War on Poverty

Eugene Foley's most significant advance in affirmative action was his ambitious plan to promote the start-up of African American businesses. He was primarily interested in the advancement of minority enterprise but was quick to sense that "poverty was in the air" when he took over as administrator.[20] Foley expanded his minority enterprise program by wedding it to the War on Poverty. The high hopes of 1964, however, soon gave way to disillusionment. The program suffered from bureaucratic bickering, budgetary restrictions, internal opposition, an agency financial crisis, and above all, a naive optimism in the agency's ability to groom entrepreneurs among the disadvantaged.

Foley first became involved with African American business during his days at the Commerce Department. In July 1961, Asa Spalding, president of North Carolina Mutual Life, asked Secretary of Commerce Luther Hodges to hold a conference on Negro business. Spalding argued that the federal government could no longer afford to neglect the needs of black business. Hodges agreed to sponsor a conference in late November and sent Foley to act as his deputy. The meeting attracted a diverse group of business owners, academics, and government officials.[21]

The political climate had changed considerably since the last conference on Negro business in 1946. Energized by the civil rights movement, the conferees rejected the "separate-economy" philosophy of the past and focused on ways to integrate African American business into the economic mainstream. The decline of a segregated market meant that black business owners needed to seek new opportunities outside their communities. The conferees agreed that black businesses should consider relocating and hiring white employees to compete more effectively in an integrated economy.[22]

Conference speakers also discussed black business's role in the Cold War. The chairman of the conference, Representative Charles C. Diggs Jr. (D-Mich.) stated that the Kennedy administration was "including us in the drive . . . to help in the Nation's global struggle with the Sino-Soviet block" (*sic*). Asa Spalding believed that black entrepreneurs served as role models for the Third World; they were capitalist success symbols for the "underprivileged peoples and underdeveloped nations." Other speakers saw an opportunity to combine politics with profit making. LeRoy W. Jeffries, the vice-president of Johnson Publishing Company, noted the business opportunities in the newly independent nations of Africa. But, equally important, black business owners could act as economic ambassadors to Africa: "Who can be a better salesman of democracy in Africa," he asked, "than an American Negro businessman with some worthwhile product or service to offer?"[23]

In 1961, African American business leaders made few demands upon the federal government. They continued to emphasize self-help and embraced a color-blind model of business–government relations. Their goal was one of equal access to existing services, rather than the creation of separate programs for African Americans. The conferees were aware of white racism and its negative impact on black business. For example, African American firms were not welcome in most national trade associations; consequently, they lacked access to technical and managerial aids. The conferees therefore urged the Commerce Department and SBA to publicize the financial and managerial assistance available from the government. There was also discussion of a proposed "Marshall Plan" to raise venture capital through a national nonprofit foundation, but the concept of government financing never arose. The general consensus was that African American businesses would have to rely upon the private sector.[24]

During the early 1960s, several government officials proposed establishing a separate program for black enterprise, yet the SBA initially rejected their proposals. In May 1961, Ross Davis wrote a memorandum to John Horne urging him to increase assistance to African American business, but Horne was uninterested. One year later, the Drexel Institute of Technology contacted the agency's regional office in Philadelphia with a proposal to promote small businesses run by members of "certain socio-economic groups," but the agency declined their proposal. The Executive Director of the President's Commission on Equal Employment Opportunity, John Feild, also sought SBA sponsorship for a pilot project to aid black business. When Horne rejected his request, Feild turned to the Area Redevelopment Administration (ARA), where George H. Robinson, Special Assistant for Minority Affairs, had conceived similar plans of his own. In June 1963, the ARA joined with several Philadelphia groups—including the Drexel Institute, the city government and the Philadelphia Fellowship Commission—to establish a Small Business Opportunities Corporation (SBOC). The ARA granted technical assistance to the SBOC, but the new corporation lacked financial support.[25]

Eugene Foley was enthusiastic about the SBOC project. On 28 January 1964, he held a press conference in Philadelphia announcing the creation of a new microloan program under SBOC auspices. Participants received management training and a $6,000 loan with a six-year maturity. These "6-by-6" loans were open to all businesses, but Foley made a special effort to reach the black business community, which the agency had long neglected (according to an informal survey, the SBA had made only seven loans to black businesses in Philadelphia during the previous ten years). Although the program was technically color-blind, Foley spoke of "Negro loans" and "jobs for minorities."[26]

There was a huge demand for these low-interest loans. In the first month of operation, the SBOC received more than one thousand applications. Most of the initial demand came from white applicants, but the number of applications from African Americans quickly and substantially increased. During 1964, the agency approved nearly one hundred loans to black businesses in Philadelphia. The early statistics looked good—the regional office reported "absolutely no delinquency" in the first six months. Encouraged by his success, Foley set up additional pilot loan programs in San Francisco, New York, Washington, and Camden, New Jersey.[27]

The Philadelphia project had a dual mission: to generate jobs for the poor and to create symbols of African American success in business. It was not enough to increase the number of black firms—the Philadelphia area already had over four thousand; the SBA wanted to elevate the standing of the business owner in the black community. Agency officials held a low opinion of black business. Randall Tyus lamented that the "Negro businessmen do not . . . represent very useful models" for African American youth. Foley characterized the typical black entrepreneur as "a very small businessman—who is generally not a very good businessman and, frankly, not a very significant factor in the Negro community." The federal government, he argued, was the only institution capable of improving upon this dismal record of entrepreneurial failure.[28]

The microloan program gained a big boost from the Johnson administration's War on Poverty. In March 1964, President Johnson submitted legislation to Congress creating an assortment of antipoverty programs, with the Office of Economic Opportunity (OEO) as the chief coordinating body. The War on Poverty stressed opportunity ("a hand up, not a handout") in the form of job training. But it was not enough to create jobs that lifted people barely above the poverty line; the administration raised expectations by promising upward mobility. Hubert Humphrey stated that "any training program calculated to make them successful janitors and housemaids for the rest of their lives is simply not going to be acceptable." Based on his brief experience with the Philadelphia project, Foley convinced Senator Humphrey to insert a small-loan provision in Title IV of the Economic Opportunity Act, the enabling legislation for the War on Poverty.[29] The agency proposed a "15-by-15" loan program with a 100 percent loan guarantee (rather than the usual maximum of 90 percent). The SBA would offer loans to people with "very low incomes" and to businesses that hired the hard-core unemployed. The sponsors of Title IV maintained that it was a profitable investment in the poor. Humphrey defended the program by stating, We are making loans to people, not because we like them, not because we feel sorry for them, but because we think they can put the money to good use." Yet the agency would have to relax credit criteria by focusing on the "character" of applicants rather than their business experience. Conservatives predicted that the Economic Opportunity Loan (EOL) program would be a money-loser for the government. If banks refused to make loans to these applicants, they asked, how could the SBA assure that they would be repaid? But the measure had the backing of liberal Republicans in the Senate, including Jacob K. Javits (R-N.Y.), who amended the bill by increasing the maximum loan amount to $25,000. Title IV passed easily and was generally disregarded in the heated debate over the War on Poverty.[30]

The SBA used Title IV funds to pursue the dual mission of creating jobs and "advancing the Negro in the business world." Foley was careful to note that poor people of all races could apply for EOLs, but an agency official later admitted that "the program was definitely oriented toward minority groups, particularly Negroes." Title IV also embodied the "community action" element of the War on Poverty. The law mandated the creation of Small Business Development Centers (SBDCs) to locate applicants for EOLs and provide them with management assistance. These community boards consisted of business owners, poor people, and social workers.[31]

The EOL program was beset with difficulties, including several acts of God. In March 1964, a massive Alaskan earthquake drained nearly $100 million from the agency coffers. A record-high demand for business loans intensified the financial strain on EOL. The situation worsened over the course of the year. In fiscal year 1965, the agency spent over $200 million on disaster aid—more than in all previous years combined—but only $10 million on EOL.[32]

One of the major problems the agency faced was the lack of personnel needed to run the antipoverty program. The Bureau of the Budget (BOB) had set a ceiling on the number of SBA employees, forcing Foley to cannibalize existing departments. The president's drive for economy in government operations made it difficult for Foley to hire the workers he needed. Foley especially wanted African Americans to work on the frontlines of EOL, but he could not locate qualified loan officers to fill these positions.[33]

The SBA's "banker culture" worked against this social experiment. Loan officers were accustomed to applying relatively stringent credit criteria to loan applications; EOL violated everything they knew about the economics of lending. These "old-line employees" did not like the new way of doing business. As one participant observed, the agency's war on poverty was defeated by "an old structure, old policies, and old methods of operation."[34]

The EOL program suffered from bureaucratic bickering with OEO and the Budget Bureau. OEO provided the funding for SBDCs but set a low priority for the small business part of the War on Poverty. Foley wanted to establish one hundred SBDCs throughout the country, but OEO limited them to cities that already had "community action" programs. Consequently, the agency had only thirty-five SBDCs in operation at the end of 1965. Furthermore, the Budget Bureau ruled that the SBA could offer EOLs only through SBDCs, thus limiting the reach of the program (Congress repealed this restriction two years later). Foley lost further control of EOL funds as cities outside his targeted areas demanded and received EOL money.[35]

Most important, the selection criteria used to judge EOL applicants were fundamentally flawed. Foley assumed that capable business owners lay "often hidden, under layers of poverty, racial prejudice, and undeveloped talent." With a little assistance, he argued, these individuals could "bloom" into successful entrepreneurs.[36] But how was the SBA to locate this undiscovered talent? The instructions to agency loan officers were sentimentally vague. The

Deputy Administrator for Financial Assistance, Logan B. Hendricks, set forth the EOL credit criteria in a memorandum to all agency loan officers. He stated that the "character" of loan applicants was more important than their business experience or assets. Loan officers were to investigate an applicant's "honesty, morality, family stability, [and] personal habits." Yet they should not automatically disqualify applicants who had a criminal record. Hendricks wrote that "poverty breeds law infractions." An applicant's "character must be judged . . . in relation to the environmental conditions that have created or established the character of the individual in the first place." Hendricks then provided a concrete example of an ex-convict accepted into the program: "a woman convicted of mail fraud was found to be an acceptable applicant because of a complimentary letter from her probation officer who mentioned the fact that the woman was a victim of an extended liaison with a man of poor character, which was contributory to her wrongdoing. The probation officer offered a favorable prognosis, too, for the woman's eventual rehabilitation."[37] Thus, guilt over poverty and racism caused agency officials to "blame the system" while excusing the bad behavior of poor people.

SBA loan officers faced a dilemma. On the one hand, they were to give applicants every benefit of the doubt. However, Hendricks warned that loans to "persons of questionable character" could result in negative public relations for the agency.[38] How could loan officers determine "character" when the system was to blame? When was an individual responsible for his or her behavior? This conundrum was symptomatic of the time—holding the poor accountable for their actions was considered "blaming the victim."[39] Little wonder, then, that loan officers thought the EOL program was an exercise in wishful thinking.

The events of summer 1965 transformed EOL from an experiment in social policy into a program designed to alleviate the "root causes" of the "urban crisis." The SBA had some forewarning of urban violence; during the summer of 1964, black rioters had clashed with police and looted hundreds of stores in Harlem and several other northern cities. And in March 1965, SBA General Counsel Philip Zeidman informed Foley that knowledgeable people were predicting a "long, hot summer of race relations." Zeidman outlined a possible role for the SBA in "future racial controversies," including the establishment of SBDCs in riot cities. Zeidman's letter was prescient. On 11 August, a routine arrest of a drunk driver in the Watts section of Los Angeles sparked a riot that lasted five days and took the lives of thirty-four people. Rioters looted and set fire to stores, as bystanders chanted, "Burn, baby, burn!" The Watts riot ushered in four "long, hot summers" of mayhem. Between 1965 and 1968, there were over three hundred riots resulting in two hundred deaths and the destruction of several thousand businesses.[40]

One week after the Watts riot ended, President Johnson sent a team of federal officials—including a representative from the SBA—to visit the riot-torn city. The White House promised substantial assistance in rebuilding Los Angeles. The president's goal was to "eliminate the deep seated causes of riots" by promising massive aid to Los Angeles and other "distressed" cities.[41] Black rioters had elicited a sympathetic response from the nation's leaders. This combination of black rage and white guilt signaled the beginning of the end for the moderate civil rights movement. Rioters learned that the police could not contain mob violence. Militants perceived that violence attracted the attention of political leaders and the media. This vicious cycle continued until the end of the decade, when the riots faded from the urban scene.

The Watts riot marked the end of Foley's tenure at the SBA. Lyndon Johnson selected him to head the newly created Economic Development Administration (EDA) within the Commerce Department. Among his duties, Foley was a "troubleshooter" in cities experiencing racial unrest. His first assignment was Oakland, California, which the Federal Bureau of Investigation designated as the city most likely to become the "next Watts." As he headed to Oakland, Foley did not conceal his sympathy for the Watts rioters. He and assistant Amory Bradford believed the riot was "a reaction of justified anger and despair." Foley used the rhetoric of black militants to justify a dramatic increase in federal aid to the cities, proclaiming that "the Negro's sounds of 'NOW!' are not irrational or threats; they are a cry of desperation; a plea for help." The only solution to the riots was the creation of "jobs with dignity." Consequently, Foley secured $23 million in economic development grants for Oakland. One year later, he left the EDA to pursue a successful career as a consultant to small companies, but he and Bradford claimed an early victory. In *Oakland's Not for Burning* (1968), Bradford admitted that "while the EDA program has not yet placed anyone in a job," it was the "real turning point" in Oakland. There was never a riot in Oakland, but if joblessness was the "root cause" of civil disorder, then the EDA contributed little to the peace, since the project produced only twenty new jobs![42] Perhaps the mere gesture of generosity forestalled violence, though similar initiatives failed to prevent other cities from burning.

Before leaving the SBA, Foley proposed merging it with EDA. He had initially refused the president's request to take over EDA, because it involved a cut in pay. Johnson promised that he would try to transfer the SBA so that Foley could retain his salary. Fierce congressional opposition dissuaded the president from delivering on his promise. Nevertheless, for nearly a year after Foley's departure, the SBA lacked an Administrator. Ross Davis served as de facto Acting Administrator, but as a career bureaucrat he lacked the imprimatur of a presidential appointment.[43]

Conclusion

The Foley years were exciting ones for the SBA. The young administrator exuded energy and enthusiasm for new ideas; he was a "policy entrepreneur" par excellence. Policy entrepreneurs "identify new missions and programs for their organizations" then cultivate external (and internal) constituencies to support their policies.[44] In the space of two years, Foley created a national network of management consultants (SCORE), waged a small-scale war on poverty (EOL), and pioneered new forms of affirmative action. He also secured a broad increase in funding for the agency's lending programs (the total volume of business loans hit a record high of $468 million in 1964).[45] He achieved these administrative successes by circumventing internal opposition and drawing upon external political support.

Foley took advantage of policy initiatives tangentially related to small business and thereby expanded his bureaucratic domain. He succeeded despite the declining salience of the traditional small business agenda. The "bread-and-butter" issues of small business (financing, management assistance, taxation) receded into the background for the duration of the 1960s, as president and Congress grappled with more pressing problems, including civil rights and the War on Poverty. Yet Foley successfully exploited these issues and turned them to his advantage.

Like other bureaucratic entrepreneurs, Foley saw a "window of opportunity" develop as the political climate turned in favor of activist government. During this period, President Johnson won an impressive series of legislative victories by engaging in the "politics of overpromise." The Eighty-ninth Congress created innumerable agencies and enacted countless laws addressing everything from poverty to pollution. James Sundquist notes that, in the space of two years, the liberal view of government's potential went "from gloom to euphoria." The affluence of the 1960s contributed to the "hope and hubris" of Great Society liberalism. Expectations were high, and public faith in the government's ability to deliver on its promises was equally high.[46]

This optimism and "can-do" attitude imbued Foley and his associates at the SBA. He, too, pledged to attack poverty and racism through lending programs and new racial preferences. But by promising to do so much, Foley raised the stakes for the SBA. Could the agency deliver in so many unrelated areas? Or would the bureaucracy buckle under the strain of too many responsibilities? How much internal support did Foley really enjoy? Most important, could the agency adapt to the ever-changing circumstances of the 1960s? Or would future administrators be locked into programs that showed initial promise but soon outlived their usefulness?

Policy entrepreneurs are often admired for their boldness and willingness to represent the "voiceless," but as political scientist James Q. Wilson observes, "Such a process . . . can result in programs that do not work well, or work at all."[47] In addition, zealous policy innovators frequently lack the administrative skill or desire to carefully implement and monitor new programs. Foley relinquished this role by creating a new Office of the Executive Administrator but failed to construct an effective organizational structure.

Foley also ran into a bureaucratic culture leery of change, a problem that worsened with time. SBA lending officers maintained a "banker's mentality" and were skeptical about the social programs initiated by Foley and his associates. Employees of the Financial Assistance Division were accustomed to following formal rules concerning eligibility and loan criteria; their perceived mission was to keep loss rates low. On the other hand, the agency's poverty warriors bent existing rules to achieve social change as rapidly as possible. The two factions served different interest groups: loan officers had built a clientele of firms with well-established credit histories, while the poverty officials reached out to African American groups. These two conflicting subcultures—tightfisted "bankers" and social activists—coexisted uneasily. The tensions between them increased as the "urban crisis" worsened in the late 1960s.[48]

The SBA took part in a civil rights revolution that turned the "plain meaning" of the Civil Rights Act on its head.[49] Swiftly and self-consciously, SBA officials abandoned the color-blind tradition of the civil rights movement by classifying applicants according to race. How could such an unpopular policy—opposed by conservatives and liberals alike—become the de facto law of the land? Part of the answer is administrative pragmatism. The SBA began informally collecting racial statistics on borrowers as early as 1964. These statistics provided agency administrators with a crude measure of civil rights compliance and highlighted the importance of reaching out to the minority community. But the numbers also sanctioned a color-consciousness that was previously unimaginable. For nearly a century, civil rights activists had held to a philosophy of color-blindness embodied in Justice John Marshall Harlan's famous dissent in *Plessy v. Ferguson* ("There is no caste here. Our Constitution is color-blind, and neither knows nor tolerates classes among citizens").[50] Nonetheless, the practical administrative logic of record keeping overcame ideological scruples. The SBA, like the EEOC and other federal agencies, simply lacked the personnel needed to monitor civil rights compliance on a case-by-case basis. Although the record keeping of the Foley era did not produce "hard and fast" quotas, it did inject a new race-consciousness into the agency's operations.

The EOL program, with its emphasis on "Negro loans," reinforced this tendency. The color of an applicant's skin now mattered, because it represented victimhood. But if African Americans were victims, how could the SBA distinguish between those who had the ability to succeed in business and those who did not? Would SBA officials let sentiment impair their judgment? Certainly, the admission of ex-convicts did not bode well for the future success of the program. Were good intentions enough? Could the agency simply wish away the harsh realities of a competitive economy?

Agency officials still had not decided whether the program's aim was one of integration or separation. The "Negro loan" program attempted to achieve two contradictory aims. On the one hand, Foley insisted that firms catering to a segregated market had a "limited future." The black business owner had to "cut racial ties and move his enterprise out into the mainstream." Yet the SBA sought to create role models within existing black neighborhoods, thus intensifying their reliance upon a "Negro market."[51] If the goal was integration (i.e., creating success stories in the larger business world) the agency would have to encourage the "best and brightest" African Americans to start their own businesses, but SBA officials made no attempt to do so. Moreover, the government's affirmative action programs worked at cross-purposes: federal agencies and government contractors recruited college-educated managers from African American businesses and offered them better pay and benefits; few were willing to exchange the security of a salaried position for the risks of starting a small business.[52]

Administrative pragmatism only partly explains the changes in the agency's civil rights policy. Before 1964, SBA officials recognized legal limits on their ability to enforce nondiscrimination in hiring. The success of sit-ins, the March on Washington, and the passage of the Civil Rights Act changed the tenor of the movement by raising expectations for immediate progress. These exhilarating victories quickly transformed American liberalism. In the early 1960s, liberal supporters of the civil rights movement had admired the "amazing patience" of African Americans, who had endured centuries of racial oppression. By 1965, there was a new emphasis on achieving "equality as a fact." Many moderate civil rights advocates, like Eugene Foley, were now liberals in a hurry. Patience and perseverance gave way to haste in the execution of policies that were untried and unproven. Foley's personal ambition contributed to this change in attitude, but the agency also faced pressure from the White House and the various civil rights agencies.

Foley's abrupt departure in August 1965 left the agency leaderless and adrift. The SBA had nearly exhausted its financial resources as well as its employees. But with Foley gone from the scene, agency officials had time to ponder the legacy of his administration. Foley's eventual successor reorganized and reformed agency operations, just in time for another round of policy entrepreneurship in response to the terrible riots of 1967–1968.

4

CRISIS AND CONSOLIDATION

"The Sixties" conjures up images of a nation torn nearly asunder by racial and political conflict; popular memory flickers with televised footage of police brutality and riots, assassinations and antiwar demonstrations. The years between 1965 and 1968 were among the most tumultuous of this crisis-filled decade. The easy, can-do confidence of the early sixties gave way to over-heated rhetoric and apocalyptic predictions of race war, yet America survived the upheavals of this period.

This was similarly a period of crisis and consolidation for the SBA. The "urban crisis" forced the agency to expand its affirmative action programs and make them explicitly race-based. The SBA's interest-group representation became more heterogeneous as officials increased size standards to bail out SBICs and rescue one of the nation's largest corporations from bankruptcy. Through it all, the agency's traditional programs expanded and grew more reliant upon the private sector. In short, the SBA emerged from the crucible of the late 1960s far different from the agency that entered the decade.

Time of Troubles

For nearly a year after Eugene Foley's departure, the SBA lacked an administrator. This continued uncertainty produced a crisis of confidence. On 4 May 1966, Executive Administrator Ross Davis called a meeting of area administrators and regional directors to discuss the agency's mission. He and others questioned the rationale of the SBA's direct loan program. The agency found it difficult to "weed out" creditworthy borrowers who sought SBA loans in lieu of bank financing. Davis also criticized the "irrationality" of subsidized interest rates—the agency should charge higher rates on money lent to high-risk borrowers. An agency economist, Padriac Frucht, echoed this concern over the unsound economics of direct lending. He further noted that below-market rates created an insatiable demand for agency funds. Frucht predicted that if current trends continued, the agency would soon be "using billions and billions of taxpayer dollars with no limit in sight with a tremendous vested interest block [*sic*], a strong Congressional group, and no apparent means of [budgetary] control. . . . This is a terrifying thought." Looking back on the rapid growth of the Horne-Foley years, Frucht declared that "we are getting into the big leagues. We are on the edge."[1]

SBA officials also questioned the agency's role in the War on Poverty. The early flush of success gave way to disillusionment with a program that pleased no one. By the end of 1965, nearly one-third of the original "6-by-6" loans were delinquent or in liquidation. The head of the EOL program, Benjamin Goldstein, reported that "we've had a tremendous amount of complaints—from [SBDCs], from Negro businessmen, from Congressmen, from everybody." Regional directors especially hated EOL, because the credit standards were "exceptionally low"; they did not like making loans to "extremely small businessmen" with little or no collateral.[2]

These controversies highlighted the need for a strong administrator to impose order on agency operations and give the SBA a sense of direction. In May 1966, President Johnson selected Bernard Boutin to become the next head of the SBA. A strong-willed, effective administrator, Boutin had served as head of the General Services Administration (1961–1964) and later as Deputy Director of the OEO (1965–1966). Loyal to Johnson and on good terms with Congress, the White House counted on Boutin to "shake up SBA" from top to bottom. His appointment heartened congressional small business advocates and put to rest the lingering rumor of a hostile takeover.[3]

Boutin's no-nonsense management style contrasted sharply with that of his predecessor. Unlike Foley, he believed in a hands-on approach to agency administration. It was clear that the SBA desperately needed new leadership. Within months of taking his post, Boutin notified the White House that the agency was "almost completely adrift," morale was "at an all time low," and the organizational structure was "chaotic." Moreover, serious personnel problems existed, with job training "practically nonexistent." Employees arrived late to work and took long "Martini luncheons." The bureaucracy was riddled with "political hacks" who contributed little to the organization. In short, the SBA was "knee-deep in incompetence."[4]

Reversing recent trends, Boutin centralized responsibility for loan liquidation, procurement, and computer data gathering. He also imposed "internal discipline" on malingering employees, especially those at the higher ranks. Boutin reassigned workers to positions for which they were qualified and instituted job training for those who needed to upgrade their skills. The goal, according to Boutin, was to put "square pegs into square holes," an elementary task that the agency had avoided for much of its existence.[5]

SBICs and the Redefinition of "Small"

Boutin's greatest challenge was to revive the moribund SBIC industry. These venture capital companies had never recovered from the stock market crash of 1962. Several SBA-sponsored studies showed that SBIC investment had increased the profits, sales, and net worth of client companies, yet the SBICs continued to report losses. They remained plagued by high operating costs, illiquidity, and a lack of investor confidence. Consequently, many SBICs had become inactive and were holding money in cash accounts rather than investing in new ventures.[6]

The summer of 1966 saw persistent rumors of corruption in the industry erupting into a full-fledged scandal. The SBA official responsible for policing the SBICs, Deputy Administrator Richard Kelley, had overlooked serious violations of agency regulations. In July, Boutin reported to Congress that there were more than two hundred "problem" companies, and he suspected that many of them were guilty of criminal activity. He estimated the agency would lose approximately one-sixth of the $300 million it had invested and pledged to "clean out the mugs" to salvage what remained of the industry's reputation.[7]

Boutin ordered a massive investigation of SBICs. He dedicated all of the SBA's auditors to the effort and borrowed an additional one hundred investigators from other federal agencies. Their findings were shocking: nine out of ten SBICs had violated agency regulations, and dozens of companies had committed criminal acts, including money-laundering for organized crime and "sweetheart deals" with companies owned by individuals sitting on their board of directors. Most of the "problem" companies were small, privately held SBICs ("one-man operations").[8]

Officials in the SBIC industry feared that Boutin's investigation might result in the elimination of the program. Yet, despite the demonstrated failure of the SBIC program, Congress never seriously considered abolishing it, because doing so might hurt small business. Instead, Congress strengthened the SBA's police powers by authorizing the agency to issue cease-and-desist orders against violators and to revoke licenses of companies that "knowingly breach the law." Congress also raised the ceiling on SBA financing of a single SBIC to $10 million and increased the ratio of government-to-private financing. A "small" firm could now have up to $5 million in assets and still be eligible for SBIC investment. The reformers hoped to encourage the formation of large SBICs in place of the small companies that then dominated the industry.[9]

The fundamental problem with the SBIC program was that politicians did not understand the economies of scale inherent in the venture capital market. Ignorance produced unintended consequences. In their study of politics and bureaucracy, William Mitchell and Randy T. Simmon observe that often those "who believe themselves to be promoting the public interest are led by an invisible hand to promote other kinds of interests." In the case of the SBIC program, the original goal was to aid small business, but it had become, as William Proxmire feared, a "medium-size or even a big business" subsidy.[10]

The early history of the SBICs also illustrates how government growth sometimes results from efforts to deal with the failure of existing programs. In 1958, the sponsors of the Small Business Investment Act described the program in terms of self-help. They predicted that the government would eventually "work itself out" of the SBIC industry. During the 1960s, however, Congress reacted to each crisis by expanding the government's role and making SBICs more dependent on SBA assistance. Scandals might seem to favor advocates of retrenchment, but this is rarely the case. Once programs are created, their existence is no longer debated, and the range of policy options narrows considerably. Liberals must contend with the inefficiencies and unintended consequences of their policies, while conservatives recognize that a program, once created, is here to stay; therefore, they too seek to reform rather than abolish. Thus, the ideological debate over the SBIC program gave way to "rationalizing policies," defined as a "government-led search for solutions to government's problems."[11]

The effort to reform the SBIC industry highlighted two continuing themes of the agency's history: first, the paradoxical expansion of the SBA's role in the credit markets despite evidence of its incompetence; and second, a redefinition of "small" business to include companies much larger than the "very smalls" for whom Congress originally intended the program. Thus, the "smalls" grew bigger, as did their federal representative.

Boutin's reforms strengthened the SBIC industry by removing the weakest firms. The stock value of the survivors underwent an amazing turnaround in late 1967. In June, the business press had dismissed the SBIC program as a "flop" and "the Dream that Failed"; six months later, *Forbes* reported that SBICs were back in favor with speculative investors—stock values were "going up, up, up." In 1968 and 1969, the industry produced "extraordinary" profits. However, the boom was short-lived—during the next two years, the SBICs lost nearly all of the ground gained in the bull market of the late 1960s. The overall rate of return for the 1960s was a disappointing 5 percent, far less than the 10 to 15 percent earned by commercial finance companies. The SBA made money on the program because the costs were "exceedingly small," but the interest paid by borrowers hardly justified such a high-risk venture.[12]

By the end of the 1960s, the private venture capital market had eclipsed the

SBICs. Between 1966 and 1970, private venture capitalists created 119 investment firms, compared to only ten new SBICs. Aggressive growth mutual funds also entered the market. These firms provided clients with equity, whereas the SBICs continued to make loans. Private venture capitalists grew confident in their ability to meet the needs of speculative investors. Their trade association recommended tax and securities reform as a substitute for SBICs and called for the eventual elimination of federal financial assistance to the industry.[13]

Sizing up Small Business

Bernard Boutin generally opposed policy innovations because he wanted to avoid promising what the agency could not deliver. Thus, he rejected proposals for a White House Conference on Small Business, because it "could raise demands for new programs." Similarly, he opposed creating preferences for Vietnam veterans, because he was "leary [*sic*] of programs that when announced carry a lot of promise and then . . . do not even begin to fulfill that promise. This agency has suffered from this type of thing too many times in the past." In 1966, Boutin made one notable exception by expanding the definition of "small" business to admit the financially troubled American Motors Company (AMC) into the agency's set-aside program. The SBA adopted new size standards for the automobile and tire industries based on market share (a "small" company had less than a 5 percent market share). AMC had only a 3 percent share of the automobile market but was huge in absolute terms, with over 30,000 employees and almost $1 billion in sales. Boutin defended his action by stating that the new size standard "represents the world of today, not the world of the early fifties." The Congressional Small Business Committees raised no objections to the expansive new definition; in fact, they had long urged the SBA to scale the standards upward.[14]

The AMC decision exposed the confused state of the agency's interest-group representation. The economic rationale was sound—the SBA was supposed to promote competition in highly concentrated industries—but AMC offered a poor test case. Boutin devised the new standards to bail out an uncompetitive company. Furthermore, the announcement of this policy revealed what Washington insiders already knew—that the SBA served medium- and large-sized companies. This revelation threatened to undercut popular support for the agency. The policy may have also violated the Small Business Act, which limited SBA assistance to companies that were "independently owned and operated." Yet, except for William Proxmire, the congressional small business advocates acted disingenuously by supporting a definition of "small" that departed so sharply from their speeches, which were often peppered with references to "Mom-and-Pop" grocers and corner druggists.

The SBA had historically operated in the gray area between the smallest and the largest businesses in the country. Surveys showed that most Americans thought a small company had fewer than 25 employees (less than 3 percent thought that a "small" business might exceed 100 employees).[15] On the other hand, Americans thought a "big" business had 5,000 employees or more, thus leaving a great middle section of the economy that the SBA could describe plausibly as "small" or "not big."[16] Yet the AMC decision violated any reasonable conception of smallness and left the agency open to the charge that it ignored the needs of the "truly small" businesses.

In 1967, as a follow-up to the AMC decision, Boutin established a task force to study ways of incorporating competitiveness into the agency's definition of small business. The existing arbitrary size standards pleased no one. Critics charged that the standards were too high, while relativists argued for even bigger size standards in concentrated industries. One year later, the task force sputtered out of existence and an agency historian commented that "it has not been possible to develop small business size standards . . . in a way that is satisfactory to everyone, or to a high percentage of those most interested." This issue continued to bedevil the agency into the 1980s and beyond.[17]

Bernard Boutin tendered his resignation on 27 June 1967, citing financial considerations as his primary reason for leaving government service (his position as SBA administrator did not pay enough for him to support a family of ten children, several of who were then in college).[18] He left the agency in a much stronger position to deal with the administrative challenges posed by its various programs. During his thirteen months at the SBA, Boutin never promised more than he could deliver. Subsequent events—including the worst riots of the decade—forced his successors to raise expectations once again, with disastrous consequences for the agency's reputation.

The Urban Crisis and Affirmative Action

Boutin selected Deputy Administrator Robert C. Moot to be his successor. Moot was a military procurement officer before arriving at the SBA in 1966 to inherit an agency that was still growing. In calendar year 1967, the SBA's business loan volume hit a record $600 million. A new "Simplified Blanket Guaranty Plan" boosted the percentage of business loans guaranteed by banks, thus leveraging agency funds and securing the political backing of the banking community. The SBIC industry was beginning a two-year upswing. *Reader's Digest* published an article on SCORE, and the program "took off like a runner hyped up on steroids."[19] The U.S. economy was booming. In short, the future looked bright for small business and the SBA.

This rosy picture did not extend to America's inner cities, which were enduring the worst civil violence in a half-century. Black rioters looted and burned thousands of buildings—mostly small businesses—and clashed with police, the National Guard, and the federal troops sent to quell the disorder. The extent of the rioting was enormous; in the summer of 1967, there were 176 disturbances. The total number of riots for the year numbered well over 200, with 71 major riots occurring in 82 cities. The worst riot of the decade took place in Detroit, just days after Robert Moot took office. A police raid on a "blind pig" (illegal after-hours bar) sparked a violent upheaval that took the lives of 43 people and resulted in the partial or total destruction of 2,500 stores.[20]

The cause of the riots was widely debated. Conservatives blamed the unrest on a breakdown in "law and order." They argued that the looting was done "mainly for fun and profit." By responding paternalistically to the riots and refusing to take a hard line against violence, liberal policymakers spawned a self-fulfilling prophecy that encouraged self-destructive behavior. In effect, rioters were granted a moral holiday and their neighbors paid the price.[21]

Black militants and their white sympathizers, on the other hand, considered these "rebellions" a form of political violence aimed at forcing concessions from governmental authorities. The rioters were "political dissidents" who targeted "hated examples of outside oppression and exploitation." They allegedly embraced a "riot ideology" based on the use of "negative political power."[22]

The dominant liberal explanation incorporated the riot ideology and stressed a "revolution of rising expectations." The "root cause" of the violence, they argued, lay in a lack of "good" jobs; therefore, liberal policymakers responded by promising aid to the cities. Improving conditions in the inner city would, Johnson argued, "make us all a happier and more guilt-free people." Consequently, an increasing percentage of federal antipoverty dollars went to the ghettoes, thus turning the color-blind War on Poverty into a series of "black-oriented" programs.[23]

The riots also challenged the taboo against public discussion of racial preferences. Advocates of affirmative action considered it "the price society had to pay to prevent further violence." Politicians of all stripes advanced race-conscious policies to address the causes of the riots. The "elite wisdom" of the time was fast moving away from the color-blind consensus of the early 1960s toward racial redistribution of jobs and government benefits. Though many Americans disagreed with this "soft" response—half of those surveyed thought that shooting looters was "the best way" to deal with riots—policymakers were intent on formulating a more benevolent response to the violence in the cities.[24]

The civil disorder forced the SBA to expand its commitment to Economic Opportunity Loans (EOLs) even as officials admitted publicly that the program was foundering. SBA employees were making loans without carefully evaluating credit records or the borrower's prospects. The agency financed new businesses in fields already crowded with competitors. Political commentators from the left and right criticized the impracticality of the program. The *Wall Street Journal* editorialized that "if a man who wants to start his own business is a good bet to go broke, saying 'no' may be the most charitable response a lender can give." Likewise, a writer for the *Nation* observed that very small businesses had a high failure rate and that the hard-core unemployed did not make good business owners. It was not an issue of money—the agency spent the Lilliputian amount of $30 million a year on the program—but of insuperable obstacles to success. Nearly everyone agreed that spending more on the program was a waste of taxpayers' dollars.[25]

The primary impetus for expanding the program came from African American activists and white officials responding to the riots. Bernard Boutin had initially resisted their demands for racial preferences. In July 1966, he expressed "complete disagreement" with Padriac Frucht's suggestion that the agency make more "Negro" loans. Boutin maintained a color-blind approach to civil rights, stating that a "major emphasis on loans to minorities . . . borders on reversed discrimination." He told Frucht that "all programs of SBA will be equally available to all American small businessmen . . . but never one race to the exclusion of another." Yet, apparently, many agency officials still considered EOL a "Negro" program. At a conference of area administrators and regional directors, Boutin reproached those who "don't seem to understand what is meant by being disadvantaged. You don't have to be Negro or Chinese, you don't have to be a Mexican-American, or any other nationality or race. You have to be disadvantaged!" He urged the administrators not to be blinded by racial consciousness or to ignore rural poverty.[26]

Nonetheless, the pressure for race-based loans continued to build. Boutin directed SBA employees to "go out into the ghettos" and assigned African Americans to work on EOL teams. But this was not enough to please black militants. Stokely Carmichael and Charles Hamilton, in their book *Black Power* (1967), denounced the SBA as a representative of the "white power structure." By denying African American businesses a fair share of loans, the SBA embodied "institutional racism" and perpetuated "economic colonialism."[27]

Traditionally conservative figures also demanded that the SBA do more for black business. The National Business League (NBL), for example, transformed itself into a supplicant for federal aid. Established by Booker T. Washington in 1900 as a self-help organization for African Americans, the NBL abandoned Washington's philosophy once government aid became available.[28] To capitalize on the growing concern with the inner city, League President Berkeley Burrell adopted the militants' rhetoric. The SBA's failure to help black business owners was an "expression of racism in its most rabid form."

The income restrictions on EOLs rendered the program a "phony, fraud, and hoax." If the SBA was interested in creating role models, Burrell argued, it should help existing black business owners rather than "go down to the unemployment compensation boards to find entrepreneurs standing in line." Burrell's criticisms had the desired effect. Boutin responded by creating an "EOL-II" program for those with higher incomes who "have been disadvantaged by factors beyond their control," a thinly veiled reference to race. Meanwhile, in 1967, Congress doubled the EOL loan appropriation to $60 million. Thus, the pressure to "do something" about the urban crisis overwhelmed the well-founded concern that the program was unworkable.[29]

The year 1968 witnessed the apotheosis of the riot ideology. After leaving the Commerce Department, Eugene Foley published *The Achieving Ghetto* to promote a massive "Marshall Plan" to develop America's inner cities. Besides jobs programs, he recommended "an aggressive small business program for the ghetto," including a dramatic expansion of EOL and establishment of race-based set-asides in government contracting. This "self-help" was preferable to welfare because it provided "local, neighborhood success symbols." Foley touted his book as the "first word" on black business, but it was not the last.[30]

In February, the president's National Advisory Commission on Civil Disorders, chaired by Otto Kerner, issued its famous report on the riots. The Kerner Commission blamed "white racism" for the uprisings and declared ominously that the U.S. was "moving toward two societies, one black, one white—separate and unequal," ignoring the economic and educational gains of African Americans in the 1950s and 1960s. Furthermore, the Kerner report enshrined the liberal riot ideology: rioters were not to blame for the conditions that caused them to riot. The civil disorders were regrettable but understandable; they were essentially a "political act of protest by the powerless." Thus, along with jobs programs and welfare spending, the commission recommended giving "special encouragement to Negro ownership of business" by expanding the EOL program.[31]

Meanwhile, African American leaders grew increasingly militant in their demands for government assistance, including aid to black business. Jesse Jackson declared that "the black ghetto must be controlled by black people." There would be no peace, Jackson warned, if "the colonial powers—the white owners" continued to "take profits and leave poverty" in the ghetto. (This colonial metaphor was de rigeur in radical circles—African Americans allegedly lived in an "internal colony" and worked in a "*de facto* slave economy").[32] A few black businessmen urged self-help and warned of becoming too dependent upon the government but were drowned out by the loud, angry voices seeking racial entitlements.[33]

Advocates of black business continued to criticize the SBA for its alleged indifference to the ghetto. Of course, many borrowers were grateful for their Economic Opportunity Loans.[34] But, in the eyes of its critics, the agency could do nothing right. They attributed delays in loan processing to racism, because "whites seem to get their money much faster." Critics accused loan officers of condescending to African American applicants and treating them disrespectfully. When Charles Kriger, the New York Regional Director, made a "visual demonstration" of black loan officers before the Senate Small Business Committee, he was called on the carpet by a New York city official who took "great exception" to the public display of these "Hertz Rent-A-Negros." The chief complaint was that the SBA was too conservative in its loan criteria. Proponents of minority enterprise invoked the urban crisis as justification for relaxed standards. And a Newark official voiced the typical sentiment that "these are emergency days, and we must provide emergency solutions."[35]

The presidential election of 1968 underscored the growing importance of minority enterprise. In April 1968, Republican candidate Richard Nixon announced a "black capitalism" agenda for the ghetto. In a radio address entitled "Bridges to Human Dignity," Nixon echoed the militants' demand for a "piece of the action." He proposed federal assistance to create new businesses and expand existing ones. In his August acceptance speech at the Republican national convention, Nixon reiterated his commitment to "black capitalism," noting that African Americans did not want to exist as "a colony in a nation." They wanted an "equal chance" to own businesses and homes, and he promised them "new programs which will provide that equal chance."[36]

Was Nixon motivated by political opportunism or a sincere belief in racial preferences? Critics charged that Nixon's program was nothing more than a "star-spangled hustle," a campaign gimmick. There is some evidence that Nixon hoped to split the labor movement along racial lines and attract black votes in the process (the AFL-CIO denounced "black capitalism" as "apartheid, antidemocratic nonsense"). He sought southern white votes (by opposing forced integration of schools) while also promising "more black ownership, black jobs, black opportunity." But although Nixon failed to sway many African American voters with his proposal—he received only 3 percent of the black vote—his vision of "black capitalism" struck a chord with liberals and conservatives alike. The *Wall Street Journal* hoped that the new policy would make Republicans out of rioters. William F. Buckley Jr., the conservative editor of *National Review*, also approved of the plan. Racial preferences in lending and contracting would soon become controversial, but in the tumultuous year of 1968, "everybody seemed to be for it."[37]

Political factors cannot entirely explain Nixon's motivations. He sincerely believed in racial preferences to promote the economic advancement of minorities. During the 1950s, as chair of the President's Committee on Gov-

ernment Contracts, Nixon advocated "limited preferential hiring" of minorities.[38] The idea appealed to him *because* he could expect no appreciable gains
in the African American vote. Nixon considered himself a moderate
"unbeholden to the major pressure group involved," who could do the "right
thing" by bridging the gap between the races. It would later be said that "only
Nixon could go to Communist China"; similarly, in Nixon's eyes, only he
could breach the great racial divide in America. Contemporary critics focused
on his "southern strategy," an overt attempt to court southern white voters,
but ignored this other side of Nixon's civil rights policies. As for "black capitalism," it was, according to biographer Stephen Ambrose, "an idea he had
adopted enthusiastically, and one that he would stick with."[39]

Nixon's "black capitalism" speech forced his Democratic opponent, Vice
President Hubert H. Humphrey, to accelerate the implementation of his own
minority enterprise program. In March, Humphrey had established an interagency task force to develop a "National Program for Promoting Minority
Entrepreneurs." The task force concluded that the riots were sparked in part
by "Negro bitterness at being economically dominated" by white business
owners. Therefore, the new minority enterprise program should emphasize
ownership, rather than job creation. During the next several months,
Humphrey offered proposals that were similar to those advanced by Nixon,
with an emphasis upon creating role models in the ghetto.[40]

One member of the task force, Undersecretary of Commerce Howard J.
Samuels, was keenly interested in controlling the new program. Samuels, an
ambitious, self-made millionaire, was active in the civil rights movement. In
June 1968, Samuels proposed an aggressive program of aid to black business.
He convinced President Johnson to appoint him SBA administrator to carry
out his vision of black capitalism (Robert Moot was leaving to become Comptroller of the Defense Department). Consequently, on 1 August, Samuels took
over the SBA, announcing that he wanted it "to become known as the Federal
Agency that made the greatest contribution to social change" in the 1960s.[41]

On 13 August, Samuels introduced Project OWN, an ambitious attempt to create twenty thousand new minority-owned businesses a year. His
ultimate goal was to close the gap between white and minority business ownership by the end of the 1970s. Samuels estimated a total annual cost of $500
million to reach this seemingly unattainable goal. His unbridled enthusiasm
was reminiscent of the Foley years, when hope triumphed over reality. In speaking before the National Business League, Samuels declared that the SBA was
writing "a new page in world history." The agency was once again "on the
move. We've got a new religion, a new motivation, a new commitment."[42]

Samuels offered every conceivable justification for a new round of racial
preferences. First, he argued that white Americans owed minorities, especially

African Americans, compensation for past and present discrimination. Hence, he spoke of "compensatory capitalism" as the basis for Project OWN. Equality under the law was insufficient because it perpetuated existing inequities. Second, Samuels cited the statistical disparity between white and minority business owners; minorities were 15 percent of the population, but owned only 1 to 3 percent of the nation's businesses and accounted for less than 1 percent of total business receipts. Third, he maintained that minorities were "like the inhabitants of an underdeveloped nation" and therefore deserved "foreign aid." But the chief political appeal of "compensatory capitalism" was as a response to the riots. Project OWN, Samuels argued, would "help turn the tide of lawlessness."[43]

But Project OWN was fraught with difficulties. The agency abandoned any pretense of "mainstreaming" minority businesses into the larger economy and focused entirely upon establishing minority businesses in the ghetto. Business prospects were extremely poor in the ghetto even before the riots broke out, and the violence and a soaring crime rate exacerbated the plight of inner-city business owners. The SBA had to lower its loan criteria to reach a greater number of prospective entrepreneurs. Samuels insisted unrealistically that the loss rate would not exceed six or seven percent.[44]

The SBA revised its standards in other ways, one of which was reversing its longstanding policy against financing "buy-outs" of existing businesses— the new goal was to get "whitey" out of the ghetto by replacing him with a black business owner. This zero-sum strategy created no new jobs and may have created a *less* productive local economy, because the new owners lacked business experience. Samuels also overturned the existing ban on loans to liquor stores and bars, a touchy issue that angered members of Congress and threatened to inflame hostilities in the ghetto (liquor stores were the number one target of rioters).[45]

The linchpin of Project OWN was its emphasis upon guaranteed loans— the only way the SBA could finance $500 million a year in new loans to minority-owned businesses. In fiscal year 1969, the agency quintupled the amount of guaranteed EOLs to $22 million, a sum that fell woefully short of the $500 million goal. Banks were unwilling, even with a 90 percent government guarantee, to risk their capital on such high-risk ventures. According to Samuels, these loans made good economic sense, but the businesses with the greatest expertise in this area—the banks—disagreed.[46]

Samuels tried unsuccessfully to appease African American critics, who complained that the SBA stood for "Stop Black Advancement." First, he established two advisory councils on Black Economic Development and Spanish American Economic Development. Declaring that the SBA must become "black conscious," he hired African American employees to work in the ghetto.

Samuels also ordered the agency's Minority Enterprise Teams to undergo "Sensitivity Training" to overcome stereotypical attitudes toward people who lived in the ghetto (ironically, the trainers discovered that white team members were more sympathetic toward minority loan applicants than were the black team members). Yet, despite the agency's best efforts at outreach, the carping of the critics continued.[47]

During his brief tenure at the SBA, Howard Samuels introduced one innovation in minority enterprise policy that had a lasting impact: the Section 8(a) program for minority contractors. This provision of the Small Business Act authorized the SBA to take prime contracts and let them out to small companies. Section 8(a) lay dormant until 1967, when a Defense Department official suggested that the agency use it to help minority business. Samuels immediately saw its potential for promoting minority firms. The original goal of the program was to benefit minority business enterprises in areas of high unemployment. White-owned corporations could sponsor minority firms by providing capital and management assistance but were to relinquish control once these companies were on a solid footing. There was some concern that the 8(a) companies would become permanently dependent upon the government; therefore, the agency required each applicant to formulate a "program for future independence from SBA assistance." The agency also realized that the 8(a) program could undercut small, white-owned contractors; thus 8(a) officers were to select contracts for goods and services previously produced by the government or by large corporations. The initial output of 8(a) was modest—the SBA awarded eight contracts in 1968—but it soon became the largest, and most controversial, program benefiting minority business.[48]

During the "long, hot summers" of the 1960s, few public officials were willing to voice their doubts concerning the effectiveness of the government's "black enterprise" policy. However, critics within the Budget Bureau did point out the flaws inherent in this approach. In August 1968, the economist V.L. Broussalian wrote a progress report on the various minority enterprise programs of the SBA. He concluded that low-income people made poor entrepreneurs. The most ambitious and talented individuals were taking salaried positions in large corporations and government agencies, a direct result of affirmative action. Furthermore, it was hard to justify major expenditures on "black capitalism," given the economics of the ghetto. The SBA's experience with EOL confirmed the commonsense belief that ghetto enterprise was difficult to sustain. The agency had succeeded only in creating a class of business owners permanently dependent upon government support.[49]

Two months later, another Budget Bureau economist, Bob Weinberg, offered similar criticisms of EOL and 8(a). He noted that the real purpose of "black capitalism" was to overcome the alienation of ghetto residents, but these programs had backfired by producing conspicuous failure rather than success. Ghetto entrepreneurs experienced "personal misfortune" when their businesses folded, the community blamed the SBA for their failure, and the general public lost faith in the government's ability to deal effectively with the urban crisis. Racial hostility was compounded by the resentment of rejected loan applicants who accused the SBA of racism. While the critics clamored for more aid to black business, Weinberg concluded that the SBA was already in danger of "moving too fast" with a program that was a "catastrophe."[50]

There were early signs of opposition to the conspicuous racial preferences embodied in "compensatory capitalism." The authors of an SBA-sponsored study admitted that Project OWN constituted "*discrimination in reverse*," yet, they wrote, "the notion of compensatory capitalism is now firmly rooted in our society" (italics in original). But the question was far from resolved. A *Time* magazine writer observed that the consensus favoring racial preferences resulted from emergency conditions and that whites were "bound to complain that such aid gives Negroes an unfair competitive advantage." Similarly, Bob Weinberg advised the White House that "antidiscrimination law works both ways"—de jure preferences violated the rights of white business owners, although informal targets were "probably legal."[51]

The House Small Business Committee was adamantly opposed to "reverse" racial discrimination, for a variety of reasons. Representatives Laurence Burton (R-Utah) and James Corman (D-Calif.) did not want the SBA to "ghettoize the ghetto" by limiting loans to black businesses in the inner city. Other committee members complained that the SBA had ignored the rural poor, black and white. But the chief objection was moral: by making racial distinctions in lending, the SBA undermined the principle of equal protection under the law. Thus, in its final 1968 report, the committee warned that "if any such 'discrimination in reverse' policy is permitted to develop, the reputation of the agency for fair dealing could become tarnished." Samuels and other agency officials responded that EOL was legal because it was theoretically open to all races; in practice, however, the SBA applied lower standards to applications from minorities. This tactical dodge offered the agency a legal defense but did not end the controversy surrounding racial preferences, a debate that raged on into the 1970s.[52]

Conclusion

The publicity associated with "black capitalism" masked the steady growth of the SBA's traditional loan programs. The agency was more "black conscious" than ever, but most of its loan dollars still went to white-owned firms (in fiscal year 1969, minority enterprises received 75 percent of the EOL budget but only 15 percent of total loan dollars approved). The SBA approved general business loans amounting to $550 million (excluding EOL), up from $420 million just four years earlier.[53] This growth rate was much more modest than in the Horne-Foley years but still significant.

The SBA's growth did not come at the expense of the private sector. On the contrary, the agency privatized portions of its financial and management assistance programs. In fiscal year 1969, loan guarantees accounted for 70 percent of general business loan dollars, up from less than 20 percent in fiscal year 1965. The absolute value of direct business loans (excluding EOL) declined from $285 million to $110 million.[54]

The SBA also relied upon SCORE to provide management counseling to small businesses. The earliest studies found that the volunteers boosted client companies' sales and profits. But the paperwork required to run this "free" service initially overwhelmed the agency's management assistance officers. In 1967, the SBA solved the problem by turning over administrative responsibilities to SCORE, which created a formal organization made up of local chapters. SCORE was a rare example of genuine self-help operating successfully within the loose confines of the federal government.[55]

In his history of government growth, *Crisis and Leviathan*, the economic historian Robert Higgs stresses the importance of crisis and ideology.[56] There is no better example of this crisis-ideology effect than the government's response to the "urban crisis." Many high federal officials succumbed to the riot ideology. The authors of one survey found that "a majority or near-majority of influentials in each of these [government] agencies felt that violence was advantageous to social change."[57] Consequently, they responded to the riots by increasing assistance to the ghetto. Reform-minded administrators at the SBA shared this belief in a riot ideology and used it as a pretext for expanding the "black capitalism" programs. The SBA also officially recognized "black" and "brown" capitalists as a separate interest group served by their own programs. Unfortunately, this approach was counterproductive; it locked agency officials into futile policies that ostensibly appeased rioters but did little to enhance black enterprise. In fact, the EOL program played a cruel joke on poor African American entrepreneurs, who often lost their entire life savings. In one of the earliest studies of EOL, the economist Timothy Bates reported that the delinquency rate for new businesses was a shocking 70 percent. Worse, delinquent borrowers remained responsible for their SBA loan payments even after liquidating their businesses. Bates concluded that EOL was "a device for perpetuating rather than alleviating poverty among low-income, disadvantaged entrepreneurs."[58]

By attempting to "gild the ghetto," the SBA overlooked the far greater opportunities for black enterprise in the economic mainstream. In one of his earliest essays, the economist Thomas Sowell analyzed the shortcomings of separatist economics. The concept of "keeping money in the community" was foolhardy, he wrote, if African Americans found better business prospects elsewhere.[59] The key to African American business success was integration, not separation. Advocates of "compensatory capitalism" viewed blacks as helpless victims of discrimination who could not compete without government aid. They failed to realize that the decline in racial discrimination opened up new opportunities in high-growth fields, including manufacturing and business services. The educational gains achieved by African Americans in the 1960s enabled them to exploit these business opportunities in subsequent decades. But the resulting black business boom did not take place overnight; it was built upon the hard work of individuals pursuing their own self-interest. The loud, impatient cry for immediate results concealed the steady progress made throughout this period.[60]

Advocates of "black capitalism" adhered to what Thomas Sowell has called the "anointed vision" of the policymaking elite. Good intentions substituted for hard thinking about the limits of public policy and the dangers inherent in romanticizing violence and sanctifying a new form of race-consciousness. The initial promise of EOL was a "hand up," not a handout, but it soon evolved into a racial entitlement, joined by the Section 8(a) program in 1968. SBA administrators denied the obstacles to success and downplayed the losses, both to the agency and the prospective beneficiaries. They proclaimed the righteousness of their cause and refused to evaluate the empirical evidence demonstrating the failure of their policies. "Doing good" ultimately became an end in itself.[61]

Meanwhile, the SBA failed to help the real victims in the inner-city—small business owners who experienced the triple threat of urban renewal, rioting, and a soaring crime rate. By equating disadvantage with skin color, the riot ideology privileged one group of small business owners while marginalizing others.[62] These unseen "others" were the forgotten men and women of the 1960s.

The immediate legacy of the urban crisis was to leave the incoming president Richard M. Nixon with a "Pandora's box of civil rights questions."[63] Nixon promised to restore "law and order" to the cities. He also pledged to promote "black capitalism" through the SBA. During the next several years, the agency navigated between the Scylla and Charybdis of black militancy and white resentment of "reverse discrimination." Yet the 1970s brought not only a continuation of old conflicts but the emergence of new issues, including deregulation, the rise of a powerful small business lobby, demands by women business owners for a "piece of the pie," and scandals galore.

5

THE AGONY OF HILARY SANDOVAL

President Richard M. Nixon had high hopes for achieving policy successes through the Small Business Administration. The agency catered to small business, an important constituency in Nixon's "Silent Majority." The SBA also provided a showcase for the administration's highly visible "black capitalism" initiative. Nixon's unusually keen interest in small business ensured the survival and growth of the SBA into its third decade.

Unfortunately, the spotlight of media attention illuminated the failings of SBA leadership. Nixon's choice of administrator, Hilary Sandoval, was sick and ill-equipped to manage a government agency. The SBA subsequently became embroiled in scandals that undermined agency morale and created organizational chaos. Furthermore, a white backlash against "reverse discrimination" set the tone of debate over affirmative action. An interest-group rivalry also simmered between Hispanics and African Americans, both claiming status as "disadvantaged" business owners. Consequently, the SBA found it more difficult than ever to define whom it represented.

Nixonomics and the Politics of Small Business

When Richard Nixon took office, contemporaries characterized him as a "conservative" who would reverse the liberal domestic policies of his predecessor. Instead, the Nixon years ushered in another era of government growth. Nixon's partisan attacks on the Great Society had misled many into thinking that he opposed big government. Philosophically, Nixon was ill-disposed to wage an assault on the welfare state. Throughout his career, he identified with the moderate wing of the Republican Party and despised "far right conservatives." Furthermore, as a political strategist, Nixon believed that voters would always choose the Democratic Santa Claus over the Republican Scrooge. He therefore adopted a philosophy of "relaxing and enjoying the inevitable" tendency of Congress to spend more money on domestic programs. Simultaneously, Nixon courted conservative voters, who were the backbone of the Republican Party. Consequently, his domestic policies were a mishmash of liberal "zigs" and conservative "zags" appealing to both ends of the ideological spectrum. Political pragmatism took precedence as Nixon sought to construct a new coalition cutting across traditional liberal-conservative lines.[1]

Nixon's economic policies were likewise incoherent. Though disdaining economics, he realized that his political support rested on continued prosperity. As the economy stumbled, Nixon lurched from one policy to another to save his presidency. At different times, he embraced monetarism, Keynesianism, laissez-faire, and wage-price controls. He practiced what one writer called "the most comprehensive economics in the history of the world"! At the end of his first term, Nixon went on a spending spree to boost the economy before the election, a move that greatly benefited the Small Business Administration (see chapter 6).[2]

Nixon's preference for small business was the one constant in his political economy. His father owned a small grocery and taught Nixon to value economic independence and distrust large corporations. Presidential economic adviser Herbert Stein recalled that Nixon was "no fan of big business." Conversely, small business fit Nixon's conception of the "Silent Majority." An aide later wrote that small business owners were "our constituency"—they were "'grassroots' people" who "oppose massive street demonstrations and riots." Nixon believed that it was the government's responsibility to aid and protect these "independent" enterprisers. This sympathetic attitude made the Small Business Administration a natural vehicle for increased spending.[3]

The SBA also benefited from Nixon's unwavering commitment to "black capitalism." Despite congressional opposition, Nixon persisted with a controversial program that promised little short-term political gain. He institutionalized a form of affirmative action that might have withered in the face of such strong resistance. Ultimately, by the end of the Nixon presidency, racial preferences had become a permanent feature of agency operations.

Hilary Sandoval, 1969–1970

Given the SBA's high profile, the selection of an administrator was important, particularly after the high turnover of the past few years. Nixon blundered by appointing Hilary Sandoval, a Mexican American businessman from El Paso, Texas, to head the SBA. The president chose Sandoval to please his congressional backer, Senator John Tower (R-Tex.) and to reward Sandoval for gathering support among Mexican Americans. Unfortunately, Sandoval lacked leadership skills and was suffering the debilitating effects of a stroke, a condition that he covered up with the assistance of a few trusted aides. His irrational behavior resulted in one of the most agonizing periods in the agency's history.[4]

Several White House aides expressed strong opposition to Sandoval's appointment, alleging that he was not competent to run a government agency. Leonard Garment, the presidential aide responsible for minority enterprise, observed that Howard Samuels had turned the SBA into "one of the most sensitive agencies—technically and politically." We can expect "major trouble," Garment wrote, if we do not make "bullet-proof appointments" to the "black capitalism" agencies. What the SBA needed was a take-charge leader who would be "very aggressive in pushing a dead bureaucracy." Other White House staffers echoed this assessment of Sandoval's abilities and noted that he had suffered some unknown illness. Furthermore, they emphasized that the appointment of a Mexican American to an agency responsible for "black capitalism" was bound to upset African American leaders. But Nixon insisted that he owed Senator John Tower this appointment. The SBA would have to live with the consequences of this presidential decision.[5]

Personal insecurity and health problems contributed to Sandoval's paranoid distrust of agency employees. He declared, "I am new to government—I do not quite understand it," and therefore surrounded himself with people whom he felt he could trust, including a personal priest who had an office in SBA headquarters. Sandoval had no administrative experience, other than running his small magazine business in El Paso, and the SBA bureaucracy overwhelmed him. Moreover, Sandoval was recovering from the effects of a stroke that had paralyzed his right hand. He underwent violent mood swings and suffered severe insomnia. It was later revealed that Sandoval had a malignant brain tumor.[6]

The new administrator, an "Arch-Republican," distrusted Democrats and tried to purge them from the agency. He ordered a record number of "reassignments, reclassifications, and transfers" of employees. This organizational shake-up sent agency morale plummeting. Union membership doubled in the first year of Sandoval's administration. The National Federation of Independent Business (NFIB) and the Small Business Committees were up in arms over the confusion at the SBA.[7]

Meanwhile, the president's decision to hand leadership of "black capitalism" over to the Commerce Department embittered relations between that agency and the SBA. Secretary of Commerce Maurice Stans was Nixon's chief campaign fundraiser and one of his closest advisers. Stans was excited about "black capitalism" and persuaded the president to hand him authority over the new program. On 5 March 1969, Nixon issued an executive order establishing the Office of Minority Business Enterprise (OMBE) within the Commerce Department. The OMBE was set up to help "blacks, Mexican Americans, Puerto Ricans, Indians, and others" deprived of the opportunity to own their own businesses. Lacking any resources of its own, OMBE coordinated the activities of other federal agencies, including the Small Business Administration. SBA officials resented this arrangement because their agency provided most of the services to minority business but received little of the credit.[8]

The creation of the OMBE renewed congressional concern over a possible Commerce Department takeover of the SBA. On 5 March, Secretary Stans appeared before the National Press Club and stated that "by definition" the SBA belonged within his department. Stans's comment caused an uproar among congressional small business advocates. The Small Business Committees were jealous of any encroachment on the agency's responsibilities; they feared that the OMBE represented "an ever present danger to SBA's independence." The White House realized Congress would never allow a merger, but absent a presidential statement to the contrary, rumors of a takeover lingered through the end of Nixon's first term.[9]

The president hoped that the SBA would focus its attention on minority enterprise, but the agency was embroiled in one embarrassing incident after another. In March, Sandoval confirmed the reinstatement of Charles Kriger as Regional Director in New York. Howard Samuels had fired Kriger in late 1968 because he allegedly resisted making loans to minority-owned businesses. His dismissal angered Representative John J. Rooney (D-N.Y.), Kriger's mentor and chair of the House Appropriations subcommittee overseeing the SBA budget. Two days before Sandoval took office, Acting Administrator Howard Greenberg reinstated Kriger. Fearful of Rooney's wrath, Sandoval let the reinstatement stand, thus provoking criticism that the Nixon administration was not serious about minority enterprise.[10]

The Kriger fiasco coincided with revelations that the SBA had lent money to mobsters. During the early 1960s, Charles Kriger approved nearly $500,000 in loans to a company partly owned by the teenage son of "one of the country's most vicious loan sharks." In 1966, the Federal Bureau of Investigation (FBI) informed SBA officials of the "hoodlum domination" of the company, advising them not to take action until the investigation was complete. The public disclosure of these Mafia ties in March 1969 embarrassed the SBA, as critics accused the agency's New York office of being more generous toward mobsters than minorities.[11]

In response to these revelations, Hilary Sandoval instituted procedural reforms to screen out loan applicants with mob ties. SBA auditors uncovered two-dozen borrowers with underworld connections and turned their cases over to the Justice Department. Still, stories of Mafia influence continued to appear. In 1974, a *New York Times* investigation revealed that the New Orleans office had made loans to Mafia figures. An anonymous employee alleged that these mobsters had offered bribes to SBA loan officers. The mafiosi reportedly used SBA loans to finance their "front" businesses.[12] Unfortunately, the agency's decentralized field structure prevented the Central Office from detecting these abuses.

The mob scandal took place on Sandoval's watch, but he was not accountable for loans made in the past. However, he was responsible for selecting Albert Fuentes to be his special assistant. Fuentes, a Sandoval crony, used his influence within the SBA to secure a large loan for an El Paso firm. Fuentes and his partner, Eddie Montez, demanded company stock as compensation. In April 1969, the FBI launched a probe when the owner complained of extortion. Fuentes argued that he was only trying to help a minority enterprise, a defense that outraged Representative Henry Gonzalez (D-Tex.), who chided Fuentes for exploiting his "la raza" (race). Fuentes held press conferences denying his guilt and calling Gonzalez an "unmitigated liar." The resulting congressional outcry forced Sandoval to dismiss his troublesome aide on 20 May. Six months later, a jury convicted Fuentes and Montez of conspiracy.[13]

An angry challenge from black activists followed the Fuentes fiasco. The Black Advisory Council established by Howard Samuels included such notable figures as Ralph D. Abernathy, Whitney Young, Dick Gregory, Marion Barry, and Jackie Robinson. These African American leaders did not trust the Nixon administration to keep its commitment to "black capitalism." In late May, they asked to meet with Sandoval, but he refused, stating that the Council had been created "mainly for show purposes." Council members reacted by holding a press conference in the lobby of SBA headquarters to protest Sandoval's abrogation of their organization. A spokesperson for the group declared that the SBA was "the greatest menace" to the minority enterprise program, because Sandoval failed to follow through on Samuels' annual pledge of $500 million in minority loans. Marion Barry appeared dressed in African garb to demand Sandoval's resignation. This turn of events caused great distress to the White House. The head of the Urban Affairs Council, Daniel Patrick Moynihan, informed the president's advisers that Republican members of Congress were "up in arms on the whole SBA situation" and that the White House might have to take action soon to contain the damage.[14]

The White House was embarrassed again in July 1969 when the head of the SBA Office of Minority Entrepreneurship, Philip Pruitt, resigned, allegedly in protest of Nixon's refusal to approve the agency's request for $200 million in direct loans to minority businesses. Pruitt accused the president of offering "rhetoric, rhetoric, rhetoric, but no support." In truth, Pruitt was denied clearance by the Civil Service Commission. Moreover, during his six months in office, Pruitt faced unrelenting criticism from African American leaders. There were strong partisan overtones to their criticism. NAACP official Charles Evers asked Pruitt, "How could you as a black man sit in that [Nixon] administration?" Clearly, Democratic civil rights activists were not going to give Nixon the benefit of the doubt.[15]

Pruitt's fiery exit prompted White House intervention in SBA management. President Nixon sent Leonard Zartman to act as SBA General Counsel. Zartman had previously worked as minority affairs specialist for Daniel Patrick Moynihan. Nixon also appointed W. Donald Brewer, an aide to Maurice Stans, as Deputy Administrator and de facto head of the agency. Because the White House feared the political consequences of firing the highest-ranking Hispanic within the administration, Brewer and Zartman were to "run the shop" while Sandoval posed as a "front man." The organizational disarray at SBA continued, however, and in February 1970, presidential advisor John Ehrlichman called Sandoval to the White House and offered him the chair of the Cabinet Committee on Opportunities for Spanish-Speaking People. Sandoval, in turn, blasted Brewer for his "arrogance" and refused to step down. Brewer remained at SBA to keep an eye on Sandoval and to warn the White House whenever another "public atomic explosion" seemed imminent. He stayed at SBA until May 1970, when President Nixon rewarded him with a seat on the Interstate Commerce Commission (ICC).[16]

The Sandoval-Brewer feud created tremendous turmoil within the SBA. Agency employees had no idea who was in charge. One employee who received conflicting orders was asked by Brewer, "Are you working for Sandoval or me?" Brewer tried to reorganize the agency, but Sandoval countermanded his orders. In a final "Memorandum for the Record," Brewer noted that the Central Office had little control over the field and that the agency used an obsolete accounting system. "It is impossible," he wrote, "to determine the true condition of the very large loan portfolio at any time." Brewer further complained that Sandoval's "emotional and intransigent" behavior had frustrated his attempts at reform. Future administrators would have to deal with the legacies of this organizational chaos.[17]

During the fall of 1970, the White House grew alarmed at Sandoval's increasingly "irrational conduct." In November, presidential aide Tod R. Hullin relayed FBI reports of Sandoval's alleged "moral indiscretions." The SBA administrator allegedly had a love affair with a woman who was "a Cuban spy presently living in South Africa" and had carried on affairs with women while on official trips. Hullin also reported that when Sandoval's family was out of town, he would host "wild parties" that lasted up to three days (there is no evidence of any such report in Sandoval's FBI file).[18] The beleaguered administrator's medical problems worsened and aides had to read to him. Hullin concluded that "Mr. Sandoval presents a scandal potential that appears imminent and incapable of being matched by any other member of this Administration." SBA Deputy Administrator Einar Johnson and General Counsel Anthony Chase urged the White House to place Sandoval on administrative leave. On November 18, Sandoval tendered his resignation citing poor health. He died of a brain tumor three years later.[19]

Sandoval's tragic tenure as administrator was a painful one for supporters of the SBA. His incompetence and inexperience contributed to a comedy of errors that made headline news. Temperamentally, he was ill-suited for a position that required diplomatic relations with the Democratic majority in Congress. His paranoid style bred hostility and mistrust within the agency, and his recruitment of old El Paso cronies brought further embarrassment to the SBA.

But Sandoval was not responsible for all of the agency's problems. Previous administrators had made a virtue of decentralization by devolving authority to the field, but the lack of central control allowed abuses to occur, such as the making of loans to mobsters. Charles Kriger typified the politically well-connected regional director who ruled his own little fiefdom and was unaccountable to his official superiors. Sandoval's predecessors had also formed close relationships with black militants, who exploited the politics of racial grievance. No action taken by the SBA was enough to appease their insistent calls for massive aid to minority enterprise. There was a subtext of interracial conflict between the organized black leadership and the Mexican American administrator. Nixon's decision to broaden "black capitalism" to include other minorities antagonized civil rights activists who thought that he was depriving African Americans of their "piece of the action."

The ultimate blame for the Sandoval saga lay with the president. Nixon had demonstrated poor judgment in selecting Sandoval to head such a politically sensitive agency. The warning signs were apparent to Nixon's advisers, yet the president refused to consider their concerns over Sandoval's health and lack of leadership ability. Once in office, Nixon was reluctant to remove Sandoval, because he was sensitive to criticism from minority groups, who were already up in arms over Nixon's controversial nominations to the Supreme Court and his foot-dragging on desegregating southern schools.

Affirmative Action Controversy

The SBA did not stand still during this scandal-ridden period; the agency evolved in a difficult environment. As the economy slumped and inflation accelerated, the Federal Reserve attacked inflation with a "tight money" policy that restricted the credit available to business. The SBA served as a safety valve by expanding its business loan volume 30 percent in 1969–1970. The agency continued to increase its reliance on guaranteed loans, while cutting direct loans by two-thirds.[20]

Responding to presidential direction, the SBA made minority enterprise a top priority. In his first proposed budget, Nixon designated 40 percent of SBA business loans to minority business. The agency concentrated this assistance in urban areas, thus maintaining the ghetto focus of the 1960s. The Economic Opportunity Loan program, theoretically color-blind, became de facto race-based. This emphasis on minority-owned companies boosted their share of all business loan dollars to 23 percent, up from six percent just two years earlier. In contrast, lending to nonminority businesses declined through fiscal year 1970.[21]

The SBA also created new minority enterprise programs. Rather than wait for congressional direction, agency officials used their administrative discretion to institute innovative policies. Beginning in 1969, the SBA guaranteed surety bonds for minority contractors, although there was no express legislative authority to do so until the following year. Likewise, the Minority Enterprise Small Business Investment Company (MESBIC) program operated informally for three years before Congress authorized subsidies for SBICs specializing in "disadvantaged" businesses.[22]

The Section 8(a) program, still in its infancy, gained a big boost when the White House advocated increased use of minority set-asides. Budget Director George P. Schultz provided the SBA with additional funds to cover the difference between the competitive bids of nonminority firms and the higher bids of 8(a) companies. Later, beginning in fiscal year 1972, Congress appropriated money to subsidize 8(a) companies. Funds were limited, however, and procurement agencies often took a loss on 8(a) contracts, a concession that made the program unpopular with Department of Defense procurement officers.[23]

Nixon's minority enterprise program drew partisan lines of support and opposition. Conservative politicians, including James L. Buckley of New York and Governor Ronald Reagan of California, praised the "boot strap" approach taken by the SBA. Groups associated with the Republican Party—including the U.S. Chamber of Commerce and the National Business League (NBL)— also backed the president's preferential programs. Under "lifelong Republican" Berkeley Burrell, the NBL secured millions of dollars in OMBE grants and dramatically expanded the organization's operations. Meanwhile, the Congressional Black Caucus, made up entirely of Democrats, blasted the Nixon administration for doing too little for African American business.[24]

The honeymoon that "black capitalism" enjoyed during the 1968 campaign soon gave way to criticism from all sides. While praising Nixon for taking up the cause of black business, Berkeley Burrell lobbied for more aid.

African Americans needed special assistance, he argued, until the day that black and white business owners sat "across the table, millionaire to millionaire." Burrell beat the drum of racial grievance by calling the U.S. a "racist country" and advocating a "Marshall Plan" for minority businesses. Burrell also reiterated the NBL's longstanding complaint that the SBA neglected the more successful African American firms. Jackie Robinson, a one-time supporter of Nixon, testified that he was "scared" of a racial civil war developing if the SBA and OMBE did not increase spending on minority business. Black Democrats were even less charitable. Representative William Clay (D-Mo.), for example, likened the SBA to the KKK: "We know better than to apply for loans with the SBA just as we know better than to apply for membership in the KKK."[25]

Nixon's advisers were frustrated at the slow implementation of the minority enterprise initiative and the resulting criticism thus generated. Privately, they berated SBA officials for failing to "get their part of the show on the road" and for engaging in a protracted bureaucratic struggle with the OMBE. The anticipated public relation benefits never materialized; instead, the administration was repeatedly embarrassed when its predictions of success turned to failure. A typical letdown occurred in June 1970, when the White House had scheduled a ceremony to commemorate the creation of the 100th MESBIC, but discovered that there were only nine in operation.[26]

The Nixon administration anticipated criticism from black activists but downplayed the prospect of a white backlash against minority enterprise preferences. Stans predicted that there would be no "severe negative impact on the majority community, as is often the case with civil rights issues."[27] On the contrary, a fierce debate over "reverse discrimination" ensued in Congress, the courts, and in public discussion of race relations. In truth, the SBA had been practicing "reverse discrimination" since 1964, but the sixties riots had submerged questions of equity. The cessation of civil disorders and Nixon's high-profile attention to affirmative action brought this controversial issue to the surface.

The Congressional Small Business Committees protested that the SBA was discriminating against nonminority small business owners by denying them access to EOLs and Section 8(a) set-asides. With Republican members dissenting, the House Committee charged that 8(a) preferences possibly violated the Civil Rights Act of 1964 and the constitutional guarantee of equal protection. The Small Business Committees were responding to the outcry of businesspeople denied direct loans and set-asides on the basis of their race. Spokespersons for the National Federation of Independent Business (NFIB) opposed "compensatory discrimination" and argued for color-blindness in SBA programs. Furthermore, businessmen and women testified that "I went to

SBA for a loan and I was told I was the wrong color" and asserted that "you can't get a loan if you aren't black." This was an exaggeration—financially strong companies were eligible for guaranteed loans—but it is true that nearly all direct loans and 8(a) set-asides were reserved for minority businesses. Thus, the minority enterprise program redistributed agency resources away from some disadvantaged white firms.[28]

In congressional testimony, Sandoval walked a fine line between defending racial preferences and denying that they existed. He declared, "We are not discriminating because of color in either direction." Theoretically, all "minority" programs were open to "disadvantaged" business owners regardless of race. Thus, when asked for the definition of "disadvantage," Sandoval responded, "The term 'minority' is a short form for the phrase 'socially or economically disadvantaged.'" He went on to say that disadvantage was not based on such an "irrational classification" as race. Agency regulations, however, stated that "in many cases," members of the following groups were disadvantaged: "Black Americans; American Indians; Spanish-Americans; Oriental Americans; Eskimos and Aleuts."[29] In theory, poor whites were eligible for assistance, but in practice, agency officials conflated race and disadvantage.

The fallacy of equating skin color with disadvantage was evident in the case of Lou Brock, a well-paid African American baseball star who received a "minority" loan in 1969. Brock used the loan to open an auto dealership in East St. Louis, Illinois. When the news media reported on this loan, the SBA responded in a confused manner, initially admitting an error only later to defend its decision. The director of the St. Louis office said, "We are concerned about creating a black example here, and we're damned enthused about it." But Brock was unaware that his application was routed to the minority program. He commented that "if they made the loan just so they'd have a 'black example,' I think it was a terrible thing to do." Agency officials faced hostile questioning from members of Congress who thought Brock was not the "disadvantaged" business owner they had in mind, but the SBA stood its ground and allowed Brock to keep his loan.[30]

The Lou Brock case revealed the dissonant definitions of "disadvantage" used by the agency. Was "social" disadvantage based on skin color enough to qualify an applicant for aid? Or was "economic disadvantage" also required? Was the goal of the minority enterprise program to make a rich black man even richer in the hope that his success would inspire the poor? A few proponents of affirmative action rationalized that the government had enriched wealthy white men, and that minority millionaires might have been more successful if they, too, had benefited from corporate welfare. Yet such cynical reasoning undermined the legitimacy of a program clearly intended to aid the underprivileged. Furthermore, the awarding of contracts and loans to well-to-do individuals displaced the assistance available to entrepreneurs who were truly disadvantaged. The controversy over "disadvantage" added a new dimension to the agency's longstanding difficulty in defining its interest-group constituency. What was a "small" business? Who was "disadvantaged"? These issues continued to plague the agency throughout the 1970s and 1980s.

The commitment of manpower to the minority enterprise program reinforced affirmative action hiring within the agency. Sandoval stated, "I don't think anyone knows the problems of the Black-American . . . better than another Black-American, a soul brother. . . . I don't think anyone knows the problems of a Mexican-American . . . better than a Mexican-American, a *compadre*."[31] There was grumbling among African American employees that Hispanics had "jumped on the bandwagon" by taking advantage of the civil rights gains of the black community.[32] Nonetheless, this form of affirmative action proved less controversial than the preferences in contracting and lending, because it was less visible and did not negatively effect the interests of white business owners.

The SBA also helped the Nixon administration impose de facto quotas on government contractors. In retrospect, it seems ironic that a Republican president and his allies in Congress instituted employment "goals and timetables" over the opposition of congressional Democrats. But Nixon was predisposed to think along racial lines. According to historian John David Skrentny, Nixon was "obsessed with the idea of diversity. He kept track of the ethnicity and gender of *all* of his political appointments, to a degree of specificity that made many in government uncomfortable." Yet, in Nixon's mind, hiring "goals" and minority set-asides were not signs of big government, because they did not require the creation of large government bureaucracies.[33]

These hiring mandates did, however, require monitoring by the Equal Employment Opportunity Commission (EEOC) and other federal agencies. The SBA was responsible for supervising the civil rights compliance of small subcontractors, a task that proved nearly impossible given the frequency with which these companies came and went on construction projects. By 1975, the agency was monitoring firms with a total of 450,000 employees, second only to the Department of Defense. More important, the SBA routinized civil rights compliance among its own clients. In the past, the agency had surreptitiously gathered racial data by noting the physical appearance of loan applicants. But during the Nixon years, the SBA's Office of Equal Employment Opportunity and Compliance began to collect racial data by distributing a Form 707 to agency clients. A gross statistical disparity between a firm's minority employment and the minority share of the local labor market could trigger an on-site review. After examining recruitment sources, agency EEO officials recommended methods to increase the minority applicant pool. Occasionally, if

the firm was still "grossly deficient" in minority employment, the SBA negotiated voluntary "goals and timetables." In rare circumstances, the agency referred possible cases of discrimination to the EEOC.[34]

The SBA considered its methods highly successful and touted the supposed overrepresentation of minorities in client workforces. In its annual reports, the SBA claimed that ethnic minorities constituted 23 percent of the
employees of SBA borrowers. Despite the fact that these numbers were skewed
by the agency's concentration on cities with large minority populations, the
SBA continued to judge the success of its EEO program by citing similar
statistics. Like the federal civil rights agencies, the SBA had become number-
conscious.[35]

Yet the agency's small business mission tempered its approach to civil
rights compliance. The EEOC's mission was to place discriminatory employers in a negative light. The Commission had the power to impose fines and
punitive measures. In contrast, the SBA's mission was to help small businesses,
not "strong-arm" them. The SBA could not afford to alienate its constituency;
therefore, it exempted very small businesses (those with fewer than fifteen
employees) from the Form 707 paperwork requirement and stressed the business benefits of widening applicant pools. Agency officials cooperated with
small employers to make them aware of any "vulnerabilities" to EEOC discrimination complaints, but the primary emphasis was on outreach and education, an emphasis that continues to this day. Even if they had wished to
punish employers who hired few minorities, agency officials had few sanc-
tions available. The SBA could conceivably revoke a loan after a lengthy procedure, but a firm could pay off the loan and seek financial assistance in the
private sector.[36]

Racial issues remained controversial long after the departure of Hilary
Sandoval, who left behind problems for the SBA in other areas. His successor
found an agency suffering from an overload of responsibilities, with severe
deficiencies in management assistance, procurement, SBICs, and disaster lending. As a presidential election approached, SBA officials enjoyed a boom in
spending, followed by the worst series of scandals in the agency's history.

6

THE SMALL SCANDAL ADMINISTRATION

Following the Sandoval debacle, the SBA desperately needed competent leadership. Sandoval's successor, Thomas S. Kleppe, improved agency operations and presided over an election-year surge in spending that reflected the political cycle of agency growth. With presidential backing, the SBA also expanded its affirmative action programs over opposition from Congress. Yet the agency still suffered longstanding problems, including a disorganized bureaucracy and a decentralized field structure that produced several scandals.

The SBA's interest-group environment was also beginning to change. Historically, the agency and its congressional allies had failed to organize small business owners into a group with strong ties to the federal government. The small business community remained a voiceless, unorganized presence outside the Broker State. During the early 1970s, however, a growing grassroots movement of small businesspeople protested big government. The SBA remained a weak advocate for these disaffected business owners, thus creating a political vacuum soon filled by the emergence of an influential small business lobby.

Restructuring a Disorganized Agency, 1971–1972

After discharging Sandoval, President Nixon was concerned with rehabilitating "an important but faltering agency." The SBA's standing with Congress was at an all-time low. By appointing Thomas Kleppe SBA administrator, the White House hoped to ameliorate relations with the Small Business Committees. Kleppe was a former member of the House of Representatives, who was well liked on both sides of the aisle. The SBA post was Kleppe's reward for agreeing to run for the U.S. Senate in North Dakota, a race that he had lost in 1970. The "peppery" westerner was a colorful figure—a rodeo rider and self-made millionaire, who displayed six-shooters in his office. He believed in decentralized management, asserting, "I am a delegator. I trust." Unfortunately, several subordinates later betrayed that trust.[1]

Kleppe devoted his first two years to overhauling the SBA bureaucracy. He first established a task force to deal with the "duplication and administrative inefficiency" that he saw as the agency's number one problem. The task force reported that there was little coordination of the various SBA divisions. During the past ten years, SBA administrators, presidents, and Congress had dumped programs into the agency without fitting them into the existing organizational structure. "Questionable promotions" and a top-heavy incentive structure had hurt employee morale, as had excessive paperwork. Administrative operations were overstaffed and there were personnel shortages in other areas. Therefore, Kleppe shifted Central Office workers to the field and granted regional and district directors greater autonomy. The danger was that these field directors were "often as loyal to their district Congressman as to the agency."[2] This conflict of interest later erupted into a terrific scandal.

Kleppe also restructured management assistance by increasing the SBA's reliance on the private sector. In 1970, the agency signed agreements with four professional associations to provide counseling to small businesses. Two years later, Kleppe established the Small Business Institute (SBI), a consortium of universities empowering business students to act as consultants to troubled firms. The SBA paid the colleges several hundred dollars for each successful case, while students received academic credit and real-world training. The SBI was an immediate success. By 1975, there were 400 colleges and 20,000 students assisting 8,000 business owners at a cost of only two million dollars.[3]

SBI represented a creative approach to the management "gap"; however, the mainstay of management assistance, the Service Corps of Retired Executives (SCORE), faced an organizational crisis. In 1971, President Nixon transferred all volunteer services—including SCORE—to the American Committee to Improve Our Neighborhood (ACTION). SCORE now served two masters; ACTION reimbursed SCORE for expenses, while SBA set policy. SCORE was the only business-oriented service under ACTION, which treated the organization ungenerously—first by denying it adequate funds, and then urging the retired executives to focus exclusively on the inner-city. Meanwhile, the SBA directed the volunteers to give up management counseling and collect the agency's bad loans. SCORE membership declined as volunteers refused to deal with "deadbeats." The SBA learned its lesson. In 1973, Kleppe returned SCORE to the Office of Management Assistance; and two years later, President Gerald Ford gave the SBA sole control of SCORE. Nevertheless, the crisis prompted SCORE officials to establish a separate organization. In 1971, they created the SCORE Council; four years later, SCORE incorporated as a nonprofit association. These moves reflected the growing independence of SCORE, because despite the lip service given to the importance of management assistance, the SBA offered little support and leadership.[4]

The SBA also failed to provide steadfast supervision of the SBIC industry. Agency funding was erratic, and turnover was a problem; the SBIC division had had twelve administrators in twelve years. The chairman of the National SBIC Advisory Committee complained that "we have all too often felt like yo-yos at the end of SBA's string." Rather than deal with fundamental problems, SBA and Congress responded in time-honored fashion by increasing the public debt available to investors. But throwing low-interest money at SBICs did more harm than good. The investment companies parked much of their capital in interest-earning accounts rather than invest it in high-risk ventures. They underperformed the broader stock market and posted substantially negative returns on their capital. Furthermore, SBICs continued to violate SBA regulations in near-record numbers. The miserable performance of the past fifteen years led the Small Business Committees to question whether the whole enterprise was worth it.[5]

The procurement program posed another perennial problem: how could the SBA boost the small-business share of contract awards when the Department of Defense (DOD) viewed the agency as a detriment to efficient procurement practices? The SBA could not coerce the DOD, nor could it change the procurement mix. The agency's Procurement Center Representatives, who barely numbered forty, matched small firms with appropriate contracts, recommended set-asides, and encouraged procurement officers to break up large orders so that small companies could compete. Yet policymakers never established a yardstick for success. Since 1947, Congress had resolved that small business was entitled to a "fair proportion" of procurement dollars but never defined what this meant. Members of Congress occasionally expressed adherence to rigid proportionalism—small firms should receive the same share of government dollars that they received in the private sector. This focus on aggregate statistics obscured the inflated set-asides used in some industries ("over 90 percent" of clothing purchases) and the minuscule share set aside in others (as low as one percent). However, in sharp contrast to the furor evoked by racial preferences, there was no debate over small business set-asides. SBA officials rarely voiced concern that small firms were too dependent on government. The universal admiration of small business muffled qualms about the equity or effectiveness of these affirmative action programs.[6]

The first two years of Kleppe's administration produced a mixed record. The Small Business Institute was an important innovation, but SCORE suffered through an ill-advised reorganization. There were no improvements in the SBIC or procurement divisions. Agency personnel were stretched thin over an ever-growing array of programs. On the other hand, employee morale recovered under Kleppe's confident leadership, and the SBA maintained good relations with Congress. The agency also enjoyed the support of a president up for reelection. Partisan presidential politics contributed to the enormous growth of SBA lending in 1972. However, once elected, Nixon reversed course and imposed fiscal restraint.

The 1972 Election

Perhaps more than any other president in the twentieth century, Richard Nixon cynically manipulated the economy in pursuit of short-term electoral gain. In 1971, he imposed wage-price controls to subdue inflation. Then, in the first half of 1972, Nixon reversed his fiscal policies to boom the economy in time for the election. According to economic adviser Herbert Stein, the president urged all government agencies to "get out and spend." The SBA profited from this fiscal ease; in 1972, the business loan volume increased 50 percent, hitting a record $2 billion. The agency made an additional $1.2 billion in disaster loans, largely in response to Hurricane Agnes. During the campaign, Nixon touted this increased spending. The president's policies seemed to work—the economy enjoyed growth and price stability—and the voters rewarded Nixon with a landslide victory over George McGovern.[7]

The president's proclivity for spending did not last beyond election day. In 1973, Nixon became a born-again fiscal conservative. He responded to a widening budget deficit by vetoing appropriation bills and impounding funds authorized by Congress. The president's policy reversal affected SBA operations. The agency significantly reduced its lending volume; by fiscal year 1975, business lending was down 25 percent. The SBA did not attain its 1972 peak again until the Carter years.[8]

Nixon's austerity measures included a major reform of the SBA's disaster loan program. The huge expense of Hurricane Agnes highlighted the need for cost savings. The SBA typically forgave the loans of needy disaster victims. In 1969, Congress granted "forgiveness" of the first $1,800 of a disaster loan. In the aftermath of Agnes, however, President Nixon approved a politically popular bill that increased the "forgiveness" amount to $5,000 and eliminated the means test. This change cost the government over $500 million in disaster grants during 1972–1973. But, after the election, when Congress passed a similar bill, Nixon vetoed it. Congress then enacted legislation requiring homeowners and businesses in flood zones to purchase subsidized insurance.[9]

Neither the president nor Congress addressed the most serious structural problem with disaster lending—the unpredictable diversion of agency personnel. The progressive liberalization of disaster aid made the program a huge potential drain on agency resources (in 1973, the SBA approved 215,000 disaster loans, *seven times* the number of business loans). SBA administrators and the Small Business Committees agreed that the program belonged in the Department of Housing and Urban Development (HUD) or in a new disaster-aid agency. Nonetheless, Congress never mustered the will to transfer the program out of SBA.[10]

The Scandals of 1973

The battle over disaster aid was a trifle compared with the scandals of 1973. During the Watergate committee hearings, Democrats charged that the White House had pressured government agencies to place contracts with companies that contributed to the Committee to Reelect the President (CREEP). The Office of Minority Business Enterprise (OMBE) raised campaign funds and awarded questionable grants to prominent African American entrepreneurs. SBA officials denied that they succumbed to similar pressure and investigators failed to prove a corrupt relationship between CREEP and the agency.[11]

The SBA did not emerge unscathed from the Watergate-era congressional investigations. In the fall of 1973, a House Subcommittee on Small Business announced a series of shocking revelations of improper White House intervention in agency affairs and internal administrative corruption. The stench of scandal led a few members of Congress to call for the abolition of the SBA, but cooler heads prevailed; the scandals did not affect the agency's bottom line. Fearful of hurting small business, Congress treated the agency with kid gloves.

The lead investigator for the House subcommittee, Curtis Prins, uncovered evidence that the White House and the SBA under Sandoval had helped black businesspeople with criminal records. The White House had ordered the Internal Revenue Service and the SBA to back off their investigation of Thomas W. Matthew, a prominent African American businessman and supporter of the president. Nixon pardoned Matthew in 1969, shortly after a jury convicted him of income tax evasion. Despite his criminal record, the SBA and other federal agencies had awarded him $1.2 million in loans, grants, and contracts. He was later caught misusing SBA loans. An agency auditor recommended prosecuting Matthew for theft of federal funds, but wrote that the White House wanted to avoid embarrassing the president. This was not the first time the White House had intervened on behalf of a convicted black business owner; in 1969, the SBA informed presidential aide Robert J. Brown that S.B. Fuller, earlier convicted of violating the securities law, was involved in another "SEC proceeding." Brown offered White House assistance for Fuller, whom he described as "a leading black businessman and a long-time Republican."[12]

The SBA also tried unsuccessfully to rescue failing minority enterprises. African American entrepreneur J. Wallace Gaines had defaulted on $50,000 in SBA loans and lied about the financial status of his business; nevertheless, he received $800,000 in Section 8(a) contracts. Gaines's business folded after completing only one-third of its contract work. The White House and the SBA also came to the aid of the Watts Manufacturing Company, a highly publicized firm established in the aftermath of the Watts riot. The company hired the hard-core unemployed but was a business disaster. From 1966 to 1976, when the company filed for bankruptcy, it depended almost entirely on government contracts. The Nixon administration secured millions of dollars in Section 8(a) contracts to keep the company alive. The president's chief domestic advisor, John Ehrlichman, was skeptical. "The whole intention of black capitalism," he wrote, "is to put the black man into competition with the white on equal ground. The program will never be successful if the Federal Government must always provide a backstop." But the viewpoint of presidential aide Leonard Zartman prevailed. Zartman argued that "this experiment in minority business enterprise has had too much visibility to fail."[13]

These abuses resulted from institutionalized favoritism toward certain racial groups. Double standards in the distribution of government assistance produced double standards in law enforcement and the administration of this politically sensitive program. It is tempting to lay the blame on a corrupt presidency, but the abuses continued long after Nixon resigned. These cases demonstrated another problem with the minority enterprise program—the tendency to bail out unsuccessful firms. Political pressures subverted the ultimate goal of the program, which was to make these companies competitive in the open market.

The SBA was further embarrassed when the House subcommittee reported that the head of the minority enterprise program, Arthur McZier, served as director of a Bahamian bank controlled by Robert Vesco, a fugitive financier and major contributor to Nixon's reelection campaign. In 1972, the SEC charged Vesco with misappropriating $200 million from his mutual funds, and he fled to Costa Rica. During this time, McZier served as a Vesco director, before resigning his SBA post to become a full-time bank official. McZier's directorship was legal yet reflected badly on an agency that was enduring one scandal after another.[14]

The worst scandal yet rocked the agency in December 1973, when the subcommittee disclosed that Philadelphia regional director Russell Hamilton was under investigation for allegedly taking kickbacks. Six months earlier, Deputy Administrator Louis Laun had given Hamilton the option of resigning or being fired. Faced with imminent dismissal, Hamilton launched countercharges claiming that he was the victim of a mob conspiracy involving

Kleppe, the "Godfather of the Virgin Islands" and "people higher up in Government." FBI investigators debunked this conspiracy theory by confirming that Kleppe had never traveled to the Virgin Islands.[15]

Hamilton tried to further distract the Central Office by charging that the corruption in the Richmond, Virginia, district was "so wild nobody would believe it." This revelation stunned the agency. The district director, Thomas Regan, was a star employee. An investigator said that Regan was "one of the most loyal, dedicated, government people I've ever come across. Everybody loved him." But Regan operated in an intensely political environment. He described his job as one of befriending "all the politicos in the state. . . . That way, if there was any political need it would come through me." The close ties between local SBA officials, bankers, and politicians gave the appearance of a "fraternity chapter." Regan took advantage of these ties by borrowing money from banks that had dealings with his office. Regan also approved $11 million in loans to companies owned by his brother-in-law who, in turn, lent him $300,000. The House subcommittee further alleged that Regan associated with Mafia figures and that he made bad loans to individuals recommended by the White House.[16]

Kleppe took decisive action, but the damage to the agency's reputation was already done. He fired Hamilton and Regan in December 1973. A court convicted Hamilton and his chief deputy of accepting kickbacks. A jury found Regan guilty of fraud, racketeering, and bribery, and he and several of his associates received lengthy prison terms. However, the scandal continued to spread as the House subcommittee, the FBI, and the General Accounting Office (GAO) investigated twenty-two other district offices. These investigations resulted in the conviction of seventeen borrowers and five SBA employees. Kleppe contended that there were "no more Richmonds," and further investigation uncovered no new criminal cases. Yet the Milwaukee office had received an official reprimand for throwing "wild parties" and displaying a "lack of common business etiquette . . . lack of self-discipline . . . lack of quality work effort." One Milwaukee loan officer openly defied his superiors by making bad loans to meet his quotas. The committee also uncovered the widespread practice of "bank bailouts" by which banks arranged to have delinquent borrowers refinance with SBA loans. Agency financial officers allegedly looked the other way because these loans helped to meet their quotas. SBA headquarters clearly lacked control of the regional and district offices. The agency's decentralized field structure had taken on a life of its own.[17]

The unrestrained growth of the Nixon years fostered these abuses. Monthly loan quotas encouraged SBA employees to emphasize volume, regardless of the quality or legality of the loan applications. A former official later recalled that the word was to "go out and scare up as many loans as you can. If they're bad, don't worry. . . . whatever sticks to the wall [as a sound loan] is a bonus." Auditing controls were weak, and the agency lacked the personnel needed to monitor the fast-growing loan portfolio. Yet these scandals still had a certain beneficial effect—the institution of regular field audits and an increase in Security and Investigation staff. Furthermore, to prevent conflicts of interest, Kleppe and Laun created new district offices to replace those operated by Regional Offices in their home states.[18]

In August 1974, the SBA received another blow to its already sullied reputation when the Civil Service Commission (CSC) admonished the agency for making politically motivated appointments of district directors. The CSC did not charge Kleppe with wrongdoing but asserted that under his administration "political interests were allowed to influence appointments in a style that approximates a patronage system." The decentralization of the SBA meant that field officers made many of these appointments; the Central Office had little control over the hiring process.[19]

The events of 1973–1974 earned the agency a reputation as the "Small Scandal Administration." Representative Frank Annunzio (D-Ill.) stated that "prior to these hearings . . . I had always thought the initials SBA stood for the Small Business Administration. But now I believe that the initials stand for 'Superior Bagman Agency.'" Representative Ed Koch (D-N.Y.) quipped, "SBA sounds terrific, right? Always find a good name for a program, and it does not make any difference what is beneath the good name." And Senator William Proxmire (D-Wis.) included the SBA on a list of "useless agencies" that Congress should eliminate. As a consequence, Kleppe was left pleading, "It's just not true that we're all a bunch of crooks, a bunch of outlaws."[20]

Yet the scandals had surprisingly little effect on congressional relations. The subcommittee investigation merely delayed by six months the passage of a bill increasing the SBA's lending authority from $4.3 billion to $6 billion. At first glance, the congressional reaction is puzzling. Why, despite years of scandal, were critics such as William Proxmire unable to exploit these episodes of corruption? The literature on political scandal suggests that government agencies are relatively immune from punitive budget cuts when the affected constituency is considered "deserving" of continued assistance. And, indeed, Congress was unwilling to punish the small business community for the sins of the SBA.[21]

The Firestorm over Minority Enterprise

Meanwhile, the SBA's minority enterprise program grew ever more controversial. Congressional critics cried "reverse discrimination" and tried to legislate race-neutrality into programs targeted at the "disadvantaged." Supporters claimed that the programs were technically color-blind and therefore immune from constitutional challenge. This debate pitted a Republican president against congressional Democrats who opposed racial preferences. The Nixon years ended with no final resolution of this debate. It was evident, however, that the programs were doing a poor job of preparing minority firms for the real world of business.

Kleppe's inauguration coincided with a presidential drive to beef up the minority enterprise program. Nixon deposited government funds in minority banks in the hope that they would finance minority businesses. He also pressed the SBA to act more aggressively. Economic Opportunity Loans (EOLs) became less important as the SBA emphasized 8(a) set-asides, a program that did not require congressional approval. Loans to minority firms leveled off at $300 million in 1972–1973, then declined for the next several years. Section 8(a) contract dollars, on the other hand, steadily increased from $68 million to $272 million (fiscal year 1971–1974).[22]

Through his commitment to minority enterprise, President Nixon sought to build his civil rights credentials. Yet many African American critics argued that his minority enterprise agenda was insufficient. The Congressional Black Caucus (CBC) demanded a one-billion-dollar development bank, a proposal that Nixon rejected. Minority business owners also criticized the SBA for its "frighteningly inadequate" commitment of resources. The chief problem, according to these critics, was that the SBA had a conflict of interest in serving both minority and nonminority businesses. As such, the agency was forced into the unenviable position of having to take contracts away from small white-owned businesses.[23]

The SBA was caught in the crossfire between those who maintained it was doing too little and those who asserted it was doing too much. The Small Business Committees, with Republican members dissenting, complained that the agency was diverting loans, contracts, and personnel away from traditional programs to the minority enterprise division (the Republicans defended the president's program, citing racial inequalities in business ownership). Kleppe boasted that "we put about 11 times as much energy and personnel into helping the average minority or disadvantaged firm as we do in helping the average majority firm." But, the committees argued, the results were anything but positive. The EOL loss rate was 35 percent, more than ten times the loss rate on regular business loans. Furthermore, the SBA awarded millions of dollars in grants to management consultants and assigned them to minority firms that were failing rather than those with a realistic chance of success.[24]

The committees reserved their harshest criticism for the Section 8(a) program. The goal of 8(a) was to make firms competitive so that they would no longer need no-bid subsidized contracts. Participants were supposed to "graduate" within approximately three years, but there were no formal guide-lines, and only a tiny percentage ever graduated. Most 8(a) companies were not viable, because the program did not require them to compete. The few successful companies denied that they were doing well so that they could retain their government benefits. In addition, SBA officials were too busy managing the high volume of 8(a) contracts to supervise the progress of individual firms. There were other problems with the program as well. Section 8(a) was a "people-eater" that drained agency personnel from other assignments. A few 8(a) firms received the bulk of contract dollars, while others received nothing. The biggest losers were nonminority firms who lost contracts. Some of these companies survived by nominally transferring ownership to black "fronts"; others employed "fronts" to exploit the opportunity for no-bid contracts. Upon discovering that many 8(a) companies were in fact "fronts," Kleppe issued requirements that "*actual ownership* and *control* must be in the hands of the eligible minority" (italics in original), but it was difficult to prove that a black-white partnership was fraudulent.[25]

Racial discrimination was the fundamental issue raised by congressional critics. Nixon argued that white business owners shared in the overall growth of SBA business loans; therefore, they were not losing out to minority firms. But opponents considered racial distinctions odious and constitutionally suspect. The president's own Advisory Council on Minority Enterprise concluded that preferences might violate the 14th Amendment's guarantee of equal protection. The council emphasized a class-based approach to deal with the "economic insecurity of blue collar and lower-middle income whites" as well as ethnic minorities. Similarly, the Small Business Committees urged the SBA to assist disadvantaged businesses, regardless of race.[26]

Legal challenges to 8(a) led SBA administrators to declare the official color-blindness of the program, yet they admitted that only a few disadvantaged whites participated and that most of the set-asides were contracts previously awarded to small white-owned businesses. Section 8(a) officials failed to enforce regulations ensuring that current contractors were not "significantly affected adversely." Congressional hearings exposed the Orwellian rhetoric of affirmative action, as Thomas Kleppe offered evasive definitions of "disadvantage." He stated that skin color automatically qualified minorities as "disadvantaged," but that "no American is included or excluded . . . because of such an irrational classification." Kleppe cited examples of white Appalachians who might qualify as "socially and economically disadvantaged," yet remarked that, in fact, most disadvantaged individuals were minorities. In 1973, the GAO criticized the SBA for failing to develop clear eligibility requirements, but it was this vagueness that allowed the program to survive court challenges.[27]

Proponents of color-blindness confronted a race-conscious president in

1972, when Congress debated an administration bill granting the MESBIC program statutory authority. White House aides thought they were "in the favored strategic position of having proposed something to greatly help minorities which Congress flatly refuses to act upon." Democrats charged that the MESBIC program violated the Civil Rights Act and secured an amendment eliminating the word "minority" from its title. Nevertheless, the SBA continued to limit the program to racial minorities.[28]

By any measure, the various minority enterprise programs were abysmal failures. The MESBICs were small and highly leveraged; they invested most of their capital in cash and government securities. And by 1976, their net losses exceeded 50 percent of their revenue. Furthermore, minority banks invested federal deposits in government debt instead of minority enterprises. Studies by economist Timothy Bates demonstrated that SBA loans to black businesses benefited some middle-class borrowers, but lower-income blacks were left worse off. It seemed apparent that the SBA based its minority lending decisions on short-term liquidity rather than the experience and credit rating of a company. Bates concluded that the agency operated "with a time horizon which would be appropriate for a loan shark." Moreover, the 8(a) program not only failed to graduate competitive firms, it hampered government procurement. In 1973, two-thirds of the 8(a) companies were delinquent in fulfilling their contracts.[29]

The SBA and "New" Regulation

The excessive attention paid to minority enterprise concealed the emergence of an issue that soon transformed the politics of small business: the growing threat of big government. The Nixon years witnessed tremendous growth in government regulation of health, safety, and the environment. Unlike the industry-specific regulation of the New Deal era, this "new" regulation encompassed the entire economy. There was a loud outcry among small business owners complaining of the paperwork, time, and costs associated with "asinine" regulations. For example, a furniture shop owner said, "OSHA [the Occupational Safety and Health Administration] worries the hell out of me. . . . Did you know we've even got to paint the electrical outlets orange?" The Small Business Committees were sympathetic; they held hearings and authorized the SBA to make "economic injury" loans to help firms comply with the new requirements.[30]

The SBA responded slowly to the problem of overregulation. In 1970, the agency did not even testify before committees considering the Occupational Safety and Health Act. The SBA's post-hoc policies were equally inadequate. In 1974, the House Small Business Committee criticized the agency for making fewer than eighty economic injury loans. Although the SBA placed a high priority on minority enterprise, the agency failed to challenge regulations that effectively excluded minority firms from certain industries (e.g., the Interstate Commerce Commission sanctioned a cartel that barred small and minority firms from entering trucking). In 1974, Congress created a Chief Counsel for Advocacy to serve as an ombudsman for small business owners. But it remained an open question whether this new office would help the SBA live up to its self-appointed title as "Court of Last Resort" for small business.[31]

The SBA was a weak advocate partly because it felt no pressure from a strong interest group of small business owners. The National Federation of Independent Business (NFIB) was the largest small business association, but autocratic founder C. Wilson Harder dominated the group from its establishment in 1943 until his death in 1968. Members of Congress did not take the NFIB seriously.[32] But this changed in the mid-1970s as the NFIB, under new leadership, exploited widespread disaffection with big government. By the end of the decade, NFIB emerged as one of the most powerful lobbies in Washington.

Conclusion

This study of the SBA confirms the revisionist interpretation of Nixon as an "agent of change."[33] Contemporary opponents, blinded by their hatred of Nixon, failed to recognize the activist nature of his domestic agenda. Nixon was a "liberal spender" who dramatically expanded many domestic programs.[34] Motivated by partisan politics and his own presidential agenda, Nixon vied with Congress to spend more on small business. He also overcame stiff congressional opposition to racial preferences and thereby laid the foundation for modern forms of affirmative action. But Nixon left a legacy of political corruption that undermined the operation and reputation of agencies such as the SBA.

During the Nixon years, the SBA institutionalized unethical behavior in its administration of the minority enterprise program. Flagrant insubordination to the will of Congress and the open violation of agency regulations constituted a breach of professional norms. As Joseph Zimmerman notes in his *Curbing Unethical Behavior in Government*, it has become more difficult to restrain administrative agencies as the government has grown.[35] Even with congressional oversight, agency heads enjoy considerable independence. But by misusing their authority, SBA administrators undermined their credibility and reputation for fairness. Their prevaricating language belied racially discriminatory practices, which the agency could not openly defend.

The Richmond scandal highlighted the organizational weaknesses of the SBA bureaucracy. The agency's decentralized field structure rendered it vulnerable to corrupting influences. Furthermore, the tremendous growth of the SBA outstripped the Central Office's ability to supervise operations in the field. Yet, despite its operational shortcomings, the SBA remained popular with members of Congress who exploited the responsiveness of the field offices.

Essentially, in the case of the SBA, a fragmented bureaucratic structure produced an incoherent organizational culture. Management experts define "organizational culture" as a sense of community based on "shared meanings and shared values." Strong cultures inculcate "basic assumptions and beliefs" thereby fostering a consensus on the "core mission" of the organization.[36] But rapid growth, erratic leadership, and disparate program objectives prevented the SBA from developing a unified organizational culture. Lending officers and SBIC officials reflected a "banker's mentality," while minority enterprise officials—increasingly drawn from the ranks of civil rights activists—responded to the activism of their political environment. The agency's procurement specialists were retired military officers who viewed their unit as the "stepchild" of the SBA; thus, they tended to "circle the wagons" and remove themselves from the "SBA family." Likewise, management assistance officers were cloistered "academic types" who wrote agency pamphlets but had little contact with the small business community or the rest of the agency. The agency's organization along separate program lines further reinforced parochialism among the various divisions.[37] In short, the SBA contained multiple, sometimes conflicting, subcultures.

For most of its history, the SBA operated in an interest-group vacuum; small business owners remained aloof from the federal government. During the 1970s, however, organizational activity among small business owners finally took off in reaction against big government. The government's inability to deal with the severe recession of 1973–1974, coupled with the recent proliferation of regulation, fueled small business activism in the second half of the 1970s. Thus, the Ford and Carter years witnessed the rise of a powerful small business lobby supported by renewed public concern for small enterprise and growing popular disenchantment with big government. Paradoxically, the SBA continued to grow in this anti-statist environment, despite its weak advocacy of small business interests.

SMALL BUSINESS IN AN AGE
OF BIG GOVERNMENT

During the 1970s, government agencies poured forth regulations affecting nearly every aspect of business. The perceived threat of big government galvanized small business owners and fueled the rise of an influential interest group led by the National Federation of Independent Business. However, the SBA was a weak advocate for small business, largely because of its position within the executive branch. On several important issues, the SBA allied with the president against small business interests. Consequently, the agency gathered little support from the small business lobby in Washington.

This period was critical for the development of the SBA's affirmative action policies as Congress placed minority set-asides on firmer legal footing. Nevertheless, the issue remained controversial. New groups demanded "disadvantaged" status, while critics charged the SBA with "reverse discrimination." By adding disaster-struck farmers to the agency's lengthy list of constituencies, Congress made it even more difficult for the SBA to represent such a conglomeration of interest groups. The agency entered the 1980s bigger than ever, plagued with administrative problems and vulnerable to attack by a budget-cutting president.

The Ford Years, 1974–1976

On 9 August 1974, President Richard M. Nixon resigned to avoid impeachment by the House of Representatives on charges related to the Watergate affair. His successor, Gerald R. Ford, inherited an economy suffering "stagflation"—high inflation and unemployment coupled with negative growth.[1] Ford's economic policies initially derived from his economic conservatism. In the end, however, political considerations caused Ford to reverse his policy of restraint.

As a member of the House of Representatives, Ford had built a record of "consistent conservatism," voting against social welfare legislation, including the War on Poverty and Medicare. The fiscally conservative president initially accepted the theory that government deficits were responsible for both inflation and unemployment; therefore, he asked Congress to cut spending. A deadlock ensued as Congress passed spending measures that Ford vetoed.[2] However, the president could moderate discretionary spending of some government agencies, including the Small Business Administration.

Reflecting his overall philosophy of resisting special interests, Ford maintained that his macroeconomic policies benefited small business more than SBA spending. Officials at the Office of Management and Budget (OMB) shared Ford's fiscal conservatism. Not only did they repeatedly deny Thomas Kleppe's requests for up to one billion dollars in direct loans, but they considered direct loans an unwarranted interference in the financial markets.[3] The General Accounting Office (GAO) undermined the SBA's case for a budget increase by publishing reports critical of agency programs, including 7(a) loan guarantees, which suffered from adverse selection and a high delinquency rate.[4] Ultimately, SBA lending activity declined substantially in fiscal year 1975, due to Ford's austerity measures, a sluggish economy, and interest-rate ceilings that made SBA loans unattractive to banks.[5]

President Ford continued Nixon's affirmative action policies. Section 8(a) awards increased as the SBA relied heavily upon this off-budget measure. Yet maintaining the status quo pleased no one. Advocates of affirmative action demanded more assistance, and opponents cited a GAO report concluding that SBA had achieved "minimal" success in making 8(a) firms self-sufficient. The report also showed that agency officials were violating the race-neutral eligibility requirements. Remarkably, in its response to the GAO, the SBA maintained the fiction of a color-blind program and noted the danger of identifying "disadvantage" with racial status: "this principle could have sweeping implications through the social order. There might also be administrative problems in applying a purely racial or ethnic standard. Would a person who is one-quarter Indian be eligible? One-sixteenth? How is racial background proven? Who is a Spanish-speaking American?" All of these were good questions that the agency, in practice, ignored on a daily basis.[6]

As the presidential election of 1976 approached, White House aides feared Ford was losing support among small business owners. Consequently, Ford repeated the political cycle of agency growth by reversing his stringent fiscal policy and requesting a one-third increase in SBA loan guarantees. He also directed federal agencies "to pull out all stops" to help minority business. In February 1976, Ford appointed a new administrator, Mitchell Kobelinski, to replace Thomas Kleppe, whom Ford had named Secretary of Interior. Ford's selection of Kobelinski reflected his election-year concerns; he hoped that this prominent Chicago banker would attract Polish American votes.[7]

Ford's opponent, Democratic presidential candidate Jimmy Carter, also reached out to the small business voter by promising to "get the government off his back." Carter stressed his small business background and repeatedly announced that "if elected, I will be the first small-business man since Harry Truman to serve as President." Moreover, early in his business career, Carter had received an SBA loan, leading an agency administrator to later claim that without this assistance, Carter "would not have made it to become President."[8]

The Carter Years

Carter's interest in small business proved fleeting, partly because the incoming administration lacked confidence in the Small Business Administration. A transition team report noted the agency's "'cry-baby' and 'loser'" reputation, viewing the SBA as a "hostage to Congress" and a "necessary nuisance" to the executive branch. Management assistance, the team said, was "window-dressing busy-work that don't [sic] really help anyone." Furthermore, the Office of Advocacy was "run by lightweights and political appointees." Minority and nonminority business owners were bitterly divided over the 8(a) program. What the SBA needed, the team wrote, was a "Presidential 2X4 across the balky Federal bureaucracy's forehead to get—and keep—its attention." The team suggested that the president consider elevating SBA to the Cabinet or merging it with the Commerce Department (Secretary of Commerce Juanita Kreps requested the immediate transfer of SBA, but the White House decided that this was politically inopportune). Finally, the team advised the president to "get off to a flying start" by emphasizing small business issues during the first one hundred days of his term. Nevertheless, Carter paid scant attention to small business during his first three years in office, making only a few symbolic gestures, such as supporting a White House Conference scheduled for 1980. Other issues—including a "stagflationary" economy and foreign policy setbacks—crowded out any concern with small business.[9]

Carter's choice for SBA administrator was A. Vernon Weaver, a Naval Academy classmate, banker, and insurance executive from Arkansas, who was a friend of Budget Director Bert Lance.[10] Weaver's first priority was to make SBA loans more attractive to borrowers and banks. The chief gripe of loan applicants was the long delay in processing—nearly four months from application to disbursement. Bankers complained of excessive paperwork, which discouraged many from making SBA loans. The agency simplified application forms and established a pilot Bank Certification Program authorizing banks with "excellent 'track records'" to handle all the paperwork, subject to an SBA audit. The agency also eased restrictions on loan purposes and liberalized interest rates.[11]

These improvements did not assuage critics of the SBA, who noted that the Central Office had little control over the regional "fiefdoms." Agency politicos continued to base personnel decisions on party affiliation. It was also clear that the SBA had too many responsibilities ("more functions than a Swiss Army knife") and not enough employees to handle them. In addition, understaffing and failure to follow procedures resulted in "unsound loans." SCORE officials needed training in volunteer management, but SBA employees treated them as "second class citizens."[12] Furthermore, the SBA's disaster program diverted personnel away from lending and management, a problem that the Office of Personnel Management finally corrected in 1980 by authorizing the SBA to create a "cadre" of permanent disaster specialists.[13]

Most important, the SBA failed in its most basic task—defining "small" business. In a 1977 report entitled *What is a Small Business?*, the Office of Advocacy concluded that the agency had no clear idea. "Instead of focusing on competition," the report stated, the SBA "incorporated five different units of measurement into eight different definitions of a small business. Little wonder that the SBA has had considerable difficulty in conveying to the Congress and to the public, just what is meant by 'small business.'" In a follow-up study, the GAO concluded that the size standards favored mid-sized firms at the expense of smaller ones. The Senate Small Business Committee asked, "how can either SBA or the Congress determine whether the agency's programs are effective" when the SBA could not define who it was supposed to help? In response, the SBA proposed new size standards based on industry concentration, but strong opposition from vested interests prevented implementation of an economically rational plan.[14] Finally, in 1984, the SBA accepted the existing size standards based on "custom and general acceptance," while establishing criteria that applied only to future modifications. Significantly, nearly all of these modifications resulted in higher size standards; lowering standards was almost unthinkable.[15]

However, Congress was to blame for many of the SBA's problems, including understaffing and the inclusion of programs outside the agency's expertise. The disaster loan program, for example, became a major fiasco when Congress admitted farmers and lowered the interest rate on loans to 3 percent (previously, farmers were eligible only for Agriculture Department loans, which were less generous and more difficult to obtain). Farm disaster aid skyrocketed when a summer drought hit large sections of the country in 1977, with disaster loans growing from an estimated $750 million to over $3 billion. Abuses were rampant; prosperous farmers borrowed money to purchase Certificates of Deposit. Further adding to these problems was the fact that SBA employees were ill-equipped to judge the losses from crop failures. Vernon Weaver asked Congress to relieve the SBA of this unwanted burden. But the political temptation to provide benefits to constituents was strong. In 1985, Congress sacrificed the farm program only when confronted with a Reagan administration trying to abolish the SBA (see chapter 8).[16]

In sum, during the Carter years the SBA achieved modest administrative improvements by certifying lenders and establishing disaster "cadres." These successes were offset by persistent problems in management assistance and lending. Loan loss rates continued to increase, and SCORE remained an orphan within the SBA family. The farm aid program offered a prime example of Congress's predilection for dumping projects in the SBA that were unrelated to the agency's core mission. Meanwhile, the president and Congress lent official approval to the SBA's disadvantaged programs. Affirmative action finally emerged from the shadows of dubious legality, but many problems remained, including a low graduation rate and an unending stream of groups claiming "disadvantaged" status.

Affirmative Action Comes of Age

The rise of female entrepreneurs was one of the most important developments in the small business sector during the 1970s, as the number of women-owned businesses more than doubled.[17] Female entrepreneurs achieved this rapid growth without government aid, yet the women's business lobby insisted that societal discrimination was so severe that women required SBA assistance. Consequently, the agency pioneered affirmative action for women-owned businesses.

During the Ford years, newly formed associations representing female business owners demanded women's entry into the 8(a) program. The U.S. Civil Rights Commission also asked Ford to declare women a "disadvantaged" class, but SBA officials dissuaded him; the prospect of allowing half the population into the 8(a) program gave administrators pause. Notwithstanding its opposition to group eligibility for women, the SBA doubled the loans to female business owners and held special "Women in Business" workshops.[18] Despite these efforts, women business activists were not satisfied and continued to lobby vigorously for increased government assistance.

Following through on a campaign promise, President Carter established an Interagency Task Force on Women Business Owners in August 1977 to study the challenges confronting female entrepreneurs. In its final report, the task force cited "sexism" and a "history of discrimination" as reasons for the government to promote women-owned businesses. In truth, female business owners had a lot in common with their male counterparts. An SBA survey reported "their identification as small business owners beset with problems common to all small business and not inclined to think of themselves as especially affected by gender." Nor was there evidence of widespread discrimination in the credit markets; like other small business owners, women relied upon informal sources. Most of the women who applied for bank loans were approved.[19] Yet the charge of "sexism" had political appeal, because it allowed activist policymakers to "do something" for women.

The president announced a National Women's Business Ownership Campaign led by the SBA. Policy initiatives included a "mini-loan" program to serve female entrepreneurs who wanted to borrow less than $20,000. The SBA also licensed First Woman's SBIC, a company managed by a female president. (The agency was embarrassed when the company failed and a court convicted its top executives of grand larceny and conspiracy to defraud the government. The SBA lost $3 million on the venture). Furthermore, in 1979, Carter issued an executive order directing government agencies to take "affirmative action" on behalf of women-owned firms. He set a two-year goal of quadrupling the procurement dollars awarded to women-owned businesses— a "lowball" figure that was easily achieved.[20]

The Women's Business Campaign aroused no controversy, perhaps because there were no explicit set-asides excluding men. But minority assistance was another matter. The Economic Opportunity Loan (EOL) program was an open scandal. The GAO reported that only 15 percent of EOL borrowers were still in business. The default rates were phenomenal. The survivors expanded very little and employed few workers. The SBA lost $324 million (excluding interest), one-third of the total amount disbursed. Sadly, the GAO concluded that EOL borrowers "were in worse condition than before they took on small business ownership."[21]

Meanwhile, the Section 8(a) program came under attack from congressional investigating committees. In February 1977, investigators for the Senate Small Business Committee reported that SBA employees were divided between those hostile to the program and those who were enthusiastic but lacked the business expertise that 8(a) firms needed. The agency was also split over whether "race" or "economic status" determined eligibility. The committee concluded that 8(a) was "laced with problems, uncertainties, vague definitions, questionable methods and procedures."[22]

In the summer of 1977, Senator Lawton Chiles (D-Fla.), chair of a Government Affairs subcommittee, held hearings exposing widespread corruption and incompetence in the 8(a) program. SBA officials accepted, and even encouraged, the use of minority "fronts" by white-owned firms. Spurred on by the need to meet rising quotas, the SBA found corporate sponsors for minority companies, thus making them eligible for larger contracts. Many white firms lost contracts to 8(a) set-asides and were eager to recoup. In fact, SBA employees encouraged at least one contractor to "get yourself a black and get on board." Some of these fronts marketed their services to white firms, but others were "illiterate farmers or janitors" duped by their sponsors. Ineptitude also marked the administration of 8(a). The Chiles committee asserted that "SBA has a real problem in simply determining who is in the program." Minorities with political influence secured 8(a) contracts or positions as 8(a) administrators. The latter were "without exception totally unknowledgeable of small business and Federal procurement procedures." The bottom line: of the 15,000 firms that participated in 8(a), only 70 had graduated. Chiles called the program a "monumental failure." His committee recommended establishing "graduation" criteria and a net worth definition of "disadvantage," as well as requiring competitive bidding to prepare 8(a) firms for the rigors of the marketplace.[23]

Jimmy Carter was undeterred by these revelations. In September 1977, he set a goal of doubling (later tripling) minority contract dollars within two years. Carter blamed the program's past failings on the wrongdoing of a few corrupt business owners and ordered an SBA investigation to root out fraud.[24] The agency also established an 8(a) Review Board to improve the program. The results were disappointing. The SBA turned over a handful of cases to the Justice Department, but fraud was still rampant. Three years later, the review board produced an internal report conceding that 8(a) was a failure. Minority firms operated in a "sheltered business environment" and were reluctant to leave the cozy confines of 8(a). A few companies grabbed a large share of 8(a) dollars. Carter's quotas worsened the situation by pressuring SBA officials to set aside larger contracts. Small minority firms were left out in the cold. The board recommended comprehensive business development, time limits on participation, and requiring 8(a) firms to secure competitive contracts. Publicly, however, the SBA remained silent, leading Senator Chiles to comment that "the situation there is as bad as ever. I'm really concerned about a cover up."[25]

The politics of 8(a) reflected Carter's approach to civil rights. He was passionate about promoting the progress of women and minorities. Furthermore, Carter owed his victory to black votes; consequently, the Congressional Black Caucus was unrelenting in its demands for government assistance. Thus, Carter was both a "trustee" president searching for "public goods" and an appeaser of special interests.[26] He failed to convey an overarching vision of the national interest, yet his civil rights decisions established precedents for future presidents.

Congressional response to the 8(a) scandals was mixed, but abolition of the SBA loomed as a serious option. Senator William Proxmire (D-Wis.) revived his "final solution" for the struggling agency. The SBA's inability to reform itself exasperated many longtime agency supporters. Gaylord Nelson (D-Wis.), chair of the Senate Small Business Committee, stated that if the agency did not soon improve, he would propose "getting rid of every single office in the U.S.," to which Vernon Weaver responded, "If we can't straighten it out, I'll join with you." Yet no one really believed Congress would abolish its pet agency. The White House debated transferring the SBA to the Commerce Department but feared a congressional backlash and the prospect of Republican gains among small business voters.[27]

Other members of Congress fought to expand minority set-asides and formalize group eligibility. During the Nixon and Ford years, Democrats had contested racial preferences but came to terms with quotas under a Democratic president. In 1977, Representative Parren Mitchell (D-Md.), chair of the Congressional Black Caucus, inserted an amendment in the Public Works Employment Act setting aside 10 percent of contract dollars for businesses owned by "Negroes, Spanish-speaking [sic], Orientals, Indians, Eskimos, and Aleuts." The Economic Development Administration was responsible for managing these set-asides. This was the first congressional act since 1854 designating beneficiaries by race, yet there was virtually no discussion or debate.[28]

Nineteen seventy-eight was a critical year for affirmative action policies, particularly with respect to minority set-asides. On 28 June, the U.S. Supreme Court upheld the principle of racial preferences in Bakke. This landmark decision inspired hard-line advocates of affirmative action. Parren Mitchell introduced amendments to the Small Business Act creating a "rebuttable presumption" that blacks and Hispanics were "socially disadvantaged." The Senate Small Business Committee argued that a "rebuttable presumption" violated constitutional guarantees of equal protection; therefore, the Senate bill directed the SBA to consider disadvantage on a "case-by-case" basis. Mitchell accused the Senators of "neo-racism," and ultimately his version found its way into PL 95–507, signed by President Carter on 24 October 1978.[29]

PL 95–507 established a "three-track system" to determine 8(a) eligibility. The SBA considered Black, Hispanic, and Native American applicants socially disadvantaged but could disqualify them if they were not also economically disadvantaged. Other groups could petition for presumptive eligibility by showing that "prejudice, bias, or discriminatory practices" had resulted in "economic deprivation." Lastly, individuals regardless of race were eligible if they proved social and economic disadvantage (the final Conference Committee report stated that a "poor Appalachian white person" could conceivably qualify for 8[a] status).[30]

This new system left many questions unresolved. When was a presumptive candidate disqualified on the basis of economic advantage? Two years later, Vernon Weaver admitted that "It boils down to a judgment call. . . . I must have spent a hundred hours with my general counsel . . . discussing: What the hell is 'economic disadvantage?'" It is not surprising then that minority millionaires took advantage of 8(a). PL 95–507 also did not affect loans. Weaver had to remind his employees that the Carter administration's policy of targeting direct loans to the disadvantaged did not mean "'no money for white male owned firms.'"[31]

The admission of new groups into the 8(a) program proved contentious. In 1980, the SBA developed a formal application process that became "the most copied model for affirmative-action programs around the country." Group eligibility depended upon a variety of factors, including "low income," "unfavorable location," and "limited education." In an illuminating article, George R. LaNoue and John C. Sullivan concluded that there was no consistent rationale for group admission other than a vague "'people of color' ideology." In 1980, the SBA began admitting immigrant groups (Tongans and Sri Lankans) who had just arrived in this country and therefore had no record of past discrimination. But the agency rejected an application from Iranians, because this group was "too narrow" and had not been in the country long enough. The SBA originally denied a request from Asian Indians because they were overrepresented in business, but accepted a second application that stressed their dark skin color. Likewise, Indonesians enjoyed above-average income and education but were admitted when they stressed their "yellow" skin. Disabled veterans were entitled to 8(a) status before Congress passed PL 95–507, but the agency denied their application for readmission. In short, 99 percent of 8(a) business owners were "people of color," ignoring the high percentage of whites who were also "disadvantaged" (and also ignoring the wide variance in self-employment among the so-called "white" ethnic groups).[32] The unintended result of admitting so many dark-skinned immigrant groups was the steady erosion of the African American share—the group for whom 8(a) was originally designed.[33]

But these events lay in the future. In the short term, the Carter administration had to deal with claims by Asians, women, and Jews that they, too, were "disadvantaged." In 1979, Asian American senators lobbied for a new 8(a) category of "Asian and Pacific Americans." In fact, studies showed that self-employed Asian business owners were not disadvantaged; they outperformed white and black businesses. Nor was there any evidence of credit discrimination against Asian businesses. Their entry was due to their political pull and their pre-1978 status as a preferred category under 8(a).[34]

During the late 1970s, some advocates of affirmative action sought to build a coalition of the disadvantaged including women and minorities.[35] In reality, these two groups fought bitterly over the status of women. As early as 1977, Weaver informed the White House that "a confrontation was developing between Blacks and Women over the 8–A program. Blacks think that the 8–A program belongs to them and Women want in on the program." The Carter administration had promised to help both groups; now it found itself in a no-win situation. An African American lobbyist stated that "if white women join [8(a)], we can just wrap it up and go back to the plantation." Washington *Post* columnist Jack Anderson voiced the opinion of female entrepreneurs who complained that the SBA was "giving women the business figuratively but not literally." Deputy Administrator Patricia Cloherty lamented that women and minorities were "each other's worst enemies. Every time you propose something for one group, it gets knocked out of the park because the other thinks it'll be bad for them. . . . We may end up with a program that's of no use to anyone, and it can't create anything but bad feelings." In the end, the Congressional Black Caucus prevented women from entering the program.[36]

The White House was also caught in the crossfire between Hasidic Jews and the Black Caucus. The Hasidim presented a strong case of social and economic disadvantage and had the support of many members of Congress. SBA General Counsel Edward Norton was ready to rule for the Jews but feared setting a precedent that would allow other groups to enter the program. The zero-sum mentality of the Black Caucus defeated the Hasidim's efforts to enter 8(a). Parren Mitchell was "sympathetic to the economic conditions of the Hasidic Jews. . . . But there's a limited pie." Consequently, Norton reversed his position by noting the "establishment-of-religion problems" that might ensue if the agency granted status to a religious group.[37]

These ethnic conflicts were the bitter fruit of a race-conscious program. In the world of 8(a), some disadvantaged groups were more equal than others. Yet the widespread belief that 8(a) offered "something for nothing" belied the negative impact it generally had on a firm's competitiveness. However, Section 8(a) served well the purposes of politicians catering to their ethnic constituencies. The politicization of 8(a) also extended to the placement of contracts with well-connected firms. Thus, the idealism that originally motivated the creators of 8(a) gave way to divisive racial politics.

The Rise of the Small Business Lobby

During the Carter years, a powerful interest group of small business owners finally emerged in response to the perceived failure of big business and big government. The National Federation of Independent Business (NFIB) exploited the disaffection of business owners "fed up" with inflation, taxes, and government regulation. The NFIB and other business associations disregarded the SBA, because the agency failed to voice the antigovernment concerns of these small business owners.

The late 1970s witnessed an amazing transformation in the public image of small business, from dying anachronism to dynamo. Throughout the 1950s and 1960s, social commentators had extolled a "big-is-better" myth of the economy, ignoring the important contributions of the small business sector. For example, in his best-selling *New Industrial State* (1967), the economist John Kenneth Galbraith asserted that large corporations were nearly invincible because they controlled production and manipulated consumer demand through advertising.[38] The economic crisis of the mid-1970s shook public confidence in the invincibility of big business. Opinion surveys revealed widespread public distrust of large corporations and a counterposing confidence in small business. Writers across the ideological spectrum praised the virtues of smallness. In *Small is Beautiful* (1973), the New Left economist E.F. Schumacher offered small enterprise as an antidote to the alienation produced by a "monster economy." The conservative *National Review* agreed that "small is beautiful" because small firms created new jobs; therefore, "what was good for small business was good for America."[39]

This last theme—small business as "engine" of economic growth—captivated policymakers searching for solutions to stagflation. Contemporary studies found that small firms produced a disproportionate share of jobs and technological innovations. In pioneering research, the economist David Birch claimed that very small firms (those with fewer than twenty employees) created two-thirds of net new jobs, while large firms (over five hundred employees) created less than 15 percent. The economic and political circumstances of the 1970s were ripe for a new small business ideology, one that promised to counter the downsizing of large corporations and reinvigorate the American dream of entrepreneurship. This new ideology stressed the economic benefits rather than the moral character of small enterprise. Small business was now a means to an end.[40]

Yet policymakers confronted a paradox: if small business was so productive, why was it losing market share? Between 1963 and 1977, medium-sized firms (those with 20–499 employees) maintained their share of Gross National Product (GNP), but smaller companies (0–19 employees) lost substantial ground. In the retail and service sectors, firms with fewer than five employees lost one-third of their sales share. Zero-employee retailers ("Mom and Pops") lost 50 percent. The rate of small business innovation also slowed considerably.[41] This decline coincided with a wave of governmental activism, leading many to blame big government for the deteriorating fortune of small business. The new small business ideology held that these firms could only achieve their full potential if freed of government regulation. In short, small business was a dynamo in chains. This paradox contributed to a crisis mentality: the future of small business—and thus the American economy as whole—was either bright or inauspicious, depending upon the policymaking decisions made in the late 1970s.[42] This revival of crisis rhetoric, after decades of relative calm, helped small business advocates plead their case.

The image of the small business owner "beset, bothered, and beleaguered" by big government was a staple of the business and popular press during the Carter years. Small business owners complained loudly of inflation, high interest rates, rising payroll taxes, and "ridiculous" regulation. The regulatory burden fell especially hard on small firms that lacked the wherewithal to meet the requirements of OSHA and other government agencies. Many entrepreneurs complained of the "mental burden" of having to fill out paperwork. The appeal of self-employment was "being your own boss," but increasingly government encroached on the business owner's autonomy.[43] The aggrieved small businessperson served as a useful symbol for the conservative critique of the welfare state, yet she also appealed to moderates and liberals. There was no better example of the transformation in liberal thinking than the mea culpa offered by John Kenneth Galbraith. The Harvard economist now noted the dynamic potential of small business and advocated exempting small companies from government regulation.[44]

However, the SBA was an ineffective advocate for deregulation, because the Carter administration forced it to defend positions that conflicted with the perceived interests of small business. In 1977, for example, the White House supported a labor reform bill backed by unions but opposed by small business groups. The administration also endorsed the creation of a Consumer Protection Agency, another measure unpopular among small business owners. In both cases, the SBA Office of Advocacy issued critical reports, but Weaver squelched the findings and reported that they did not represent the agency's official position.[45]

Clearly, small business owners needed to organize to defend their interests. Their growing disaffection with government made this possible. As late as 1975, the conservative political commentator Irving Kristol described the small businessperson as "The New Forgotten Man," whose voice was unheard in Washington. But the threat of regulation soon galvanized small business activists at all levels. The phrase "mad as hell" described their feelings about big government. They wanted government to "leave us alone." One small manufacturer complained that "we have been badgered, intimidated, stonewalled, and ignored by government." Politicians jumped on the small business bandwagon en masse. Governor Richard Lamm (D-Colo.) declared, "There is a tidal wave behind me. Its name is small business. And any politician who does not look over his shoulder at that wave will be a politician out of a job." By the end of the decade, small business was the "'in thing'" in Washington.[46]

Antigovernment sentiment fueled the growth of small business lobbies, with NFIB membership doubling to 600,000 during the 1970s. Under the direction of James D. ("Mike") McKevitt, a former congressman, the NFIB grew increasingly sophisticated in its lobbying, including the creation of a Political Action Committee to fund candidates and a Research Department to study policy issues. The NFIB also enlarged its Washington staff and employed lobbyists in every state, using its ratings of voting records to reward allies and target opponents for defeat. But the chief advantage of the NFIB was its grassroots influence. The NFIB provided members of Congress with its membership surveys, listing how individual business owners voted. A lobbyist observed: "You give a Congressman a list of people in his district, he invariably looks down it to see whom he knows. He knows the prominent business people in his district. He can't ignore them." Other business lobbies, including the U.S. Chamber of Commerce, enjoyed similar gains in membership and political clout by emphasizing small business issues.[47]

The emergence of a powerful small business lobby posed a problem for the Carter administration. Many observers considered the NFIB a "conservative Republican operation" (a White House aide called it the "enemy camp"). Furthermore, small and big business lobbies displayed unprecedented unity in opposition to the labor reform bill and the Consumer Protection Agency, two measures defeated in Congress. The business lobby also overcame presidential opposition to a massive capital-gains tax cut. Political commentators stressed the important role of small business in achieving these legislative victories. To overcome congressional suspicion of big business motives, corporate lobbyists worked closely with small business activists. As one writer put it, "These days the big guys may actually need the little guys more than vice versa."[48]

The political influence of small business culminated in January 1980, with the long-awaited White House Conference on Small Business. The theme of the Conference was clear: Arthur Levitt Jr., chair of the White House Conference Commission, stated, "We are here to petition for less. . . . We're looking for less interference and less harassment." The conferees recommended tax cuts, regulatory reform, and capping federal spending at 15 percent of GNP (a substantial reduction from the then-current 22.5 percent). They scarcely mentioned the SBA, other than asking for a dramatic expansion of advocacy activities.[49]

The White House Conference kicked off a banner year for small business advocates as both the president and Congress responded to the crescendo of complaints about big government. Carter directed federal agencies to reduce the regulatory burden on small firms.[50] Meanwhile, Congress passed three acts making it easier for small companies to deal with the federal government. The Regulatory Flexibility Act exempted very small companies from some new regulations. The Equal Access to Justice Act ordered agencies to pay the legal costs of firms that successfully challenged their rulings. The Prompt Payments Act required government agencies to pay their bills within thirty days or be liable for late charges.[51] A fourth act established Small Business Development Centers (SBDCs) as clearinghouses of technical expertise for small companies.[52]

These political triumphs did little to brighten the economic outlook for small business. By the summer of 1980, double-digit interest rates and inflation squeezed profits, depleted capital, and increased business failures. The economy was the number-one issue in the fall election. President Carter cited SBA lending and regulatory relief as evidence of his administration's concern for small business. In the opposing camp, Republican presidential candidate Ronald Reagan pledged to dramatically reduce the size of government through tax and budget cuts, deregulation, and "sunset laws." A survey of small business executives found two out of three supported Reagan. He also had the support of the leading small business associations, including the NFIB. Reagan's rhetoric appealed to small business owners fed up with big government. His candidacy promised them a "revolution" in the relationship between business and government. By reducing the state role in the economy, Reagan hoped to unleash the "animal spirits" of businesses large and small.[53]

Looking Backward: 1970–1980

The Carter years closed a decade of growth for the SBA. The agency participated in the "federal credit explosion" of the 1970s. Between 1970 and 1980, new loan guarantee commitments increased from $450 million to $3.6 billion. By the early 1980s, the SBA provided 40 percent of intermediate-term small business credit. Economists argued that loan guarantees and subsidies distorted the credit markets and weakened monetary policy, yet the political virtues were irresistible. The chief appeal of SBA loan guarantees was the leveraging of agency resources and the cooperation of bankers who were once hostile to the agency.[54]

Other SBA programs also enjoyed substantial growth. Two new management assistance programs—the Small Business Institute and the Small Business Development Centers—expanded the services available to small firms. The 8(a) program mushroomed from $22 million in contract awards to $1.3 billion in 1980.[55] In addition, congressional liberalization of disaster aid produced a spectacular increase in spending.

Paradoxically, the agency's expansion paralleled rising discontent with government. The small business lobby was the immediate beneficiary of this grassroots movement against big government. The rise of the NFIB confirmed

James Q. Wilson's thesis that business associations enjoy their greatest growth during times of crisis, such as the Great Depression or the regulatory outburst of the 1970s. Thousands of small business owners reacted by joining the NFIB and other trade associations, thus establishing a strong interest-group presence in Washington, D.C., and the various state capitals. It is important not to exaggerate the extent of small business activism, as even after the impressive membership gains of the 1970s, the NFIB and the U.S. Chamber of Commerce represented less than 10 percent of business owners. In fact, we know surprisingly little about the political attitudes of small business owners; the subject deserves further investigation. Nevertheless, those who were politically active held a laissez-faire view of government. They were, as historian David Horowitz describes them, "populist insurgents" against the centralized power of big government.[56]

The new small business ideology embodied elements of laissez-faire. In the past, small business ideologues blamed big business for the decline of independent enterprise. They sought government aid—including antitrust prosecutions and financial assistance through the SBA—to preserve a traditional way of life. Economic arguments were secondary; small business owners were worth protecting because they embodied independence, considered key to the maintenance of democracy. By the 1970s, however, Americans had grown accustomed to big business and no longer viewed it as a fundamental threat to American democracy. An emerging literature depicted small business as potentially the most vibrant sector of the economy, if only freed of government regulation. This interpretation turned the older view upside down: small enterprise was dynamic, not dying, and needed less, not more, government intervention in the economy.

The Reagan presidency tested the small business lobby's commitment to laissez-faire. By first reducing and later proposing the elimination of the SBA, the Reagan administration challenged NFIB members to act on their principles. Not surprisingly, the White House's economy drive met fierce opposition from the Congressional Small Business Committees. The presidential assault on the SBA provides a valuable study of the difficulties faced by budget-cutters in a modern welfare state.

ETERNAL LIFE

In 1979, Ronald Reagan told an audience of small business owners that "a government program . . . is just about the nearest thing that we know of to eternal life."[1] As president, Reagan tried unsuccessfully to abolish the SBA, thus illustrating the apparent inevitability of government growth. Yet this episode also underscored the agency's weak interest-group support; small business owners were indifferent to the fate of their federal representative. In other areas, such as affirmative action, Reagan abandoned his commitment to limited government by expanding quotas. In short, the Reagan years offered a mix of principle, pragmatism, and political expediency. During the years that followed, the agency continued to grow, making the Reagan Revolution look even less impressive in retrospect.

The Reagan Revolution, 1981–1984

In his inaugural address, Ronald Reagan announced the theme of his "revolution" by stating that "government is not the solution to our problem; government is the problem." On domestic policy, Reagan pledged to cut taxes, deregulate the economy, and reduce government spending. His economic advisers shared Reagan's staunch conservatism. For example, Budget Director David Stockman had once penned an essay describing the federal government as a "social pork barrel" doling out unneeded benefits to large blocs of middle-class voters.[2]

The Reaganites applied their laissez-faire theory to small business assistance. The chair of the Council of Economic Advisers, Murray Weidenbaum, advocated eliminating all federal credit subsidies, including SBA loans. "Government credit . . . is no free lunch," Weidenbaum wrote, because it crowded out private borrowing and raised overall interest rates. Thus, "the small business sector would be a great deal healthier without [SBA subsidies]." Simi-

larly, a transition task force on small business recommended ending *all* preferences for small and minority-owned firms, leading a Republican congressional
aide to wonder at this "blue-sky, ivory-tower kind of stuff."[3]

Reaganomics produced significant budget cuts at the SBA. In Reagan's
first fiscal year, business loan approvals declined 50 percent, from $3.5 billion
to $1.8 billion. An Interagency Task Force on Small Business Finance ratio-
nalized that SBA lending was less important, because private sources of credit
had substantially improved. President Reagan argued that his massive tax cuts,
passed in 1981, benefited small business more than SBA loans. The National
Federation of Independent Business (NFIB) supported the tax cuts and did
not oppose the reduction in SBA spending.[4]

In his second budget, Reagan proposed eliminating direct SBA loans. A
muckraking series by the *St. Louis Globe-Democrat* bolstered the president's
case. The newspaper reported that the agency lost one-third of the money it
lent to borrowers but covered up the damaging statistics by offering gratu-
itous deferments. Perversely, the direct loans left many disadvantaged borrowers worse off, a fact not lost on SBA loan officers. Phoenix District Director
Thomas Trimboli stated that "putting many of these people into business in
the first place is like putting them in the ring with Muhammad Ali. Once they
start to take a beating, there's not much we could do." Even before Reagan
took office in October 1980, a nationwide gathering of field representatives
recommended abolishing all direct loan programs. Congress held hearings on
the issue and subsequently approved deep cuts in direct lending.[5]

The White House selected Michael Cardenas, a prominent Hispanic
businessman, to head the SBA, primarily because of his ethnicity and strong
financial background. Cardenas had the unenviable task of carrying out the
first significant budget cuts in the agency's history. He abolished lending "quotas" and spent less than Congress authorized. In line with his economy drive,
Cardenas emphasized advocacy, management assistance, and further "whole-
saling" of loans through an expanded Lender Certification Program.[6]

However, Cardenas's budget cuts caused less controversy than his personal management of the SBA. Internal critics charged that he micromanaged
the agency by personally approving routine matters. Supporters considered
him "bright" and "capable" but a poor public relations person. Cardenas angered the women's business lobby by remarking that "having special programs
for women is discriminating." His attempt to clean up the 8(a) program added
to his unpopularity. When Cardenas blocked an improper contract award to a
politically well-connected African American firm, the owner accused him of
placing the contract with a Mexican American business in Cardenas's home-
town (the SBA Inspector-General cleared Cardenas of all charges). His refusal
to award a contract to another 8(a) company, Wedtech, may have provoked

the White House to demand his resignation in February 1982, though it leaked that he was "incompetent" to run the agency.[7]

One of Cardenas's staunchest critics, associate administrator James Sanders, replaced him as SBA head. Sanders was a retired businessman and friend of deputy White House chief of staff Michael Deaver. At his nomination hearing, Sanders expressed a desire to serve as a "conduit" between Congress and the Reagan administration. In practice, however, Sanders had no access to the president and sided with Congress in opposing further cuts in the SBA budget. He reduced the agency workforce and restricted direct lending but dramatically increased loan guarantees, leading conservative critics to charge that he subverted the Reagan Revolution.[8]

The severe recession of 1982 strengthened the hands of those who argued for more government spending on small business. During the election campaign, congressional Democrats tried to capitalize on the widespread misery in the small business community.[9] Meanwhile, Republican supporters of the SBA cited political factors as reason to reverse the budget cuts of 1981. James Sanders argued that the OMB's "stubborn opposition" to agency funding requests was doing political damage. Within the Reagan administration, Elizabeth Dole, head of the Office of Public Liaison, wrote a memorandum entitled "Big versus Little: A Strategy for Small Business," which she promoted throughout 1982. Dole characterized the months leading up to the election as "this Administration's 'Valley Forge.'" There was a widespread perception that "this Administration favors the 'bigs over the smalls,'" even though small business provided the president with "a huge block of supporters" in 1980. Dole promoted a range of initiatives to demonstrate concern for this neglected constituency, but the president offered only token gestures. Nonetheless, with congressional support, the SBA significantly increased its lending activity between 1982 and 1984, regaining much of the ground lost in 1981.[10]

Overall, Ronald Reagan's first term in office produced no rollback of government. Real spending increased due to congressional opposition and the president's reluctance to demand sacrifice from various interest groups. In this context, the SBA budget cuts were particularly harsh, especially since Republicans considered small business one of their key constituencies. James Sanders believes that Reagan took small business for granted; the Democrats, with their "big government" reputation, were unappealing to groups like the NFIB. Yet ideological factors played a larger role in determining Reagan administration policy toward the SBA. OMB officials displayed a visceral hatred of the SBA, which to them represented all that was wrong with the federal government. In fact, as early as 1982, the OMB contemplated transferring the SBA to the Commerce Department but deferred doing so until a more politically opportune time.[11]

Reagan Champions Quotas

The SBA budget debate was mild compared with the controversy surrounding racial preferences in government contracting. The election of Ronald Reagan aroused legitimate fear among civil rights activists that he would do away with minority set-asides and other forms of affirmative action. During the campaign, Reagan voiced strong rhetorical opposition to racial preferences. He appointed opponents of affirmative action to the Justice Department and the Equal Employment Opportunity Commission (EEOC). Yet the Reagan administration was deeply divided. Conservatives urged the president to repeal the prior executive orders underlying race-sensitive programs. Moderates, including Secretary of Labor William Brock, Elizabeth Dole, and her husband, Senator Robert Dole (R-Kans.), argued to retain preferences. They had the support of corporate executives who had learned to live with affirmative action. Small contractors, on the other hand, opposed set-asides. Ultimately, the Reagan administration eschewed color-blindness and expanded contracting quotas. The administration hoped that set-asides would attract minority voters or, at the very least, defend Republicans from charges of racism. Thus, the president sacrificed his small business supporters and chased the chimera of black Republican votes.[12]

President Reagan had an ideal opportunity to renounce set-asides both on principle and on practical grounds. By the early 1980s, there was a considerable literature documenting the shortcomings of the 8(a) program.[13] The Reagan administration also faced political pressure from small business associations to eliminate minority set-asides. The White House received many letters from small contractors describing the losses they endured as a result of 8(a). One such writer, Louisiana contractor Kirk Fordice, wrote to Representative Trent Lott (R-Miss.) pleading, "We've got to get this to the President. We both know that he couldn't condone this affront to free enterprise if he knew the details and the mortal harm being done to [those small business owners] who supported him so staunchly." In a separate letter to the president, he wrote that 8(a) "is snowballing along with quotas doubling and tripling as though there had been no election." Obviously, Fordice and others expected Reagan to deliver on his promise of color-blind government.[14]

The president faced countervailing pressure from administration moderates to show "compassion" for the disadvantaged. Elizabeth Dole's Office of Public Liaison lobbied for more minority set-asides. Dole argued that the "'lack of compassion' issue" had hurt the president's image not only among African Americans and Hispanics but also "the elderly, women and moderates of all parties." The Justice Department's opposition to affirmative action "antagonized" minority groups and "caused the President to be perceived in a negative manner." Set-asides benefited business, the only minority group with Republican political potential. Dole therefore urged Reagan to "make concessions in order to gain increased support."[15]

In December 1982, over the opposition of his conservative advisers, Reagan announced a three-year procurement goal of $15 billion. He also required federal grant recipients to award $6 billion in contracts to minority firms. According to historian Nicholas Laham, this order "represents perhaps the most sweeping expansion in the minority set-aside program ever undertaken by any president." In January 1983, he signed the Surface Transportation Act, a bill that established a 10 percent quota for "disadvantaged" businesses. Six months later, he issued an executive order directing federal agencies to establish annual "objectives" to increase minority procurement. These measures were necessary, Reagan declared, because the slow-moving "economic train" of the 1970s had deprived minorities of their chance to achieve the American Dream. Minority set-asides were "designed to get the train moving again."[16] Thereafter, Reagan touted his support of set-asides, proudly announcing that "we've put our money where our mouth is."[17]

Conservative administration officials were upset at the president's continuing support for quotas. Three years later, the White House squashed a Civil Rights Commission report calling for the elimination of minority set-asides. Commission chair Clarence Pendleton Jr. protested that "the administration has to make up its mind whether it wants opportunities for all or preference for some, and stop speaking with a double voice." The liberal *New Republic* also noted the irony of an anti-quota president who was "an enthusiastic promoter" of the "spectacularly corrupt" 8(a) program. The journal dubbed 8(a) "affirmative action for the rich."[18]

The presidential initiative boosted 8(a) contract dollars by 30 percent in fiscal year 1984. The SBA added five hundred new firms to the program, the largest cohort since 1969. But the continued commitment to 8(a) did not render it any more manageable. All attempts by Cardenas and Sanders to reform the system met with howls of protest from the Congressional Black Caucus. For example, one of the agency's chief goals was to "graduate" firms to make room for new entrants. In 1980, Congress directed the SBA to set "fixed program participation terms." And in 1981, Cardenas established terms that varied from one to five years, depending upon the viability of the firm. The SBA also conducted size determinations to remove companies that had grown beyond the agency definition of "small." Representative Parren Mitchell (D-Md.) responded by denouncing Cardenas's "heartless attack" on minority business. He thought that the 8(a) firms needed up to twenty years of benefits to become viable.[19]

The situation did not improve under Sanders' administration. In July

1982, the GAO ruled that the SBA had to expel two-dozen firms that had grown too large for the 8(a) program. The White House feared the public relations consequences of this order. Elizabeth Dole recommended administrative changes to delay the inevitable. After losing on appeal, Sanders issued a six-month stay-of-execution, which ran out on 14 February 1983. African American leaders, including Parren Mitchell and Jesse Jackson, termed this the "St. Valentine's Day Massacre" and attacked the SBA for waging "economic genocide" on black Americans. Ultimately, through creative rule-bending and a nod from minority enterprise officials, most of the companies remained in the program.[20]

The Wedtech Scandal

Reagan's racial politicking contributed to one of the greatest scandals of the 1980s, a fiasco involving the Welbilt Corporation (later renamed Wedtech). This 8(a) firm exemplified the worst defining features of minority set-asides: contracting based on race, rather than merit; political connections substituting for performance; minority "fronts"; and a president and SBA bureaucracy willing to look the other way in the name of a good cause. The scheme collapsed when muckraking journalists exposed the web of corruption surrounding the company. Congress passed legislation reforming the 8(a) program, but fundamental problems remained.

South Bronx businessmen John Mariotta and Fred Neuberger established the Welbilt Corporation in 1970. Five years later, they learned of the 8(a) program and decided to "milk Mariotta's Hispanic heritage for all it was worth." The two partners each owned 50 percent of the company but drew up a falsified document stating that Mariotta owned two-thirds. The SBA approved their 8(a) application in September 1975.[21]

As late as 1980, Welbilt was little more than a small metal-stamping company, but the partners had grand ambitions to secure multimillion dollar 8(a) contracts. Realizing that they could not compete with established firms, the partners exploited the political appeal of helping a struggling company in "bombed-out" South Bronx. In 1980, Reagan had made a campaign stop in the Bronx promising to revive the inner-city economy. Welbilt's slogan, "Off Welfare, On Welbilt," appealed to Reagan's conservative sensibilities. In January 1982, presidential aides invited Mariotta to a White House conference and sat him beside the president, who was deeply impressed with Mariotta's welfare-to-work vision. Two years later, at a campaign fundraiser, Reagan toasted the success of Welbilt, stating that "people like John Mariotta are heroes for the eighties." Thus, Welbilt became a symbol of the Reagan Revolution in the inner-city.[22]

Welbilt based its success entirely on political influence. The company corrupted procurement officers, accountants, members of Congress, SBA officials, and White House aides. Welbilt's partners in crime included Representative Mario Biaggi (D-N.Y.), a "Hero Cop" turned "congressman on the take." Biaggi reportedly had a "solid hold" over the New York regional office of the SBA. Representative Robert Garcia (D-N.Y.), former chair of the Congressional Hispanic Caucus, had a reputation as "one of the city's last honest politicians," yet he, too, peddled his influence to Wedtech. Two associates of presidential counselor Edwin Meese III—friend E. Bob Wallach and deputy James Jenkins—received stock, cash, and promises of post-government work for pleading the company's case. Welbilt also employed former presidential speechwriter Lyn Nofziger as company lobbyist.[23]

With help from its friends in government, Welbilt secured 8(a) contracts that it could not perform and on which it lost money. The Ponzi scheme depended upon the acquisition of ever larger contracts. Initially, Michael Cardenas stood as an obstacle in the company's path. In January 1982, two presidential aides attended an SBA meeting to discuss Welbilt's $30 million bid for an engine contract. Army officials informed Cardenas that Welbilt's price was too high and that the company was not qualified to fulfill the contract. Therefore, despite presidential pressure, Cardenas denied Welbilt the award. Several weeks later, the White House demanded his resignation. Deputy Administrator David Gonzalez recalled that "afterward, we both looked at each other and said, 'What did we do wrong?' Reagan hired us to clean the [SBA] up. We tried to do that, and they fired us."[24]

White House intervention continued under Sanders' administration. In May 1982, presidential aide James Jenkins convinced Sanders to award the engine contract to Welbilt. One year later, Welbilt changed its name to Wedtech and became the first 8(a) firm to go public. The company maintained its 8(a) eligibility by conducting a phony stock deal giving Mariotta a majority share. In 1984, Sanders set aside a $134 million pontoon contract for Wedtech, the largest set-aside in SBA history. Later, despite failing to deliver a single pontoon, the Navy awarded the company another $51 million contract. By now, the SBA had too much at stake to let Wedtech drown in its own incompetence. The agency failed to graduate the company, because it "made the whole 8(a) program look good." As one SBA official put it, "We weren't looking for a way to say no. We were looking for a way to say yes."[25]

The end seemed near in late 1984, when House Small Business Committee chairman Parren Mitchell caught wind of possible misdeeds at Wedtech. Mitchell sent a list of twelve questions to the SBA. Wedtech had Peter Neglia, New York Regional Administrator, prepare a carefully crafted response that covered up Wedtech's tracks (the company rewarded Neglia with a job at the Biaggi law firm). Wedtech also offered bribes to Parren Mitchell's nephews,

Clarence and Michael, which they readily accepted. Soon thereafter, the House committee dropped its probe.[26]

This sordid state of affairs might have continued indefinitely but for the work of investigative reporters at the *Wall Street Journal* and the *New York Daily News*. In February 1986, the *Journal* reported that Mariotta's partners had fired him and that he owned only 23 percent of company stock. This revelation forced the SBA to begin 8(a) decertification procedures. Rather than fight the agency, Wedtech withdrew itself from the program. Before the news hit the street, company officials dumped $5 million worth of stock. In October, the *Daily News* ran a series of articles exposing the full extent of Wedtech corruption. Two months later, the company filed for bankruptcy.[27]

Juries convicted the principals on numerous counts of bribery, racketeering, tax evasion, and fraud. Clarence and Michael Mitchell were convicted of mail fraud and impeding a congressional investigation, but their uncle escaped prosecution and retired from Congress in 1986. He continued his work with the Minority Business Legal Defense Fund, an organization he founded to defend set-asides against court challenges. Independent Counsel James McKay investigated Meese's role in the affair but found no evidence that Meese knew of E. Bob Wallach's financial ties to Wedtech. Nevertheless, the cloud of scandal reportedly led Meese to resign his post in August 1988.[28]

Congress reacted to the Wedtech scandal by passing reform legislation in 1988. The SBA pushed for tough reforms, including mandatory term limits and a "business-mix" requirement that 8(a) firms acquire non–8(a) business. The original bill contained a strong "business-mix" provision, but the Senate accepted Lowell Weicker's (R-Conn.) plea for flexible "targets" rather than mandatory goals. The final bill required competitive bidding only on contracts exceeding $3 million ($5 million for manufacturing contracts). The act also directed the SBA to establish net worth limits for "economic disadvantage"; new agency regulations set three-phase limits of $250,000 (Phase 1); $500,000 (Phase 2), and $750,000 (Phase 3). The SBA was unhappy with the weak business-mix and competitive bid requirements. Deputy Director of Congressional Affairs Joan Bready lamented, "We want [firms] to work in the world outside of 8(a), and a lot of them can't."[29]

The 1988 reforms did not eliminate the abuses or longstanding problems with 8(a). Ten years later, the SBA official who wrote the new agency regulations was still not optimistic about achieving real reform. Likewise, James Sanders believes that the problem of corruption is "almost unsolvable," given the political dynamics. The abuses continued as 8(a) officials failed to enforce the eligibility and net worth requirements. "Fronts" remained a fact of life. A few large firms reaped the lion's share of contracts, while a majority of 8(a) companies received no awards.[30]

Wedtech was not an aberration; it was the embodiment of the corruption inherent in the 8(a) program.[31] The original goal of 8(a) was to promote "black" and "brown" capitalism, but program incentives encouraged companies and SBA officials to merely play at capitalism by showering a few favored firms with contracts. Prodded by quota-minded presidents, 8(a) officials considered only volume; they did not develop these firms into competitive companies. Not surprisingly, business owners with political connections thrived in this artificial environment. Politicians wrapped themselves in the mantle of minority enterprise, presumably a good cause that excused the program's shortcomings.

President Reagan's enthusiastic embrace of minority set-asides and his refusal to repeal affirmative action call into question his reputation as a principled conservative who placed ideology above party interests. Faced with opposition in his own party, Reagan appeased the moderates and abandoned conservatives. Critics on the left depicted Reagan as a cynical politician who sought white votes by trying to "turn back the clock" on affirmative action.[32] However, there is no documentary evidence to support this interpretation. More important, these critics ignore his set-aside policy, which "represents perhaps the most obvious and blatant racial quota of any federal affirmative action program." In fact, opponents of racial preferences were deeply disappointed with Reagan. For them, it seemed as if nothing had changed. One such critic, Nicholas Laham, concludes that Reagan was "just another shrewd, pragmatic, and even unprincipled, politician."[33]

Reagan also failed to challenge procurement preferences for small business. Set-asides accounted for half of all small-firm procurement dollars. These preferences decreased competition, benefited larger firms, and encouraged companies to act as "fronts" for big corporations. In many fields, small businesses were competitive and therefore did not need set-asides. Yet there was no movement to reform small business set-asides as there was with race-based affirmative action. Thus, it is not surprising that Reagan left these set-asides intact. On the other hand, he signed the Small Business Innovation Research Act (1982), despite opposition from congressional conservatives. This act set aside 1.25 percent of research-and-development grants for small business, a percentage that steadily increased over time. Although politically popular, the SBIR grants supplanted private R&D investment and produced "the illusion of success but no real economic gains." In short, the revolutionary rhetoric of 1980 gave way to political pragmatism. Quotas and social engineering thrived during the height of the "Reagan Revolution."[34]

For conservatives, Reagan's first term was discouraging. His landslide victory in 1984 renewed their hopes for a counterrevolution against big government. In 1985, Budget Director David Stockman made a desperate last stand for deep budget cuts and received the president's go-ahead to abolish the Small Business Administration. The SBA thus enjoyed the dubious distinction of being one of the few agencies targeted for elimination. Contemporaries considered the SBA battle a test case for the "Reagan Revolution." If the president could not kill an agency with such a checkered past, then truly the conservative crusade for limited government was futile.

The Battle to Abolish the SBA, 1985–1987

Reagan's reelection coincided with an economic upturn that altered the social and political environment of small business. During the mid-1980s, fears of a small business crisis dissipated as smaller companies enjoyed faster-than-average growth. Judging from the contemporary literature, this was a golden age of small business. Economists, business writers, and politicians of all stripes praised small firms for creating jobs and advancing technology. Clearly, as economist Bennett Harrison puts it, "Small was bountiful. Small was beautiful. Small was *in*."[35]

The political implications of the new small business ideology were ambiguous. Democratic small business advocates sought more government spending, arguing that it was "better to lend than spend" to create new jobs. But Reagan exploited the laissez-faire element of the ideology. In his view, small business substituted for welfare and government job creation. "It's small business . . . not the Federal Government," he declared, "which created four out of five new jobs. . . . It's small business, not the Federal Government, which can best rebuild our inner cities." Freed of government interference, small business was a dynamo unbound. Small business was thriving, Reagan maintained, because his administration was "getting the Government out of the way."[36]

Reagan's landslide victory in 1984 emboldened budget-cutters determined to reduce the growing federal deficit by attacking domestic programs. They considered 1985 "the make-or-break year for a second-term Reagan Revolution." OMB Director David Stockman compiled a list of programs that "could be attacked on principle"; the SBA was at the top of his "hit" list. James Sanders was aware that OMB officials considered SBA "the worst of all the agencies" but was taken aback when told of White House plans to eliminate his agency. Although Sanders promised to support the president's decision, he publicly made it clear that he opposed abolition. Meanwhile, the threat of termination did not faze most agency employees, who thought that Congress would never allow it.[37]

Stockman launched a cogent attack on the rationale for SBA lending. He termed the SBA a "billion-dollar waste—a rathole" that benefited only a tiny percentage of small businesses. In February 1985 congressional testimony, he argued that SBA loans crowded out private-sector borrowing and reallocated funds "from more creditworthy to less creditworthy firms." Most SBA loans went to companies in low-growth sectors, rather than the "sunrise industries." In the concentrated industries, SBA lending was *"virtually non-existent"* (italics in original).) High loss rates rendered the SBA a "money-losing bank." The original rationale for SBA loans—a "credit gap" in small business financing—no longer existed; private credit sources were abundant. Disaster loans were also unnecessary, because homeowners and businesses could get federal disaster insurance. Stockman estimated that selling the SBA loan portfolio would raise $3 billion in revenue. He favored retaining SCORE and transferring it to the Commerce Department, which would henceforth represent all businesses, large and small.[38] Later studies of SBA loan programs confirmed elements of Stockman's critique.[39] President Reagan meanwhile characterized the SBA as "another example of government poking its nose into areas where it has no business." "If programs like these can't be cut," he declared, "we might as well give up hope of ever getting government spending under control."[40]

While expressing support for the president's proposal, Sanders testified that many SBA programs were successful, including loan guarantees and the SBICs, which provided small businesses with long-term financing. Sanders defended the agency from Stockman's "slander" and disputed his assertion that SBA loans "crowded out" private lending. In April, he told the *Washington Post* that Stockman was "an embarrassment" to the White House. The Budget Director was "surrounded by fanatics [who] have no real life experience." Sanders was clearly determined to survive Stockman's onslaught.[41]

The struggle over the SBA exposed the agency's lines of support and opposition. Opponents included federal procurement officials, who were "almost unanimously" in favor of abolishing the SBA. They resented SBA interference and opposed set-asides. Two leading business groups—the National Association of Manufacturers and the Chamber of Commerce—also backed Stockman's plan. Hard-core support came mostly from conservative activists, who favored total elimination of the SBA rather than gradual cutbacks, because they feared the agency would later regain lost ground. A Heritage Foundation spokesman stated that the SBA was "like a cancer—if you don't cut it out altogether, it will grow back in a year."[42]

The NFIB was ambivalent. A 1984 survey found that two out of three NFIB members favored "ending all lending activities of SBA." An even larger majority opposed SBA programs for "disadvantaged groups." The NFIB followed this unscientific survey with a representative poll that was less devastating. Still, most respondents were unfamiliar with agency programs; the SBA was the "Great Unknown" to small business. Apathy and indifference typified the attitude of most business owners. Very small businesses (gross receipts under $100,000) supported SBA programs, while the "not-so-smalls" opposed them, thus confirming Richard Hamilton's earlier findings (see chapter 1). When asked what the government should do for small business, the majority endorsed tax incentives, competitive bidding, management assistance, and strong advocacy of small business interests. The Federation leadership withheld its support from Stockman until April, when he agreed to a compromise measure eliminating all lending programs but maintaining the SBA as an advocate for small business.[43]

Support for the SBA came primarily from banks and Congress. The attitude of bankers had turned completely around since the 1950s, when the American Banking Association opposed SBA intervention in the credit markets. What transformed the banking community from enemy to ally was the agency's use of loan guarantees. SBA guaranteed loans were profitable and nearly risk-free, and an active secondary market allowed banks to turn over their portfolio rapidly. A GAO survey of bankers found that 82 percent would have refused to make some loans to small business borrowers or would have imposed more difficult terms without the loan guarantee.[44]

The SBA enjoyed overwhelming congressional support, with only a few exceptions. Senator William Proxmire (D-Wis.), a longtime critic, characterized the SBA as one of "Washington's 10 Worst Boondoggles." In the House, Representative David Dreier (R-Calif.) introduced a bill to "sunset" the SBA, but not one Republican senator sponsored companion legislation. At the same time, the Small Business Committees mounted a vigorous defense. In March, they held hearings to rally support for the SBA. The House Committee gathered a petition signed by all former SBA administrators opposing the "junking or crippling of a useful Government agency." The chair of the Senate committee, Lowell Weicker, put the party leadership on notice that "they were going to have a war" if they tried to eliminate the SBA. Regardless, in April the White House negotiated an omnibus budget bill that included a provision abolishing the SBA. With the agency forced to the brink of extinction, Weicker offered an amendment authorizing deep cuts in SBA spending over three years. Reagan needed Weicker's tie-breaking vote to pass the omnibus budget and therefore relented. The final legislation cut $2.5 billion in SBA spending over three years, but most of the savings came from programs that were not central to the agency mission, such as farm disaster loans. Weicker stated that "frankly, it hasn't been cut very heavily at all."[45]

Thus, the SBA survived its first near-death experience, but the Reagan administration still planned to eliminate it. In January 1986, tired of fighting the White House, Sanders announced his resignation effective 31 March. The president then installed conservative activist Charles Heatherly as his "hit man" in the SBA. Rather than face a Senate confirmation hearing, Reagan appointed

Heatherly acting administrator. Heatherly was the editor of *Mandate for Leadership*, a 1981 manual considered the "bible" of the Reagan administration. *Mandate* stated that "it is possible to remove all or most of the personnel and functions from a given organizational unit, thus making it much more amenable to control, dispersal, and eventual elimination." Heatherly carried out this destroy-from-within policy at the SBA. On 1 April, his first day in office, Heatherly fired six regional administrators who opposed Reagan's death sentence ("If they're not supporting the President, they shouldn't be there"). Critics termed this the "April Fool's Day Massacre" and called Heatherly the "Angel of Death." On 2 April, he sent a memo to SBA employees directing them "to prepare the agency for an orderly transition to . . . the Department of Commerce." He spoke of "transfer," rather than elimination, noting that all agency functions except lending were moving to the Commerce Department.[46]

Not surprisingly, Heatherly's blunt and brash manner antagonized members of Congress. In newspaper interviews, he labeled Congress as being "without discipline and without guts." The SBA lending programs were "just middle-class entitlements the nation can no longer afford." In committee hearings, Weicker and his colleagues berated Heatherly for his "mean-spirited comments" and "smug or sarcastic" attitude. Heatherly apologized for his "facetious or lighthearted" remarks, but the damage was done. By June, the White House realized that Congress was not going to surrender. Furthermore, the ongoing public relations fiasco threatened to embarrass the president at a forthcoming White House Conference on Small Business scheduled for August. Therefore, two days before the conference, Reagan announced that he would name a permanent SBA administrator. Four months later, he chose former U.S. Senator James Abdnor (R-S.Dak.) to head the agency. Abdnor took office in March 1987, thus ending a critical chapter in the history of the SBA.[47]

James Abdnor's two years in office (1987–1988) were relatively uneventful. The main controversy concerned SBIC attempts to privatize their industry. During the 1980s, the SBICs suffered high interest rates, low rates of return, serious regulatory violations, and a declining presence in the booming venture capital market. The SBICs were frustrated with SBA red tape and the unstable budgetary environment; consequently, as early as 1983, they sought the creation of a federally chartered Corporation for Small Business Investment (COSBI). The Reagan administration opposed COSBI, because it authorized SBICs to borrow funds from the Treasury Department and provided weak supervision of an industry long plagued with violations. Citing the recent savings-and-loan debacle, Abdnor warned that "when a regulator is weak and the credit is too easy, there are going to be attempts to take advantage of that." Thus, the COSBI bill languished in Congress.[48]

Abdnor lobbied for the president's agenda of lower guarantee rates and higher user fees on SBA services but admitted that "Congress won't buy it." The Reagan battle for budget cuts was over. The Small Business Committees now fought to regain lost ground. During fiscal year 1988, business loan approvals inched upward to $3.3 billion.[49]

What "Revolution"?

The failed attempt to abolish the SBA provides a valuable case study in the political bankruptcy of the "Reagan Revolution." After a sustained attack lasting eighteen months, the president secured only modest cuts in the SBA budget. Contemporary observers considered the SBA's survival "a metaphor" for the failed experiment in conservative governance. "As the case of the SBA seems to show," wrote *National Journal* writer Jonathan Rauch, "the heady days of the Reagan Revolution . . . are over." The chair of the Senate Budget Committee, Pete Domenici (R-N.Mex.), also called it a "bellwether. . . . If you cannot get rid of [the SBA] when you have this kind of [deficit] problem . . . it sort of tells us something about . . . our willingness to really cut." More generally, conservative and libertarian activists were bitterly disappointed with the president's inability to eliminate agencies such as the SBA. While liberals bemoaned the supposed rightward turn in politics, conservatives questioned whether their quixotic crusade against big government would ever achieve results.[50]

Why was the Reagan Revolution such a failure? Some of Reagan's revolutionaries blamed administration moderates for betraying the cause. They argued that entrenched bureaucrats also sabotaged their best efforts to repeal government programs. Paul Craig Roberts sums up this view: "The first year of the Reagan Administration was a struggle between a few people in government who wanted change and a government full of people who did not." Within a year, those favoring the status quo had gained the upper hand. In a postmortem on his sojourn in government, Charles Heatherly cited shortcomings in personnel management. The bureaucracy was the "permanent embodiment of the liberal agenda"; therefore, the loyalty of political appointees was crucial. Too often, Heatherly lamented, agency heads "go native" by becoming "defenders of their own little fiefdoms." Heatherly and Roberts agreed that Reagan delegated authority to people opposed to his revolution. His primary concern was with preserving party unity. Always a minority, even within the Republican Party, conservatives were left carping from the sidelines.[51]

According to this interpretation, moderates kept Reagan "from being Reagan." The "real" Reagan waged rhetorical assaults on big government. Yet, in reality, Reagan was a pragmatic politician. He never seriously contemplated sweeping reductions in government. Eliminating the SBA was Stockman's idea, not the president's. In 1986, *New Republic* columnist Fred Barnes noted that Reagan had spoken favorably of the SBA in the past. Moreover, he "never demonizes it in his speeches. He scarcely mentions it." In his bitter memoir, Stockman acknowledged that "ridding Big Government of the SBA was not on the President's real agenda after all."[52]

Several commentators emphasized the influence of an "iron triangle" consisting of the Small Business Committees, the SBA bureaucracy, and "tiny businessmen interested in latching on to the loot."[53] Yet small business support for the agency was notoriously weak, even among borrowers, who lost interest once they received their loans. The NFIB actually supported Stockman's plan; the association was more interested in economy-wide measures such as deregulation and tax cuts than defending loans that benefited relatively few firms. The SBA bureaucracy was in the hands of abolitionist Charles Heatherly. Thus, two of the three triangle legs supported elimination of the SBA. A history of scandals and an extensive body of literature critiquing various SBA programs strengthened the intellectual case for abolition. In short, far from being a typical example of an "iron triangle," the SBA offered a good scenario for determined budget-cutters.

But Congress, the third leg of the triangle, presented insurmountable opposition. Members of Congress supported small business—and by extension the SBA—because it was held in high public esteem, second only to farming in its universal appeal. Furthermore, without the SBA, the Small Business Committees lost their primary reason for being. Unfortunately for the Reagan administration, two die-hard liberals—Lowell Weicker and Parren Mitchell—chaired the Senate and House committees. Weicker's disdain for Reaganomics was well-known ("the trickle down idea is a bunch of bananas," he said in 1981). His vote played a crucial role in rescuing the SBA from Stockman's chopping block.[54]

Blaming a liberal Congress for Reagan's defeat would be misleading, however. The conservative chronicler David Frum wrote that the SBA "exemplified everything that's wrong with the modern state," yet conservatives failed to support the president's proposal. As one White House official put it, "They say it's an uphill battle, so why fight it?" This pusillanimous response reflected the superficial nature of congressional conservatism. Like their president, Republican members of Congress feared being perceived as "mean" by proposing deep budget cuts. In an apt phrase, Fred Barnes described Republican leaders as "big government conservatives" who had come to terms with leviathan. Conservative officeholders succumbed to the temptations of power. Herbert Stein observed that "a revolution can hardly be engineered from outside the government, and even conservative governments when in office do not want to limit their own powers. So the radical conservative revolution is the dream of conservatives out of office, but not the practice of conservatives in office."[55] Thus, Stockman and Heatherly were on a fool's errand; abolishing the SBA was not within their grasp.

The Bush-Clinton Years

The Reagan legacy looks even less impressive in retrospect. Reagan's successor, George Bush, brought a government-friendly attitude to the White House. He declared that "I do not hate government. . . . A government that serves the people . . . is a good and needed thing." During the Bush years, nondefense spending grew rapidly. The SBA more than doubled its business loan approvals, from $3.3 billion to $7.2 billion. Bush also established a "microloan" project to "empower" the poor. However, those who remembered the failed Economic Opportunity Loan program cautioned against high expectations.[56]

The SBIC industry collapsed during the recession of 1991, resulting in several hundred million dollars in losses to the government. The economic downturn compounded longstanding problems of a high debt burden and lax oversight. In 1992, Congress passed legislation tightening up licensing requirements and creating a new "participating security" similar to preferred stock. The early results were promising, although the rush of new money into the SBIC industry was no doubt related to the sizzling stock market of the 1990s.[57]

The Clinton years brought further growth in SBA lending; business loan approvals hit $9.5 billion in 1994. With the election of a Republican Congress, a few conservatives advocated eliminating the SBA, but the Republican "revolution" of 1994 was no more real than the Reagan Revolution. The SBA continued to increase its general business loans, approving a record $11.4 billion in 1999. The president's proposed budget for fiscal year 2000 would raise this figure to $14 billion, nearly five times the level when Reagan left office.[58]

The Section 8(a) program remained mired in difficulties. Although minority businesses made tremendous strides, 8(a) helped few of them.[59] A 1990 survey of "disadvantaged" businesses reported that they were disappointed with government assistance. The typical respondent thought procurement preferences only "helped a little," and many thought that the programs did not help at all. Obsessed with meeting numerical goals, the SBA provided little practical assistance. Not surprisingly, 8(a) firms experienced high postgraduation failure rates. Meanwhile, the original target beneficiaries, African Americans, steadily lost their share of 8(a) to Asian American business owners, who were better capitalized and better educated than their black *and* white counterparts. Nevertheless, the program was politically inviolable; there was no serious move by Congress or the president to repeal 8(a).[60]

Minority set-aside programs did face court challenges. In two important cases, *Croson* (1989) and *Adarand* (1996), the U.S. Supreme Court subjected local, state, and federal set-asides to a "strict scrutiny" test. The Court ruled that government agencies must document past discrimination before establishing set-asides. These decisions gave birth to an industry of consultants producing studies offering crude statistical disparities to "prove" that discrimination existed. President Clinton's promise to "mend, not end" affirmative action amounted to similar stonewalling. Denying that 8(a) was based on race, Clinton claimed that the program was theoretically color-blind and therefore not subject to the strict standards set forth by the Court. In practice, however, 8(a) was explicitly race-conscious; no white person, no matter how "disadvantaged," had a fair chance of being admitted to the program (in 1996, there were only eight white women in the program).[61]

In 1996, two presidential candidates—Republican Robert Dole and Democrat Bill Clinton—were implicated in embarrassing incidents involving SBA minority enterprise programs. Dole campaigned for an end to 8(a), stating that "it has been abused." Yet *Washington Post* reporters alleged that he was one who had abused the program. In 1988, Dole's office pressured the SBA to award 8(a) contracts to a firm run by John Palmer, a former aide. Several years later, beginning in 1994, an independent counsel investigated charges that Clinton pressured David Hale, owner of a MESBIC, to illegally lend $300,000 to Susan McDougal, a woman who was hardly "disadvantaged" (she and her husband had a net worth exceeding $2 million). Hale charged that McDougal used the loan to purchase land for the Whitewater Development Corporation, an enterprise owned by the Clintons and the McDougals. Juries convicted the McDougals and Hale of fraud in 1996; the investigation of the president continues as of this writing. Regardless of the outcome, the fraudulent loan was fresh proof of the corruption associated with the minority enterprise programs.[62]

Regulation surged upward in the Bush-Clinton years, renewing small business complaints about heavy-handed government. Previous reforms, including exemptions for very small businesses and cost-benefit analysis, failed to reduce the burden on medium-sized companies. The NFIB and the U.S. Chamber of Commerce continued to attract new members by railing against big government. In 1993, they played a pivotal role in defeating President Clinton's proposed national health care plan (pushed unconvincingly by the SBA). The Republican "revolutionaries" of 1994, led by Representative Newt Gingrich (R-Ga.), strongly associated themselves with small business. The small business lobby also benefited from the bipartisan belief in the job-creating powers of small business. By 1997, the NFIB ranked as the most powerful business lobby and the fourth most influential lobby overall.[63]

It would be wrong to overstate the benefit or harm the federal government does to small business. The enterprise of millions of businessmen and women will determine the future of small business. As these business owners enter the twenty-first century, they face new challenges—global competition, Internet commerce, and an aging workforce. As always, there are advantages and disadvantages to being small. There is no guarantee that small business will flourish in the years ahead, yet the lesson of the twentieth century is that rumors of its death were greatly exaggerated.

CONCLUSION

The history of the Small Business Administration is a microcosm of American government in the last half of the twentieth century. From the partisan budget battles of the 1950s to the Reagan Revolution of the 1980s—with stops along the New Frontier, the War on Poverty, and the populist backlash of the 1970s—the agency participated in the broader movements of the American body politic. This concluding chapter considers important historical themes and the changing relationship between small business and government.

Interest-Group Representation

The modern American state is premised on the notion that government can and should serve as a broker between organized interest groups. In the twentieth century, groups claiming to represent both the "special" and "public" interests sought to advance their agendas through governmental programs. Once regarded as a necessary evil, interest groups became a public good when tied to the pluralist model of political equilibrium. Democracy thus became a "product of group conflict." The increased role of government in American life, in turn, provoked additional interest groups to organize and defend themselves against perceived threats.[1]

However, the Small Business Administration does not fit this Broker State theory. Unlike other government agencies, the SBA represents no strong client; rather, it embodies a public sentiment favoring small enterprise, an ill-defined interest group. One of the ongoing problems the SBA has faced is that the intellectual expression of this sentiment has changed over time. The original Jeffersonian ideology extolled the virtue of self-reliance; independent enterprise was a bulwark against an overreaching state. But in the late nineteenth and early twentieth centuries, fearing the imminent decline of small business, antitrusters necessarily sought government assistance to counter the "trusts." The Small Business Administration evolved from this antitrust tradition; Congress hoped that positive assistance to small business would "level the playing field." In the past quarter-century, the public has come to appreciate the resiliency of small enterprise. Pundits now praise the economic dynamism of small business, while politicians in both parties proclaim "small is beautiful."

Yet, even after the establishment of the SBA in 1953, policymakers contested the small business ideology and debated the existence of a "small business interest." Conservatives, including President Dwight D. Eisenhower and David Stockman, considered this form of federal aid to "free enterprise" a contradiction. Commerce Department officials, meanwhile, disputed the concept of an arbitrary line separating "small" and "big" business. Preferences for one class of business owner, they argued, placed others at a disadvantage. How, then, did congressional supporters of the SBA reconcile government assistance with the supposed independence of small business, the very basis for its popular appeal? Earlier generations argued that small firms were victims of "institutionalized discrimination" in the marketplace and government; the SBA countered the effects of such discrimination. More recently, members of Congress have characterized SBA loans as a sound investment in a growing sector of the economy.

Nonetheless, the symbolic value of the SBA—as the embodiment of public support for the "little guy"—was undercut by the agency's inability to define "small" business. SBA size standards were arbitrary and susceptible to political pressure from members of Congress.[2] More important, the size standards deviated sharply from the public definition of small business, thus lending support to Senator William Proxmire's criticism that the SBA is "a medium-size or even a big business administration." Little has changed since the 1950s, when one author wrote that "discussions of 'small business' almost always turn out to be about medium-sized business."[3] The SBA's definition of "small" encompasses nearly 99 percent of the business population, from sole proprietors to corporations with thousands of employees. An extreme example of this bias toward the "not-so-smalls" was the awarding of small business status to auto giant American Motors Corporation. Periodic efforts to lower the size standards faltered because of congressional opposition. In short, the SBA and the Congressional Small Business Committees benefited from misplaced public support.

This expansive definition of "small" business had important policy consequences. The agency devoted much of its resources to the "not-so-smalls," the segment of the small business community least in need. Firms with more than twenty employees maintained their market share, while the very smalls, especially those with fewer than five employees, lost significant ground. "Mom and Pop" have seen better days.[4]

How well does the SBA represent its constituency? Does small business now have an influential voice within the Broker State? For most of its history, the SBA, together with the Small Business Committees, acted as the small business lobby in Washington. But the agency was a weak advocate for small business. During the 1960s, SBA administrators failed to represent the interests of small firms affected by urban renewal and the riots. The following decade witnessed a small business backlash against government regulation, but the SBA frequently placed itself on the side of big government. Congress created an Office of Advocacy to take independent stands on controversial issues, but SBA executives vetoed position statements that conflicted with those of the incumbent administration.

The emergence of a powerful small business lobby, led by the National Federation of Independent Business (NFIB), filled this interest-group vacuum. Since the late 1970s, the NFIB has been an effective advocate for small business interests. Unlike most organized interest groups, the NFIB was indifferent to the fate of its representative agency; the association supported Ronald Reagan's attempts to eliminate all SBA functions except advocacy. Politically active small business owners were as conservative as their 1950s counterparts. Their antigovernment animus overcame the "free rider" problem inherent in organizing a large, heterogeneous group. It bears stressing that small business is not a conservative monolith. Our knowledge of small business attitudes toward government is limited. Richard Hamilton's study of small business in the 1950s and early 1960s remains the only in-depth analysis of this important issue.[5] Further research is needed to clarify whether NFIB members represent the norm or whether small business owners divide along income or size lines. A Gallup poll taken in 1995 found no significant differences between the attitudes of NFIB members and the general small business population, although the survey questions dealt only with SBA programs. A second Gallup survey found small business owners were strongly Republican and conservative, but the report did not break down responses by income class.[6]

The Reagan administration's battle to abolish the SBA showed that the agency's strongest support—its real constituencies—were the Small Business Committees and the nation's banks, not the organized small business lobby. The SBA socialized the risks of small business finance, thus turning banks from staunch opponents into avid supporters of government lending. The political appeal of investment guarantees was obvious: Congress could magnify the apparent government contribution to small business investment and co-opt a leading opposition group. Loan guarantees also concealed and deferred the costs to the taxpayers.

Why was Congress so interested in small business and the SBA? Many members were sincerely interested in small business issues. Others used their committee membership to strengthen ties with the business community. The SBA was a useful conduit for the constituent work of the Small Business Committees, a dumping ground for politicos, and a "petty cash drawer" for the pet schemes of Congress. The agency's extensive field structure served many congressional districts; the field directors were "often as loyal to their district Congressman as to the agency."[7] It is little wonder, then, that Congress was so fond of the SBA.

The Small Business Administration also served the political needs of various presidents. Dwight D. Eisenhower used the agency to deflect criticism that he favored big business. John F. Kennedy backed the SBA to challenge the notion that he was "antibusiness." Richard M. Nixon had the agency promote his vision of "black capitalism." Yet presidential support has been uneven. Presidents Johnson, Ford, and Carter paid little attention to the SBA. Ronald Reagan's administration tried unsuccessfully to eliminate it.

In sum, the SBA was a highly politicized agency that served the interests of politicians in both parties. However, the agency's support among small business owners was notoriously weak. Even with the great expansion in loan guarantees, the SBA reached a tiny segment of the small business community. Thus, thirty years after the agency's establishment, the SBA was still the "Great Unknown" among small businesspeople.

Affirmative Action

Few Americans are aware that the Small Business Administration pioneered racial preferences. Inspired by the March on Washington, SBA administrator Eugene Foley launched a pilot loan project targeted at African Americans. Foley inserted his "Economic Opportunity Loan" (EOL) program in the enabling legislation for the "War on Poverty." The goal was to combat poverty and create role models in the ghetto. The riots of the mid-1960s transformed EOL into a "black-oriented" program to deal with the "root causes" of the urban crisis. Unfortunately, rather than create success symbols, EOL highlighted the failure of poor entrepreneurs. The program left borrowers worse off than before they entered business. This failed experiment illustrated the naivete of SBA officials who let idealism and guilt cloud their thinking about social policy.

The history of 8(a) contracting preferences demonstrated that affirmative action made for strange bedfellows. This controversial program was originally a response to the inner-city turmoil of 1968. A crusading administrator, Howard Samuels, exploited the urban crisis by advocating "compensatory capitalism." Under Section 8(a) of the Small Business Act, Samuels began to "set aside" no-bid contracts for minority firms. President Richard M. Nixon dramatically increased the use of these set-asides. Theoretically color-blind but practically race-conscious, 8(a) bred dishonesty and deception in a program designed for the "socially and economically disadvantaged." Ironically, the Republican Party, now a rhetorical opponent of affirmative action, made explicit racial quotas in government contracting. Congressional Democrats denounced this "reverse discrimination," but by the late 1970s, they too were promoting the new racialist regime. Ronald Reagan, who preached "color-blindness" in government, betrayed his conservative supporters by further expanding 8(a) set-asides.

The consequences of the 8(a) program were perverse. A few well-connected firms received the bulk of the set-asides, while others received nothing. Obsessed with quotas, the SBA provided little practical assistance; indeed, its minority enterprise officials, many of them former civil rights activists, lacked business experience. Not surprisingly, most 8(a) firms never developed into viable enterprises. In a classic case of robbing Peter to pay Paul, the SBA took contracts from some of the least advantaged white companies and gave them to minority firms. The agency also applied its eligibility criteria inconsistently, admitting affluent immigrant groups with dark skin and denying the applications of disadvantaged light-skinned peoples. The program provoked conflicts among African Americans, whites, women, Jews, and other ethnic groups. Political favoritism and corruption were rampant.

Polls taken in the U.S. and Europe show strong opposition to explicit preferences based on race or gender. Two leading students of the subject conclude that "proposing to privilege some people . . . on the basis of a characteristic they were born with, violates a nearly universal norm of fairness."[8] Nevertheless, despite repeated scandals and failure to meet its objectives, the 8(a) program is entrenched as a racial pork barrel used by Democrats and Republicans alike to demonstrate their civil rights credentials. The massive resistance to adverse court decisions reflects the ingrained nature of affirmative action. Liberalism has become its opposite: where once it stood for equality before the law, now it defends "benign" violations of that principle. Conservative politicians, fearful of being tagged racists and eager to attract minority votes, have sent a mixed message: expressing public opposition to preferences but implementing them once in office. This hypocritical stance has won them neither the respect of their opponents nor the admiration of their supporters.[9]

Minority businesses were not the only beneficiaries of procurement preferences; small firms benefited from set-asides, too. In the late 1950s and early 1960s, advocates of small business advanced arguments for preferential treatment that bore striking resemblance to later justifications for minority set-asides. They argued that small firms deserved a "fair proportion" of government contracts equal to their share of private-sector sales. The underrepresentation of small business was prima facie evidence of past and present discrimination by procurement officers, large corporations, and banks. The discrimination against small business was subtle, often unconscious and pervasive; therefore, it could not be corrected with educational campaigns. Quotas and set-asides countered institutional discrimination and promoted "economic diversity."

The rationale for size-based preferences was dubious. Congress exaggerated the underrepresentation of small firms by relying on crude statistical disparities. Aggregate statistics obscured the SBA concentration of set-asides in industries already dominated by small business; consequently, size preferences did not affect very large corporations. The chief victims of this well-intentioned program were the "not-so-small" companies, large by industry standards but small in comparison to the national economy. A third party—the not-so-small company—lost business to compensate for the alleged discrimination of procurement officials.

The parallels with affirmative action for ethnic minorities are obvious, yet policymakers took this "reverse discrimination" for granted. Virtually no one, other than procurement officers, objected to this special treatment of small business. The unquestioning acceptance of size preferences suggests that the American people and their representatives "take for granted" the inherent value of small business. The core values represented by small business—individualism and equal opportunity—legitimize "benign" discrimination favoring small companies. Is such discrimination justified? Or is this another example of unequal treatment in the name of equality? Are the losses imposed on taxpayers and medium-sized businesses worth the benefits that accrue to an arbitrarily defined group of "small" companies? Opponents of racial preferences ought to reconsider other forms of "reverse discrimination."[10]

Government Growth

Finally, this study illuminates another important theme in modern American politics: the growth of the federal government. In 1900, the federal government consisted of a handful of agencies responsible for delivering the mail, providing national defense, issuing currency, regulating trade, and conducting diplomatic relations. Since then, the federal policy agenda has expanded to include nearly every aspect of modern life. An attitudinal shift accompanied this government growth. The classical liberal abhorrence of government interference gave way to widespread sentiment that "there ought to be a law" to deal with a panoply of issues once considered private.

In his seminal *Crisis and Leviathan: Critical Episodes in the Growth of American Government* (1987), the economic historian Robert Higgs emphasizes the importance of crisis and ideology—two factors that contributed to the growth of the Small Business Administration. Congressional sponsors of the SBA believed that small business faced a competitive crisis that could only be met with government assistance. Without government aid, small firms might succumb to the market power of large corporations. Later, in the 1960s, SBA administrators exploited the "urban crisis" to justify their commitment to minority enterprise. The "stagflationary" economy of the 1970s provided yet another rationale for SBA lending. Throughout this period, SBA officials used the small business ideology to secure political support.

Nevertheless, economic and racial crises cannot explain the agency's expansion during "normal" times. Other factors, including partisan presidential politics and bureaucratic entrepreneurship, also contributed to the SBA's growth. During most presidential election years, the SBA stepped up its loan activity. Several important programs—including SCORE and the Small Business Institutes—were the product of strong administrators such as Eugene Foley (1963–1965) and Thomas Kleppe (1971–1975), thus confirming political scientist James Q. Wilson's theory that bureaucratic innovations are "heavily dependent on executive interests and beliefs." These bureaucratic entrepreneurs typically emerge during periods when public or elite opinion is favorable to government action.[11]

Agency growth also involves preserving policy gains from governmental rivals. The SBA maintained its autonomy despite takeover attempts by the Commerce Department. In his study of Bureaucracy (1989), James Q. Wilson offers several "rules of thumb" for agencies to achieve bureaucratic autonomy. Successful agencies "seek out tasks that are not being performed by others."[12] Congress created the SBA to perform a task—lending—that Commerce officials thought inappropriate. Later, the SBA took the initiative in a variety of areas, including management assistance and minority enterprise. By the mid-1960s, the SBA had outstripped its older, less innovative rival. Envious of the SBA's success, the Commerce Department tried to acquire the upstart agency but faced insurmountable opposition from the Congressional Small Business Committees.

The SBA's growth created considerable problems. Wilson advises administrators to "avoid taking on tasks that differ significantly" from their core mission and "avoid tasks that will produce divided or hostile constituencies."[13] Yet the indeterminate dividing line between "small" and "big" business produced perennial conflicts over size standards and set-asides. Disaster loans diverted personnel from the SBA's regular business programs until the agency set up a separate disaster unit in 1980. The 8(a) program was a "people eater" that drained agency resources and engendered bitter conflicts based on race, gender, and ethnicity.

The multiplication of missions—lending, venture capital, contracting, disaster aid, etc.—led the SBA to neglect functions that produced no immediate payoff, such as advocacy and management assistance. While the number of programs proliferated, the number of employees remained the same. Understaffing, lax oversight, and a highly decentralized agency structure fostered repeated scandals. The pursuit of disparate program objectives also produced a schizophrenic agency culture, with the various divisions serving different interest groups: "Mom-and-Pop" businesses, medium-size government contractors, venture capitalists, disaster victims, and groups defined by race, ethnicity, or gender.

Reinventing Government

The problems associated with government growth have raised concerns about the desirability of big, bureaucratic government. Conservatives and libertarians view the federal leviathan as a threat to individual freedom. As government grows, people become less self-reliant, more dependent, and more likely to view themselves as victims of circumstances beyond their control. Moderates and liberals have also expressed concern that government agencies become sclerotic and therefore fail to adjust to changing circumstances. Moreover, the asymmetry of government growth—with births greatly outnumbering deaths—creates an imbalance between organized interest groups and a diffuse opposition. And the fragmented structure of American government further frustrates efforts to repeal programs that have outlived their usefulness.[14]

The Reagan administration's ill-fated attempt at abolishing the SBA highlighted the difficulties faced by budget-cutters in a modern welfare state. Conservatives have long argued that the only way to reduce spending is to do it all at once. The cuts have to be deep enough so that the benefits (lower taxes) are visible to the public.[15] Yet visible cuts provoke strong responses from the affected interest groups, making them difficult to achieve. Thus, when David Stockman cobbled together programs that he could attack "on principle" he had no illusions about his chances of success. His frontal assault on the SBA—one of the few agencies targeted for elimination in the Reagan years—demonstrated the futility of the conservative crusade to cut spending and abolish government programs. Despite a long history of scandals and arguable policy failures, the SBA survived the White House challenge. Stockman was right: with one or two exceptions, there were no real conservatives in Congress. By the late 1980s, it dawned on many conservatives that, as columnist George Will wrote, "The doctrine of [limited government] is as dead as a doornail. The modern state is a sprawling, palpitating fact, and here to stay."[16]

The political center emerged stronger in the aftermath of the Reagan

Revolution. Policymakers on the left and right found their options limited to "fiddling on the margins." The goal was to "rationalize" government programs to make them more efficient and responsive to changing conditions.[17] Skeptics questioned whether government was capable of "reinventing" itself. The historian Jonathan Hughes, for example, wrote that "one can hardly become enthusiastic about government solving problems the government largely created."[18] Others expressed a more hopeful view.[19]

The SBA has a long history of reinventing itself, thus preventing it from becoming an out-and-out boondoggle, as the critics charged. Staffing limits forced the agency to do more with less. From the mid-1960s onward, the SBA increased its reliance on loan guarantees, thus shifting part of the work burden to bank loan officers. Because excessive paperwork discouraged many financial institutions from participating, the SBA established its Certified Lender programs granting banks wide latitude in approving loans. The development of a secondary market in SBA loans made them more attractive to banks and investors. These improvements in the loan guarantee program illustrate what economist Charles L. Schultze termed "the public use of private interest."[20]

Management assistance provides another good example of the SBA relying on private resources. The Service Corps of Retired Executives (SCORE) exploited the vast potential of retired business owners. The Small Business Institutes (SBIs) and Small Business Development Centers (SBDCs) drew on the expertise of university professors and students. These programs were not perfect, and the SBA often took them for granted. Nevertheless, they are widely considered successes.

The modest reinventing of the SBA is unlikely to resolve the tension that persists between small business and big government. Overall, the business community remains suspicious and hostile toward government initiatives.[21] Although pragmatic accommodation is common, business attitudes have not changed much in the past fifty years. A 1994 survey of Fortune 500 chief executive officers found overwhelming support for reductions in government spending and greater deregulation of the economy.[22] The available evidence suggests that politically active small business owners hold similar views. Moreover, the small business owner burdened by regulation is a sympathetic figure and useful symbol for opponents of big government.[23] Thirty years ago, the historian Richard Hofstadter wrote that antitrust had become "one of the faded passions of American reform." The movement against big business was over.[24] Yet many small business owners continue to battle governmental intrusion. Leviathan ruled the twentieth century. Perhaps the twenty-first century belongs to the Lilliputians?

APPENDIX A: CHRONOLOGY

1953   Small Business Administration established

1958   Small Business Investment Company (SBIC) program created.
        SBA made a permanent agency.

1961   President John F. Kennedy orders procurement quotas for small
        contractors.

1962   Stock market crash sends SBIC prices plummeting.

1964   SBA administrator Eugene Foley launches pilot loan project for
        minority businesses. Congress incorporates this concept into the
        War on Poverty by authorizing Economic Opportunity Loans.
        Service Corps of Retired Executives (SCORE) established.

1965   Watts riot fuels demands for more "black capitalism" aid.

1966   SBIC investigation reveals widespread fraud and corruption.
        American Motors Corporation declared a "small" business.

1967   The Detroit riot, the worst of the decade, results in the destruc-
        tion of 2,500 businesses.

1968   Republican candidate Richard Nixon makes "black capitalism"
        a key issue in his presidential campaign.
        SBA officials use Section 8(a) of the Small Business Act to set
        aside government contracts for minority businesses.

1969   Nixon creates the Office of Minority Business Enterprise (OMBE).

Newspapers report SBA loans to mafia figures.

Minority Enterprise Small Business Investment Company (MESBIC) program provides subsidies to investment firms specializing in "disadvantaged" businesses.

1970   Occupational and Health Safety Act mandates workplace regulations. Complaints of "asinine" regulation spark growing unrest among small business owners.

1973   Huge expense of Hurricane Agnes leads to reform of disaster loan program.

Scandals involving minority enterprise programs and Richmond, Virginia, office.

1977   President Jimmy Carter announces a National Women's Business Ownership Campaign led by the SBA.

Congressional committee, chaired by Senator Lawton Chiles (D-Fla.), investigates Section 8(a) fraud and incompetence.

1978   Public Law 95–507 establishes preferred categories for 8(a) eligibility. African Americans, Hispanics, and Native Americans considered "presumptively" eligible.

1980   White House Conference on Small Business highlights growing political influence of small business.

1982   President Ronald Reagan orders massive increase in minority set-asides.

1985   Reagan administration tries to abolish the Small Business Administration.

1986   Second attempt at abolishing the SBA.

Wedtech scandal. Congress passes weak reforms of the 8(a) program in 1988.

1992   SBIC industry collapses. Reforms spark an investment boom in the 1990s.

1994   Election of Republican Congress. Despite talk of eliminating the SBA, Congress steadily increases loan authorizations.

An independent counsel investigates charges that President Bill Clinton pressured David Hale, head of a MESBIC, to illegally lend $300,000 to one of his partners in the Whitewater Development Corporation.

2000   Clinton's proposed budget authorizes $14 billion in business loans, nearly five times the level when Reagan left office.

APPENDIX B: GRAPHING GROWTH

SBA Business Loan Approvals
$ (millions)

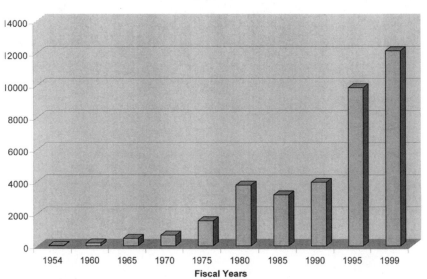

Source: U.S. Small Business Administration. These figures combine all business
lending programs (excluding SBICs and disaster loans).

SBIC Financing of Small Business
$ (millions)

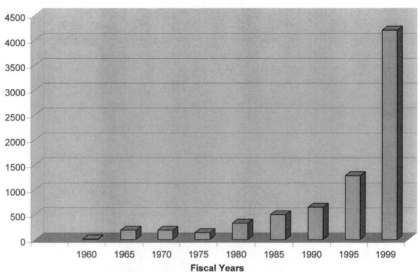

Fiscal Years

Sources: U.S. Small Business Administration, *SBIC Program Statistical Package*;
"SBA Boasts Record Lending for FY 1999," *Tax Management Financial Planning
Journal*, 16 November 1999: 295-96.

Disaster Loans
$ (millions)

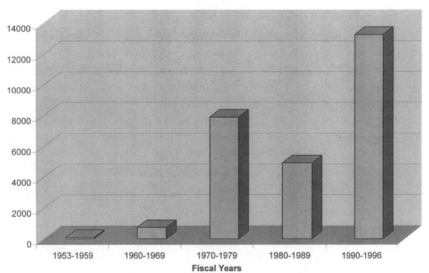

Fiscal Years
Source: U.S. Small Business Administration

Section 8(a) Contracts
$ (millions)

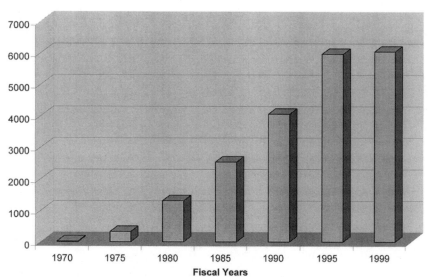

Fiscal Years

Sources: U.S. Small Business Administration; U.S. Senate Small Business
Committee, *Federal Minority Business Development Program*, hearing, 24 March
1983, table II; U.S. President, *State of Small Business* (1987), table 6.12.

NOTES

Introduction

1. "Clinton Impeached," *Washington Post,* 21 December 1998, A1; "Prosecutors Allege Scheme by Clinton," *Washington Post,* 15 January 1999, A1; "U.S. Investigating S&L Chief's '85 Check to Clinton, SBA-Backed Loan to Friend," *Wall Street Journal,* 1 November 1993: A3; "Loans for Disadvantaged Go to the Advantaged," *Wall Street Journal,* 5 November 1993, B1–2; "Whitewater Oozes Out Once More," *Economist,* 1 June 1996: 23–24; Peter Baker and Helen Dewar, "The Senate Acquits President Clinton," *Washington Post,* 13 February 1999, A1. For further discussion of the SBA loan, see U.S. Comptroller General, General Accounting Office, *Small Business Administration: Inadequate Oversight;* Stewart, *Blood Sport,* 136–38, 314–17; McDougal and Wilkie, *Arkansas Mischief,* 218–22; Coulter, *High Crimes,* 179–81. A judge jailed Susan McDougal for contempt when she refused to answer questions about Clinton's involvement with the SBA loan. However, Hale's allegation of misconduct on the part of Clinton was never proven in a court of law. President Clinton pardoned Susan McDougal on his last day in office. "Clinton's Last-Day Clemency Benefits 176," *Washington Post,* 21 January 2001: A1.

2. Thompson, *Feeding the Beast,* 275 [quote]; "Five Years of Troubles: A Chronology," *Boston Globe,* 6 July 1988: 8.

3. On the history of affirmative action, see Graham, *Civil Rights Era;* Belz, *Equality Transformed;* and Skrentny, *Ironies of Affirmative Action.*

4. See Chamberlain, "Whose State?," chap. 1 in *The American Stakes,* 11–34; Cigler and Loomis, "Contemporary Interest Group Politics."

5. Anglund, "American Core Values," 22 [quote].

6. Lowi, *End of Liberalism,* 71 [quote], 55 [quote]; Olson, *Logic of Collective Action.*

7. Surveys by the National Federation of Independent Business (NFIB) reported strong anti-union sentiment among its members. The National Association of Manufacturers also benefited from small business owners' anti-union stance. NFIB, *Attitudes of Independent Business Proprietors,* 26–28; "Favors Closed Shop Ban," *New York Times,* 25 November 1949: L39; Workman, "Manufacturing Power," 287.

8. Peterson, Albaum, and Kozmetsky, "Public's Definition of Small Business," 63–68.

9. "Table 4: Public Spending, 1890–1990," in Campbell, *Growth of American Government,* 34. "Big government" has a dual meaning. Many writers use it simply to describe

the growth of government from small to "big." For opponents of this trend, it means overly large, wasteful, or intrusive government. Here the term has both meanings.

10. Borcherding, ed., *Budgets and Bureaucrats*; Meltzer and Richard, "Why Government Grows"; Anderson and Hill, *Birth of a Transfer Society*; Larkey, Stolp, and Winer, "Theorizing About the Growth of Government," 157–220; Berry and Lowery, *Understanding United States Government Growth*; Higgs, *Crisis and Leviathan*; Vatter and Walker, *The Inevitability of Government Growth*; Hughes, *Governmental Habit Redux*; Campbell, *Growth of American Government*; Walker and Vatter, *Rise of Big Government*.

11. McClosky and Zaller, *American Ethos*; Bennett and Bennett, *Living With Leviathan*; Kaufman, *Are Government Organizations Immortal?*.

12. Graham, "The Stunted Career of Policy History," 34.

13. Harden, "What Do Federal Historians Do?," 21.

14. Stillman, "'Chinking in' a Temporary American State," chap. 3 in *Preface to Public Administration*, 42–74.

15. Bean, *Beyond the Broker State*.

Chapter 1

1. *Attention 4,000,000 Small and Independent Businessmen. Your Security Has Top Priority With Stevenson and Sparkman*, [1952], in Drexel Sprecher Papers, JFKPL, box 41, folder "Small Business Division: Chairman Materials I: 1952"); Dwight D. Eisenhower, press release, 16 October 1952, in John E. Horne Papers, JFKPL, box 2, folder "Personal Correspondence, Small Business Administration through 1953"; Glenn Davis, "Small Defense Plants Administration," *Congressional Record*, 12 March 1953, vol. 98, pt. 2:2212.

2. Cho, "Evolution."

3. Bean, *Beyond the Broker State*, 136–37; Parris, *Small Business Administration*, 14–18.

4. Parris, *Small Business Administration*, 18 [quote]; George Humphrey to Sherman Adams, 28 February 1953 [quote], in EPL, Central Files, box 228, folder "Reconstruction Finance Corporation, 1953"; George Humphrey to Sherman Adams, 2 March 1953, ibid.; "Small Business Agency," *Congressional Record*, 28 May 1953, vol. 99, pt. 11:A3042.

5. Green, "Small Business Administration," 11–12; George Burger [NFIB], testimony, U.S. Congress, House Banking and Currency Committee, *Creation of Small Business Administration*, 15 May 1953, 30; Everett D. Reese [ABA vice-president], testimony, 18 May 1953, ibid., 63–66; CASBO, Fourteenth Annual "Conference of Small Business Organizations," Resolution on Small Business Problems, 24 March 1953, in National Archives (Washington, D.C.), Record Group 46 [hereafter RG 46], Sen. 83 A-F4, Banking and Currency, Correspondence, tray, "Silver Purchase Act to War Damage," folder "Small Business"; "$$ For Small Business," *Congressional Quarterly Weekly Report*, 11 September 1953, 1143–47; J.M. Carmody to Brynildssen, 6 April 1953, National Archives (College Park, Md.), Records of the Small Business Administration, Record Group 309 [hereafter RG 309], box 17, folder "Meetings"; Zeigler, *Politics of Small Business*, 106; Republican Party Platform (1952), in *Congressional Almanac*, 772 [quote]. For more on the origin of the small business groups, see Bean, *Beyond the Broker State*.

6. George M. Humphrey, testimony before U.S. Congress, Senate Committee on Banking and Currency, *Government Lending Agencies*, 21 May 1953, 121, 123, 125.

7. SDPA, *Weekly Bulletin*, 23 February 1953; SDPA, *Weekly Bulletin*, 9 March 1953; Cho, "Evolution," 272; V.A. Votaw, *History of the Small Business Committee in the United States Senate*, RG 46, box 42, folder "History—Senate Small Business Commit-

tee," chap. 5, 16–17; Parris, *Small Business Administration*, 18–24; Charles Halleck, "Small Business Act of 1953," *Congressional Record*, 5 June 1953, vol. 99, pt. 5:6137; Walter Ploeser to Robert A. Taft, 19 February 1953, in Robert A. Taft Papers, Library of Congress (Washington, D.C.), box 1273, folder "Small Business" [quote]; Robert A. Taft to Walter C. Ploeser, 28 February 1953, ibid.; Zeigler, *Politics of Small Business*, 105–7, 111 [quote].

   8. Zeigler, *Politics of Small Business*, 104–11; SSBC, *Small Business Administration: Title II*, 2; Marcus, "Small Business Act," 143–89.

   9. Edward J. Thye, foreword, SSBC, *Small Business Administration: Title II*; William S. Hill, testimony, *Creation of Small Business Administration*, 14 May 1953, 11; Philip J. Philbin, "For Small Business," *Congressional Record*, 13 May 1953, vol. 99, pt. 4:4901–2.

   10. Hamilton, *Restraining Myths*, 248.

   11. Bean, *Beyond the Broker State*, 120–22; C.J. Judkins, "Do Associations Represent the Small Business Firm?" *Domestic Commerce*, July 1946, 15–20; HSBC, *Small Business Organizations*; U.S. Congress, House Select Committee on Lobbying Activities, *Conference of American Small Business Organizations*; Daughters, *Relationship of Small Business and Democracy*.

   12. Lipset, "Sources of the 'Radical Right,'" 196; Trow, "Small Businessmen"; Bunzel, "General Ideology"; Sutton, *American Business Creed*; Opinion Research Corporation, *Socialistic Thinking*; Opinion Research Corporation, *Free Market*.

   13. Hamilton, "Politics of Independent Business," chap. 2 in *Restraining Myths*, 33–98 [quote on 67]. A survey of self-employed Japanese Americans confirmed this split based on income, with successful business owners overwhelmingly Republican. Edna Bonacich and John Modell, "Table 7.6: Type of Firm by Political Party, Controlling for Family Income," *Economic Basis of Ethnic Solidarity*. Business writers and economists took the complaints of these small business owners seriously. See Peter F. Drucker, "The Care and Feeding of Small Business," *Harper's Magazine*, August 1950, 74–79; Adams, "Regulatory Commissions," 147–68; and Keith, "Impact of Taxation."

   14. Vinyard, "Congressional Committees," 146–47 [quotes]; Philip Jehle [Senate Small Business Committee counsel], interview with author; Walter Stults [former staff director, Senate Small Business Committee], interview with author, 5 February 1998; George Cates [Texas division manager, NFIB], interview with author; Parris, *Small Business Administration*, 167 [quote].

   15. LeLoup and Shull, *Congress and the President*, 79 [quote]; Hamby, *Liberalism and Its Challengers*, 118.

   16. "William D. Mitchell," *New York Times*, 31 July 1953, 10; Biographical Sketch, William D. Mitchell, EPL, Central Files, box 916, folder "Small Business Administration (1)"; William D. Mitchell to C.J. Rogers, n.d., ibid., [quote]; SSBC, *Weekly Staff Report*, 15 August 1953, in RG 46, box 32; SBA, *1st Semi-Annual Report*, 31 January 1954, 55; "Small Business . . . ," *Business Week*, 10 July 1954, 29; Willing, "A History," 169–71, 212.

   17. SSBC, *Small Business Administration: Title II*, 1 [quote]; Zeigler, *Politics of Small Business*, 108, 117–18; SBA, *1st Semi-Annual Report*, 8–9.

   18. SBA Loan Policy Board, minutes, 28 February 1955, in SBA Law Library (Washington, D.C.), Loan Policy Board Minutes, box 1, folder "February 28, 1955" [quote]. For insight into the continuing debate surrounding the definition of small business, see HSBC, Subcommittee No. 2, *Definition of "Small Business."*

   19. "Small Business," *Business Week*, 7 November 1953, 31 [quote]; Biographical Sketch, Wendell Burton Barnes, EPL, Central Files, box 916, folder "Small Business Administration (1)"; Jehle interview; Stults interview.

20. "Small Business," *Business Week*, 7 November 1953, 31; "Small Business," *Business Week*, 10 July 1954, 29; SBA, *1st Semi-Annual Report*, 56, 4–5; Edward Schoen Jr. to Wendell Barnes, 5 May 1954, SBA Law Library; SBA, "Public Statement of Loan Policy: Explanation of Loan Procedures," December 1953, Loan Policy Board minutes.

21. Willing, "A History," 181–82; Parris, "Organization and Administration," chap. 4 in *Small Business Administration*.

22. Paul Lodato, interview with author, 13 January 2000; Parris, "Organization and Administration."

23. SSBC, *Weekly Staff Report*, 15 May 1954; Wright Patman, "Small-Business Administration Not Effective—Small-Business Man Asks for Bread, Given a Stone," *Congressional Record*, 30 June 1954, vol. 100, pt. 7:9411; SBA, *2d Semi-Annual Report*, 31 July 1954, 46.

24. Wendell B. Barnes, "Progress Report of the Small Business Administration," 12 July 1954, EPL, Central Files, Official File, box 917, folder 258 (2).

25. Wendell B. Barnes to Sherman Adams, 27 March 1954, EPL, Central Files, box 916, folder "Small Business Administration (1)"; SSBC, *Weekly Staff Report*, 24 April 1954.

26. Sinclair Weeks, memorandum for the President, 18 December 1954, EPL, Central Files, box 66, folder "Small Business Administration"; Wendell B. Barnes, memorandum for the President, 22 December 1954, ibid.; SSBC, *Weekly Staff Report*, 14 May 1955; "Small Business Agency," *Congressional Quarterly Almanac* (1955):470; "Why Government Grows," *Nation's Business* (July 1955), 96; U.S. Chamber of Commerce, "Statement . . . On Operations and Activities of the Small Business Administration . . . ," 10 March 1955, in Joe L. Evins Papers (Cookeville, Tenn.), box 556, folder 9 ("Small Business—Correspondence and Statements"), 1–7 [quote on 1]; U.S. Commission on Organization of the Executive Branch of Government, *Report on Lending Agencies,* 71; Anonymous [Wendell Barnes?], "Background Report: Small Business Administration," 1 May 1958, EPL, Central Files, box 917, folder 258 (5), 10 [quote]; SSBC, *Weekly Staff Report*, 6 August 1955; "Small Business Agency," *Congressional Quarterly Almanac* (1955):468–70; Abraham J. Multer to Wendell B. Barnes, 14 September 1955, in National Archives, RG 309, Accession #60A-920, box 10.

27. Thomson and Shattuck, *1956 Presidential Campaign*, 36; Drexel A. Sprecher, interviewed by Larry J. Hackman, 2, 6 [quote]; Democratic National Committee, "Top Ten Issues of 1956," pamphlet, Sprecher Papers, JFKPL, box 41, folder "Small Business Division—Chairman Materials II"; Democratic National Committee, fact sheet, "The Fate of Small Business Under the GOP," 15 June 1956, EPL, Ann Whitman File, Administrative Series, box 9, folder "Dr. Arthur F. Burns, 1956–1957 (2)."

28. Wright Patman, 18 January 1956, "Is the Present Federal Small Business Policy Inadequate?" *Congressional Digest*, December 1956, 300; Abraham Multer, ibid., 312; Wright Patman to Dwight D. Eisenhower, 22 September 1956, in Wright Patman Papers, LBJPL, box 90B, folder 5; John Sparkman and Wright Patman, "The Tax Squeeze on Small Business—Tax Favoritism for Big Business," press release, 30 October 1956, EPL, Records of the Council of Economic Advisers, box 11, folder "Democratic Party Critiques re Small Business."

29. Independent Businessmen for Stevenson-Kefauver, press release, 28 October 1956, EPL, Records of the Council of Economic Advisers, box 11, folder "Democratic Party Critiques re Small Business, 1956" [quote]; Lumer, *Small Business at the CrossRoads*, 20.

30. Dwight D. Eisenhower, "Letter to Arthur F. Burns . . . ," 1 June 1956, *Public Papers of the Presidents of the United States: Dwight D. Eisenhower* (Washington, D.C.: GPO, 1956), 947; Jim Hagerty, memorandum for the President, 1 January 1957, EPL,

Ann Whitman File, Administrative Series, box 9, folder "Dr. Arthur F. Burns, 1956–1957 (1)", 1–2 [quote]; Rolles B. Kadesch, "Meeting to Plan Ways of Publicizing the White House Committee on Small Business," 14 August 1956, EPL, Council of Economic Advisers, Office of the Chairman, 1953–1960: CCSB—Personnel Matters, box 8, folder "CCSB—Publicity, 1956–1957"; Donham, "Whither Small Business?" 80 [quote]; Anonymous, "Background Report" [quote]; Arthur Burns, quoted in Hargrove and Morley, *The President and the Council of Economic Advisers*, 100.

31. Eisenhower, "Address at the Hunt Armory in Pittsburgh, Pennsylvania," 9 October 1956, *Public Papers*, 873; Eisenhower, "Telegram to Fred Herman, Chairman, Small Businessmen for Ike," 22 October 1956, ibid., 985–90; SSBC, *Weekly Staff Report*, 25 August 1956; Democratic National Committee, Small Business Division to State Directors, et al. "Funny Business About Small Business: How Republican Myth Men Play Tricks on the Public with Paid Actors," 3 October 1956, Sprecher Papers, box 42, folder "Small Business Divisions Chairman's Memos, Oct–Nov, 1956."

32. E. Burke Wilford to Sherman Adams, 15 February 1956, EPL, Central File, box 1303, folder "Small Business Administration, 1956" [quote]; Wright Patman, telegram to William S. Hill, et al., 25 October 1956, Sidney R. Yates Papers, HSTPL, box 62, folder "Small Business, 1956"; Cabinet Meeting, minutes, 16 May 1956, EPL, Ann Whitman File, box 7, Cabinet Series, folder "Cabinet Meeting of May 16, 1956" [quote]; SBA Loan Policy Board, minutes, 5 April 1956; Dwyer, *Small Business Administration*, 39; SBA, *7th Semi-Annual Report*, 31 December 1956, 1.

33. Frederick H. Mueller to Sherman Adams, 3 December 1956, EPL, Central Files, Official File, box 917, folder 258 (3).

34. "Small Business Agency," *Congressional Quarterly Almanac* (1957):677–79; "Small Business Act," *Congressional Record*, 25 June 1957, vol. 103, pt. 8:10201–46; Joseph Clark (D-Pa.), testimony, U.S. Congress, Senate Committee on Banking and Currency, Subcommittee on Small Business, *Credit Needs of Small Business*, 411 [quote]; SSBC, *Weekly Staff Report*, 29 June 1957; SSBC, *Weekly Staff Report*, 10 August 1957.

35. "Small Business Administration: 1958: Legislative Program," EPL, Ann Whitman File, Diary Series, box 29, folder "Staff Notes, December 1957"; Republican Legislative Meeting, 4 December 1957, EPL, Ann Whitman File, Legislative Meeting Series, box 2, folder "Legislative Leaders Meetings, 1957 (5)"; Anonymous, "Background Report"; SSBC, *Weekly Staff Report*, 14 June 1958; "The Small Business Administration Made Permanent," *Congressional Record*, 3 July 1958, vol. 104, pt. 10:13017; SBA, *11th Semi-Annual Report*, 31 December 1958, 29.

36. Hayes and Woods, "Are SBICs Doing Their Job?" 10; SSBC, *Small Business Investment Act of 1958*, 3–4; HSBC, *Annual Report*, H. Rpt. 2718, 85th Cong., 2d sess., 3 January 1959, 31–33; Kermit L. Culver, "Small Business Investment Companies," chap. 4 in Carson, *Vital Majority*, 61–64; "Reserve Board says Small Business Agency, Banks Fail to Aid Growth," *Wall Street Journal*, 14 April 1958, 7.

37. Vaughn, "Development," 29–30; Donham, "Whither Small Business?" 77. See also, Schweiger, "Adequacy of Financing," 323–47.

38. Schweiger, "Adequacy of Financing," 346; Brown, "Availability and Cost," 1–53 [quote on 10]; Stults interview [quote].

39. HSBC, *Annual Report*, 3 January 1959, 34–35; Vaughn, "Development," 46; Wright Patman, memorandum, 28 August 1958, Patman Papers, box 109C, folder 18 [quote]; "Small Business Investment Act of 1958," *Congressional Record*, 9 June 1958, vol. 104, pt. 8:10506 [Johnson quote], 10521 [Fulbright quote].

40. SSBC, *Small Business Investment Act of 1958*, minority report, 19–21; U.S. Congress, Senate Committee on Banking and Currency, *Financing Small Business* hearing, 85th Cong., 2d sess., 25 April 1958, 219, 301 [quote].

41. Don Rogers to Senator [Homer] Capehart, 23 May 1958, RG 46, tray Sen 85A-F4 (Correspondence), folder "Small Business Memoranda"; Memorandum to Senator Johnson, n.d., ibid.; Vaughn, "Development," 47; HSBC, *Annual Report*, 3 January 1959, 35; Hayes and Woods, "Are SBICs Doing Their Job?" 10; Neil Jacoby, quoted in Hooper, "Public Policy," 179; Dwyer, *Small Business Administration*, 42 [quote].

42. Reiner, "Transformation of Venture Capital," 302–6.

43. Paul M. Butler to Fellow Democrats, n.d., in Lyndon Baines Johnson Papers, U.S. Senate, 1949–1961: Papers of the Democratic Leader, LBJPL, box 392, folder "Policy: Democratic National Committee"; "1st Time in History: 3rd Straight Opposition Congress," *Congressional Quarterly Almanac* (1958):728–29.

44. Sloan, *Eisenhower*, 11; Deputy Director [name illegible], Bureau of the Budget to Wendell B. Barnes, 9 December 1958, RG 309; SSBC, *Review of Small Business Administration Activities, 1959–1960*, 5–6; SBA, "20 Years' Loan Approvals," *1972 Annual Report*, 6.

45. "20 Years' Loan Approvals"; SSBC, *Review of the Small Business Administration Activities, 1959–1960*, 6.

46. Hawley, *New Deal*, 473; Wilson, *Bureaucracy*, 78.

47. Dwight D. Eisenhower, "Radio and Television Address Delivered at a Rally in the Syria Mosque, Pittsburgh, Pennsylvania," 27 October 1958, in *Public Papers of the Presidents of the United States: Dwight D. Eisenhower* (Washington, D.C.: GPO, 1958), 807.

48. Parris, *Small Business Administration*, 167 [quote], 168 [quote]; Mansfield, "Congress and Economic Policy," 174 [quote]; Vinyard, "Congressional Committees," 173–75; HSBC, *Tenth Annual Report*, 2; Jehle interview [quote].

Chapter 2

1. John F. Kennedy, quoted in Fairlie, *Kennedy Promise*, 82.

2. Walter Stults [Staff Director, Senate Small Business Committee], interview with author, 5 February 1998; Philip Jehle [Senate Small Business Committee counsel], interview with author, 19 February 1998; Eugene Foley [counsel, Senator Hubert Humphrey], interview with author, 14 December 1997; Kennedy, *Compilation of Statements . . .* , JFKPL, SBA Records, box 1, no folder, 7–8.

3. Styles Bridges (R-N.H.), "The Republican Record on Behalf of Small Business—1953–1960," *Congressional Record*, 22 June 1960, vol. 106, pt. 9:13731–32; Wright Patman (D-Tex.), "Small Business and the Nation's Freedoms," *Congressional Record*, 31 August 1960, vol. 106, pt. 14:18854 [quote]; John Lesinski Jr. (D-Mass.), "Small Business," *Congressional Record*, 31 August 1960, vol. 106, pt. 14:18835; Johnson, *National Party Platforms*, 586; John F. Kennedy, campaign speeches (30 July, 17 September, 10 October, 22 October), in Kennedy, *Compilation of Statements . . .* ; John T. Burke to Theodore Reardon, 19 January 1960, JFKPL, Pre-presidential papers, Senate File, box 747, folder "Legislation File: 1960—Small Business, 1/15/60–3/29/60" [quote]; Rowen, *Free Enterprisers*, 29–30.

4. U.S. Congress, Senate Committee on Banking and Currency, *Nomination of John E. Horne*, 31 January 1961; John E. Horne, interviewed by John F. Stewart, 46–47.

5. Collins, *Business Response to Keynes*, 178; Congressional Quarterly, *Congress and the Nation: A Review of Government and Politics, 1945–1964* (Washington, D.C.: Con-

gressional Quarterly Service, 1965), 374–75; SBA, "20 Years' Loan Approvals," *1972 Annual Report*, 6; SSBC, *Small Business Administration—1961* hearing, 87th Cong., 1st sess., 21 June 1961, 6; SBA, *17th Semi-Annual Report*, 15–17; SSBC, *Fourteenth Annual Report*, S. Rpt. 1180, 88th Cong., 2d sess., 9 July 1964, 18; SBA, *1963 Annual Report*, 17.

6. Congressional Quarterly, *Congress and the Nation*, 376; SBA, *17th Semi-Annual Report*, 33; SBA, "20 Years' Loan Approvals"; SBA, "'501' & '502' Development Co. Loan Approvals," data provided to author by SBA; "Small Business Administration Training (1954–1992)," data provided to author; Marchum and Boshell, "Financing the Small and Medium-Size Business," 7.

7. Matusow, *Unraveling of America*, 100–2; John F. Kennedy, "The President's News Conference of February 15, 1961," *Public Papers of the Presidents of the United States, John F. Kennedy: 1961* (Washington, D.C.: GPO, 1962), 93; John F. Kennedy, "Statement by the President Announcing a Program of Assistance to the Textile Industry, May 2, 1961," ibid., 345–46; "Small Business Agency Cuts Interest on Loans in 101 Distressed Areas," *Wall Street Journal*, 6 April 1961, 3; John F. Kennedy, "White House Statement on a Program of Assistance to the Lumber Industry, July 26, 1962," *Public Papers of the Presidents of the United States, John F. Kennedy: 1962* (Washington, D.C.: GPO, 1963), 581.

8. SBA, *16th Semi-Annual Report*, 133–36; SBA, *1962 Annual Report*, 59.

9. Horne interview, 67 [quote], 81–82; Luther H. Hodges, 21 March 1964, interviewed by Dan B. Jacobs, 38–39 [quote on 39].

10. Vinyard, "Congressional Committees," 189 [quote]; John Sparkman, in SSBC, *Small Business Administration—1961*, 2 [quote]; Hubert Humphrey, "Small Business Administration Performing Important Service," *Congressional Record*, 19 September 1961, vol. 107, pt. 15:20224 [quote].

11. Horne interview, 84; John Kivlan to Philip F. Zeidman, 15 April 1965, Small Business Administration (Washington, D.C.), Loan Policy Board, box 1, folder "Loan Policy Board—General (1951–) [2 of 2]."

12. "Washington Versus Webster," *Wall Street Journal*, 11 December 1961, 12 [quote]; "Stretchable Smallness," *Wall Street Journal*, 4 September 1963, 12 [quote].

13. William Proxmire, in U.S. Congress, Senate Committee on Banking and Currency, *Financing Small Business*, 306; Sykes, *Proxmire*, 132 [quotes]; Proxmire, *Can Small Business Survive?* v, 139, 145, 155, 216–217. The government did not keep enterprise statistics until 1958. The smallest retail establishments (0–3 employees) saw their share of sales decline from 26 percent to 20 percent between 1954 and 1963. The smallest service establishments experienced a lesser decline. The employment share of single-plant manufacturing firms declined from 39 to 32 percent. Tables 3.6 and 3.7 in Hooper, "Public Policy," 36, 40; Vatter, "Position of Small Business," 156.

14. William Proxmire, statement in U.S. Congress, Senate Committee on Banking and Currency, *Nomination of John E. Horne and Eugene P. Foley* hearings, 88th Cong., 1st sess., 30 July 1963, 14 [quote]; Proxmire, *Can Small Business Survive?* 51–52 [quotes], 61–62.

15. "Stampede for SBICs Is On," *Business Week*, 20 May 1961, 135–36, 138; Hayes and Woods, "Are SBICs Doing Their Job?" 182, 190 [Kennedy quote]; Noone and Rubel, *SBICs*, 41; SSBC, *Twelfth Annual Report*, 3.

16. "SBICs: Rocky Road Looms Ahead," *Business Week*, 20 July 1963, 66–67; Noone and Rubel, *SBICs*, 47; Roger W. Benedict, "Shaky SBICs," *Wall Street Journal*, 16 July 1962, 1, 12 [quote]; "Double Standard," *Wall Street Journal*, 2 July 1963, 1, 16 [quote]; John E. Horne to William Proxmire, 9 July 1963, inserted in U.S. Congress, Senate Committee on Banking and Currency, Subcommittee on Small Business, *Conflict of Interest Problems in SBICs*, 7–8.

17. "SBICs Get the Pruning," 84; Hayes and Woods, "Are SBICs Doing Their Job?" 7, 16, 192; SSBC, *Operations of Small Business Investment Companies*, 3.

18. Hayes and Woods, "Are SBICs Doing Their Job?" 190 [quote], 192, 194, 198; SSBC, *Operations of Small Business Investment Companies*, 5, 20; "Congress Eases Rein on SBICs," *Business Week*, 22 February 1964, 48; HSBC, *Final Report, H*. Rpt. 1944, 88th Cong., 2d sess., 30 December 1964, 41–42; SSBC, *Fifteenth Annual Report, S*. Rpt. 635, 89th Cong., 1st sess., 20 August 1965, 13.

19. See Skrentny, *Ironies of Affirmative Action*, 37–50.

20. Suss, "Set-Asides," 429; SBA, *1964 Annual Report*, 40; HSBC, "Table XIII: Federal Government Procurement, fiscal years 1951–66 (small business share by agency)," *Status and Future of Small Business*, 81.

21. John F. Kennedy, "Economic Success of Towns Throughout the Country, July 11, 1957," in *John Fitzgerald Kennedy: A Compilation*, 534.

22. John F. Kennedy, memo for Secretary of Defense, 9 February 1961, Small Business Administration Records (hereafter, SBA Records), JFKPL, microfilm roll 1; John F. Kennedy, "The President's News Conference of March 15, 1961," *Public Papers . . . 1961*, 182–83; Robert McNamara, quoted in SSBC, *Twelfth Annual Report, S*. Rpt. 1491, 87th Cong., 2d sess., 15 May 1962, 17; Lee Loevinger to Frederick G. Dutton, 12 May 1961, JFKPL, White House Central Files, Subject Files, box 16, folder "BE 4–4 Small Business 1–1–61 to 12–31–61"; *Federal Acquisitions Regulation 14.408–6*.

23. [Frederick G. Dutton?], memorandum for Adam Yarmolinsky, 23 February 1961, JFKPL, White House Central Files, Subject Files, box 16, folder "BE 4–4 Small Business 1–1–61 to 12–31–61" [quote]; Frederick G. Dutton, memorandum for the President, 27 March 1961, ibid.; Wright Patman, "President Kennedy Appoints White House Committee on Small Business," *Congressional Record*, 3 May 1961, vol. 107, pt. 6:7249–50.

24. SSBC, *Thirteenth Annual Report, S*. Rpt. 104, 88th Cong., 1st sess., 2 April 1963, 17, 31; HSBC, "Table XIII," 81; SSBC, *Twelfth Annual Report*, 22; Anglund, "American Core Values," 155–56.

25. John Horne, memo to Frederick G. Dutton, "SBA Public Information Activity," 18 July 1961, JFKPL, White House Central Files, Subject Files, box 16, folder "BE 4–4 Small Business 1–1–61 to 12–31–61"; SSBC, *Fourteenth Annual Report*, 40; A.N. Wecksler, "Do SBA Rules Hobble Purchasing?" *Purchasing*, 11 March 1963, 76–78, 115.

26. Schrieber, "Small Business and Government Procurement," 392, 402.

27. SSBC, *Small Business Administration—1961, S*. Rpt. 1117, 87th Cong., 2d sess., 15 January 1962, 8; Gary Jackson, interview with author, 28 July 1998.

28. Henry Marcheschi [executive vice-president, Strategic Industries Association], testimony before SSBC, Subcommittee on Government Procurement, *Government Small Business Procurement Practices*, 607–14 [quote on 611].

29. Stanley D. Zemansky, "The Risks Inherent for a Small Business Taking a Contract As a Prime—or As a Subcontractor," *Journal of Purchasing* 7 (May 1971):54; Schrieber, *Defense Procurement and Small Business*.

30. John E. Horne, memorandum to Members of the White House Committee on Small Business, "Resume of Committee Meeting of November 27, 1961," 29 November 1961, JFKPL, White House Central Files, Subject File, box 207, folder "FG 754 White House Committee on Small Business."

31. WHCSB, *Small Business in the American Economy*, 11 [quote], 15 [quote]; John E. Horne, "Resume of Committee Meeting" [quote]; John E. Horne to Richard Nelson

[Council of Economic Advisers], 20 November 1961, JFKPL, White House Central File, Subject File, box 16, folder "BE 4–4 Small Business, 1–1–61 to 12–31–61" [quote].

32. HSBC, *Final Report*, 3 January 1963, 112 [quotes], 52 [quote]; WHCSB, *Small Business in the American Economy*, 14–15; John E. Horne to Richard Nelson, 20 November 1961, JFKPL, White House Central File, Subject File, box 16, folder "BE 4–4 Small Business, 1–1–61 to 12–31–61", 2 [quote]; SSBC, *Eleventh Annual Report*, S. Rpt. 51, 87th Cong., 1st sess., 16 February 1961, 5 [quote].

33. WHCSB, *Small Business in the American Economy*, 13–14 [quote on 14]; Clyde Bothmer to John E. Horne, 5 December 1961, JFKPL, White House Central File, Subject File, box 207, folder "FG 654 White House Conference on Small Business, 1–20–61 to 8–13–62"; Suss, "Set-Asides," 436; Bergmann, *In Defense of Affirmative Action*, 85 [quote].

34. John E. Horne, press release, "Address before the National Defense Committee of the National Association of Manufacturers," 8 June 1962, JFKPL, SBA Records, box 1, no folders [quote]; John E. Horne to Richard Nelson, 20 November 1961, JFKPL, White House Central File, Subject File, box 16, folder "BE 4–4 Small Business, 1–1–61 to 12–31–61" [quote]; HSBC, *Final Report*, 3 January 1963, 110 [quote]; Bothmer to John E. Horne, 5 December 1961.

35. SSBC, *Small Business Administration—1961*, hearing, 24–25; Harrison Williams Jr., "Amendment of Small Business Act, Relating to the Set-Aside Program." *Congressional Record*, 3 April 1962, vol. 108, pt. 5:5763; Philip Weaver, "Military Construction Program," *Congressional Record*, 29 June 1961, vol. 107, pt. 9:11908–11 [quote on 11911]; "Time to Call a Halt," *Wall Street Journal*, 15 February 1962, 10.

36. The AGCA continued to publicize this issue well into the 1980s, when it won a temporary exemption from set-asides. The Department of Defense reinstated construction set-asides on 17 June 1998 when the small-business share of contracts fell below the 40 percent target set by law. "Statement by the Associated General Contractors of America . . . ," in SSBC, *The Small Business Competitiveness Demonstration Program*, 132–50; "Small Business Competitiveness Demonstration Program," Title 48, Part 19.10 [48CFR19] *Federal Acquisition Regulations*, 430–32; James A. Gambardella to author, e-mail message, 5 October 1998.

37. Small Business Administration, Office of Small Business Size Standards, "In the Matter of Construction-Industry Size Standard for Set-aside Contracts (Excepting the Hydraulic Dredging Industry)," 20 February 1962, National Archives, SBA Records, RG 309, box 194, folder "Legal 2–2", 4 [quote]; John B. Henkels Jr. to Office of Small Business Size Standards, 12 February 1962, ibid., A-46–A-47; R.F. Conard to Samuel S. Solomon, ibid., A-48–A-49; William E. Dunn [AGCA official] to Samuel S. Solomon, 14 February 1962, A-52–A-53 [quote on A-52].

38. George Burger, "Statement of George J. Burger in Opposition to H.R. 10518, Which Would Eliminate Set-Asides of Construction Contracts for Small Business," *Congressional Record*, 12 September 1962, vol. 108, A6767–68; Chamber of Commerce of the United States, *Small Business: Its Role*, 32 [quote]; Irving Maness [Deputy Administrator for Procurement Assistance], "Construction Set-Asides, March 22, 1963," inserted in SSBC, *Small Business Administration—1963*, 19 [quote].

39. Irving Maness, "Small Business Administration Joint Set-Aside Program," SSBC, *Small Business Administration—1963*, 15.

40. Skrentny, *Ironies of Affirmative Action*, 13 [quote], 42–46.

41. Zemansky, "The Risks," 54.

42. See Higgs, *Arms, Politics, and the Economy* for a discussion of the noncompetitive nature of the defense sector.

43. Rowen, *Free Enterprisers*, 294 [quote], 27; Burner and Handlin, *John F. Kennedy and a New Generation*, 143; Gibson, *Battling Wall Street*, 55–67; Canterbery, *Economics on a New Frontier*, 6–7; Vogel, *Fluctuating Fortunes*, 16; Heath, *John F. Kennedy*, 42–45; Miroff, *Pragmatic Illusions*, 189, 199, 203.

44. Fairlie, *Kennedy Promise*, 240 [quote]; Reeves, *President Kennedy*, 316–17 [quote].

45. McQuaid, *Big Business*, 211 [quote], 224 [quote]; Harris, *Economics of the Political Parties*, 28.

46. Heath, *John F. Kennedy*, 29, 62–63, 50–55; Nossiter, *The Mythmakers*, 73 [quote].

47. Rowen, *Free Enterprisers*, 64–74 [quote on 74]; McQuaid, *Uneasy Partners*, 108–10; Hodges interview, 17 [quote], 26–27.

48. "Steel Crisis," *Congress and the Nation*, 378 [quote]; Fairlie, *Kennedy Promise*, 199–200 [quote on 199], 204; Heath, *John F. Kennedy*, 66–73 [quote on 72]; Reeves, *President Kennedy*, 303–4; Stebenne, *Arthur J. Goldberg*, 292–93, 496 n. (note 65).

49. "Business Men's Poll Supports President on Trade and Taxes," *New York Times*, 27 June 1962, 11; Heath, *John F. Kennedy*, 72, 74; "Steel Crisis," 378 [quote]; Stebenne, *Arthur J. Goldberg*, 298; "Steel Prices" (May 3–8, 1962), in Gallup, *The Gallup Poll*, vol. 3, 1767–68.

50. John F. Kennedy, "Address and Question and Answer Period in Tampa Before the Florida Chamber of Commerce, November 18, 1963," *Public Papers of the Presidents of the United States, John F. Kennedy: 1963* (Washington, D.C.: GPO, 1964), 864; John E. Horne, press release, "Government vs. Business: An Imaginary Conflict," address before the Harvard Business School Club of New York, 17 November 1961, JFKPL, SBA Records, box 1, no folder. Horne gave numerous speeches and held dozens of press conferences to publicize the Kennedy administration's efforts on behalf of small business. See John E. Horne Papers, JFKPL, box 2, folder "Miscellaneous—SBA Materials."

51. The final report was a revised version of a draft written by Horne in 1961. John E. Horne, *Why help small business? A Report to the White House Committee on Small Business*, 1961, JFKPL, White House Central File, Subject File [WHCSF], box 16, folder "BE 4–4 Small Business 1–1–61 to 12–31–61."

52. WHCSB, *Small Business in the American Economy*, 2, 4 [quote], 6–8 [quote on 6]; WHCSB, "Progress Report of the White House Committee on Small Business, inserted in *Congressional Record*, 30 July 1962, vol. 108, pt. 11:15080–83.

53. John F. Kennedy, "Excerpts From Annual Message to the Congress: the Economic Report of the President, January 21, 1963," *Public Papers . . . 1963*, 57–63 [quote on 63]; John F. Kennedy, "Special Message to the Congress on Tax Reduction and Reform, January 24, 1963," ibid., 77; John F. Kennedy, "Remarks to the National Advisory Council of the Small Business Administration, May 16, 1963," ibid., 404 [quote].

54. John E. Horne, "American Small Business Has an Important Stake in the President's Proposed Tax Reduction and Tax Reform Program," *Congressional Record*, 31 January 1963, vol. 109, A684; John Horne, testimony in SSBC, Subcommittee on Taxes, *Impact of Current Tax Proposals*, hearing, 29 April 1963, 28; George J. Burger Sr., testimony in ibid., 105–6; National Advisory Council resolution, footnote to Kennedy, "Remarks to the National Advisory Council," 404n; SSBC, *Impact of Current Tax Proposals*, S. Rpt. 397, 15 August 1963, 12; HSBC, *Final Report*, 30 December 1964, 99–103; Horne interview, 63; Lyndon B. Johnson, "Radio and Television Remarks Upon Signing the Tax Bill, February 26, 1964," *Public Papers of the Presidents of the United States, Lyndon B. Johnson: 1963–64* (Washington, D.C.: GPO, 1965), 312.

55. SSBC, *Fourteenth Annual Report*, 1–5 [quote on 1]; Dickerson and Kawaja, "Failure Rates," 84; Anderson and Hazleton, *Managing Macroeconomic Policy*, 31.

56. See Galbraith, *Affluent Society* and Harrington, *The Other America*.

57. Patterson, *America's Struggle Against Poverty*, 99–125; Murray, *Losing Ground*, 15–29.

58. Thernstrom and Thernstrom, *America in Black and White*, 119–51.

59. Foley interviews, 14 December 1997 and 30 June 1998; Heimlich, "Business of Poverty," 30–30n; Foley, *Achieving Ghetto*, 149 [quote]; U.S. Congress, Senate Committee on Banking and Currency, *Nomination of John E. Horne and Eugene P. Foley*, 9–11.

60. Bernard Boutin, interview with author, 21 October 1997 [quote]; Foley interview.

Chapter 3

1. Parris, *Small Business Administration*, 173; John E. Horne, interview, Oral History Collection, LBJPL, 22 July 1969, 17; Eugene Foley, interview with author, 14 December 1997.

2. Heimlich, "Business of Poverty," 69–73; SSBC, *Small Business Administration— 1963*, 2–4; SBA, *1964 Annual Report*, 62; HSBC, *Organization and Operation of the Small Business Administration (Reorganization, Curtailed Loan Program, New Small Loan Programs*, 7 April 1965, 4–5 [quote on 5].

3. Heimlich, "Business of Poverty," 31–35; "Revised Small Loan Program" [1964], Small Business Administration (Washington, D.C.), Loan Policy Board, box 1, folder "Loan Policy Board—General (1951–) [2 of 2]"; Parris, *Small Business Administration*, 109 [Foley quote].

4. Parris, *Small Business Administration*, 149; Moon, "An Evaluation," 46–58; "Where Sick Companies Can Turn for Advice," *Business Week*, 15 August 1964, 94; Foley interview, 14 December 1997; Dwyer, *Small Business Administration*, 48–50; Foley, "Address by Eugene P. Foley," A5351–52; Eugene P. Foley, "Six Months' Progress Report," 25 May 1964, LBJPL, WHCF, FG 283, box 305, folder "6/64–12/31/64." In 1968, the agency added the Active Corps of Executives (ACE), a group of consultants who were still active in business. Nellis, *A SCORE That Counts*, 64.

5. Skrentny, *Ironies of Affirmative Action*, passim [quote on 120]; Belz, *Equality Transformed*, 65–66 [quote on 65]; Glazer, *Affirmative Discrimination*, 204–5; Roberts and Stratton, *New Color Line*, 91–96; Bolick, *Affirmative Action Fraud*, 53–54.

6. Arthur M. Blacklow [Assistant General Counsel], memorandum to Fredric T. Suss [General Counsel], 5 July 1961, LBJPL, SBA Records, microfilm reel 17, Office of General Counsel, Civil Rights Files; Eugene J. Davidson [Acting Assistant General Counsel], memorandum to Jerome S. Plapinger [Acting General Counsel], "Report on Discrimination for White House Subcabinet Group on Civil Rights," 27 July 1961, ibid.; Eugene P. Foley to Lee C. White [Assistant Special Counsel to the President], 15 November 1963, ibid.; Brauer, *John F. Kennedy*, 256–57; Branch, *Parting the Waters*, 746–47 [quote on 747]; Arthur M. Blacklow to Fredric T. Suss, "Authority of the President to Direct the Withholding of SBA Financial Assistance in a Particular State," 9 April 1963, JFKPL, SBA Records, box 2, no folder; Fredric T. Suss to John E. Horne, "President's Authority to Prohibit SBA Financial Assistance in a Given State," 11 April 1963, ibid.

7. Kull, *Color-Blind Constitution*, 164 [quote], 182. Skrentny, *Ironies of Affirmative Action*, 31–33; Scott, "Politics of Pathology," 92–93.

8. Silberman, "The City and the Negro," 88–91, 139–40, 144, 146, 151–52, 154; "Is equality unfair? Negro's plea for preferential treatment," *America*, 12 October 1963, 412–13; "Preferential Hiring: Pitney-Bowes," *Newsweek*, 16 December 1963, 69; Edward T. Chase, "Quotas for Negroes?" *Commonweal*, 17 January 1964, 451–54; "Ne-

groes Preferred?" *America*, 28 March 1964, 397; Silberman, *Crisis in Black and White*, 241, 245 [quote]; King, *Why We Can't Wait*, 147 [quote], 152 [quote].

9. Thernstrom and Thernstrom, *America in Black and White*, 150; John C. Satterfield, 30 January 1964 address, in "Should Congress Enact the Employment Non-discrimination Provisions of the Civil Rights Bill?" *Congressional Digest* (March 1964), 95; Herman Talmadge, 31 July and 20 November, 1963 statements, ibid., 83; Emanuel Celler, 31 January 1964 speech, in "Should Congress Enact?" 78; Glazer, *Affirmative Discrimination*, 45, Belz, *Equality Transformed*, 24–27; Hubert Humphrey, quoted in Roberts and Stratton, *New Color Line*, 75; Skrentny, *Ironies of Affirmative Action*, 120–21.

10. Skrentny, *Ironies of Affirmative Action*, 4; Moynihan, "Negro Family," 23–37 [quotes on 28, 29]; Lyndon B. Johnson, "Commencement Address at Howard University: 'To Fulfill These Rights,'" 4 June 1965, *Public Papers . . . 1965*, 635–40 [quote on 636].

11. Skrentny, *Ironies of Affirmative Action*, 127–33; Belz, *Equality Transformed*, 27–29; Glazer, *Affirmative Discrimination*, 53 [quote].

12. SBA, *Administrative History* (1968), LBJPL, Administrative History of Small Business Administration, box 1, folder 2, 250–53 [quote on 251]; Belz, *Equality Transformed*, 24–25; U.S. Commission on Civil Rights, *Federal Civil Rights*, 579–80; SBA, "Title 13, Chapter I—Small Business Administration Part 112—Nondiscrimination in Financial Assistance Programs—Effectuation of Title VI of the Civil Rights Act of 1964," 29 December 1964, LBJPL, SBA Records, microfilm reel 17, Office of General Counsel, Civil Rights Files.

13. SBA, *Administrative History*, 253; "SBA Equal Opportunity Educational Program," 27 June 1966, LBJPL, Bernard Boutin Papers, box 26, folder "Administrator's Chronological File: 8/1–8/24/66"; Edward Dulcan, quoted in SBA *Stenographic Transcript*, Area Administrators and Regional Directors Meeting, 6 May 1966. RG 309, box 285, folder "Meetings 3–1 (FY 66)." The Civil Rights Commission praised the agency for its exhaustive compliance reviews. See U.S. Commission on Civil Rights, *Federal Civil Rights*, 691–92.

14. Howard W. Rogerson, memorandum to Civil Rights Working Group, "Assignment—Procedures for the Collection of Minority Group Data," 12 July 1965, LBJPL, SBA Records, microfilm reel 17, Office of General Counsel, Civil Rights Files; Eugene P. Foley, National Directive 335–1, "Nondiscriminatory Employment Opportunity Policy and Procedures," 8 September 1965, LBJPL, SBA Records, microfilm reel 36 [quote]. The "Asian" category included "Japanese, Chinese, Korean, or Polynesian."

15. Clarence Mitchell, quoted in Skrentny, *Ironies of Affirmative Action*, 128.

16. Rogerson, "Assignment."

17. SBA, *Administrative History*, 256–57.

18. Foley, National Directive 335–1; Randall L. Tyus, memorandum to Area Administrators, et al., "Equal Employment Opportunity," 11 February 1965, LBJPL, SBA Records, microfilm reel 17; Randall L. Tyus, memorandum to Area Administrators, et al., "Equal Employment Opportunity," 10 March 1965, ibid.; Randall L. Tyus, memorandum to the Administrator, "Equal Employment Opportunity," 24 May 1965, ibid.; SBA, *1963 Annual Report*, 54–55; Foley interview; Bernard Boutin to David S. North, 24 August 1966, LBJPL, Bernard Boutin Papers, box 26, folder "Administrator's Chronological File: 8/25–8/31/66."

19. Eugene P. Foley, memorandum to Deputy Administrators, et al., "Equalization of Employment Opportunities for Women," 12 February 1964, LBJPL, SBA Records, microfilm reel 17, Office of General Counsel, Civil Rights Files; SBA, *1964 Annual Re-*

port, 51, 63; Joe L. Evins, "Women Going Big for Small Business Loans," *Congressional Record,* 12 August 1965, vol. 111, A4496.

20. Eugene Foley, quoted in Heimlich, "Business of Poverty," 217.

21. "Negro Businessmen Ask Commerce Dept. Help," *New York Amsterdam News,* 29 July 1961, 4; Foley interview; U.S. Department of Commerce, *Problems and Opportunities,* 52–55.

22. Howard University, *Post-War Outlook for Negroes;* Commerce Department, *Problems and Opportunities,* 1, 7, 46–49.

23. Charles C. Diggs Jr., in *Problems and Opportunities,* 99 [quote]; LeRoy W. Jeffries, ibid., 9, 89 [quote]; Spalding, quoted in "Negro Businessmen." The African market appealed to black business owners in the early 1960s. One African American firm, the Simmons Royalty Company, brokered billions of dollars worth of oil leases with African nations. Walker, *History of Black Business,* 250. See also, "Eyes African Business: Business League Entertains Delegates," *New York Amsterdam News,* 10 December 1960, 7.

24. Commerce Department, *Problems and Opportunities,* 33, 73–75, 81.

25. Heimlich, "Business of Poverty," 73, 37–39; Edward N. Rosa [Regional Director, Philadelphia] to John E. Horne, 28 February 1963, LBJPL, SBA Records, microfilm reel 2; "Aiding Negro Businessmen," *Business Week,* 18 April 1964, 141.

26. Edward Rosa to Eugene P. Foley, 14 November 1963, LBJPL, SBA Records, microfilm reel 2; Small Business Opportunities Corporation, "Board of Directors Meeting, March 2, 1964," ibid.; Randall L. Tyus to John Kevlin [Office of General Counsel], 18 March 1964, ibid. [quote]; SBA, *1963 Annual Report,* 54; SBA, *1964 Annual Report,* 56.

27. SBA, *1964 Annual Report,* 55–56; Randall L. Tyus, memorandum to Edward N. Rosa, "Philadelphia Loans to Orientals," 8 March 1965, LBJPL, SBA Records, microfilm reel 2; William T. Gennetti to Randall L. Tyus, 16 March 1965, ibid.; SBA, "Statistics in Philadelphia (Pilot Loan Program) as of June 30, 1964," ibid.

28. Randall L. Tyus to John Kevlin, 18 March 1964, LBJPL, SBA Records, microfilm reel 2; Bates, *Black Capitalism,* 15; Foley, "Negro Businessman," 107–44 [quote on 115]. Foley's derogatory view of black business echoed that of E. Franklin Frazier. In his influential *Black Bourgeoisie,* Frazier derided Booker T. Washington's vision of business as a path to success for black Americans.

29. Humphrey, *Bridging the Gap,* n.p.; Eugene P. Foley, interview with author, 30 June 1998. Humphrey praised the pilot loan projects in his book *War on Poverty,* 102.

30. Heimlich, "Business of Poverty," 41–44, 53–54; Eugene P. Foley, testimony before U.S. Congress, House Committee on Education and Labor, *Economic Opportunity Act,* 379; Hubert Humphrey, "Address by Vice President Humphrey at the National Conference on Equal Business Opportunity," *Congressional Record,* 22 October 1965, vol. 111, pt. 21:28319 [quote]; SBA, *1964 Annual Report,* 60; SBA, *1965 Annual Report,* 35 [quote].

31. Foley, testimony before U.S. Congress, House Committee on Education and Labor, *Economic Opportunity Act,* 378–79 [quote]; Heimlich, "Business of Poverty," 203 [quote], 179; SBA, *1964 Annual Report,* 58, 60.

32. "SBA Curtailed Regular Program of Small Business Loans in Order to Keep Enough Money for Disaster Funding," *Wall Street Journal,* 10 November 1964, 3; HSBC, *Organization and Operation of the Small Business Administration—1966,* 29; Heimlich, "Business of Poverty," 135–37, 225; SBA, *1965 Annual Report,* 16–17, 33.

33. Heimlich, "Business of Poverty," 81–83, 132–33.

34. Ibid., 227 [quote].

35. Ibid., 103–5, 116–17, 225.

36. Eugene P. Foley, testimony before HSBC, Subcommittee No. 5, *Small Business Problems in Urban Areas*, hearing, 7 June 1965, 9.

37. Logan B. Hendricks, memorandum to All Area Administrators, et al., "Information Letter #2—Title IV—Economic Opportunity Loan Program," 21 July 1965, LBJPL, SBA Records, box 1, folder "SBA Economic Opportunity Assistance."

38. Ibid.

39. For a representative example of this mindset, see Ryan, *Blaming the Victim*.

40. Shapiro and Sullivan, *Race Riots*; Berson, *Case Study of a Riot*; "Are the Riots Planned?" *Business Week*, 9 September 1964, 34; Philip F. Zeidman, memorandum to the Administrator, "A possible role for you in future racial controversies," 15 March 1965, LBJPL, SBA Records, microfilm reel 17, Office of General Counsel, Civil Rights Files; Bean, "'Burn, Baby, Burn.'"

41. Lyndon B. Johnson, "Statement by the President Upon Announcing a Program of Assistance to Los Angeles, August 26, 1965," *Public Papers . . . 1965*, 933–34.

42. Lyndon B. Johnson, "The President's News Conference of August 25, 1965," *Public Papers . . . 1965*, 919; Foley interview, 14 December 1997; Bradford, *Oakland's Not for Burning*, 2–4 [quotes], 169, 199–201 [quote on 199]; Murray, *Losing Ground*, 37. For an in-depth analysis of what went wrong in Oakland, see Pressman and Wildavsky, *Implementation*.

43. Foley interview, 14 December 1997; John W. Macy Jr., memorandum for the President, "Economic Development Administration, Department of Commerce," 23 August 1965, LBJPL, WHCF: FG 283, box 305, folder "6/1/65–2/16/66"; Eugene P. Foley, memorandum for Joseph A. Califano Jr., "Small Business Administration and Its Transfer to Commerce," 21 January 1966, ibid. [quote]; Foley, memorandum for W. Marvin Watson, "Transfer of SBA to Commerce," 24 February 1966, ibid., folder "2/17/66–11/28/66"; Califano, *Triumph and Tragedy*, 114; John Sparkman, "The Rumored Proposal That the Small Business Administration Be Placed Within the Department of Commerce," *Congressional Record*, 4 February 1966, vol. 112, pt. 2:2124; Harrison Williams Jr., "The Talk About Abolishing the Small Business Administration," ibid., 2180; Joe L. Evins, "The Independence of SBA Supported in Statements of Leaders," *Congressional Record*, 7 February 1966, vol. 112, pt. 2:2393; Joe L. Evins, et al. to Lyndon B. Johnson, 3 February 1966, Joe L. Evins Papers (Cookeville, Tenn.), box 563, folder 2 ("Small Business—Correspondence").

44. Jameson W. Doig and Erwin C. Hargrove, "'Leadership' and Political Analysis," in *Leadership and Innovation*, ed. Jameson W. Doig and Erwin C. Hargrove, 8.

45. SBA, "20 Years' Loan Approvals," *1972 Annual Report*, 6.

46. Stillman, *American Bureaucracy*, 252–53; Samuelson, *Good Life*, 141 [quote]; James L. Sundquist, "From Gloom to Euphoria," chap. 1 in *Politics and Policy*, 3–10; Robert Collins, "Growth Liberalism in the Sixties" chap. 1 in *The Sixties: From Memory to History*, ed. David Farber, 38. In 1964, 79 percent of Americans trusted the government "to do what is right." Miller and Traugott, "Table 4.37: Trust in Government Index," in *American National Election Studies*, 272.

47. Wilson, *Political Organizations*, 345.

48. Bureaucratic theorists characterize this type of organizational culture as "differentiated" (i.e., "consensus within subcultures but . . . inconsistency and even conflict between subcultures"). For a typology of organizational cultures, see Ban, "Varieties of Organizations," chap. 1 in *How Do Public Managers Manage?*

49. The EEOC official most responsible for this change, Alfred Blumrosen, stated that his clever reinterpretation of Title VII was "contrary to the plain meaning" of the act. Graham, *Civil Rights Era*, 195.

50. Kull, *Color-Blind Constitution*, 1 [*Plessy* quote].

51. Eugene P. Foley, quoted in HSBC, *Final Report, H.* Rpt. 1944, 88th Cong., 2d sess., 30 December 1964, 126; Foley, "Six Months' Progress Report."

52. Testimony of Julius Thomas [National Urban League] and Ross Clinchy [U.S. Civil Service Commission], in U.S. Commerce Department, *Problems and Opportunities*, 41, 44. The new black middle class of the 1960s was heavily concentrated in the public sector. Heckman, "Impact of Government," 55, 78n (note 1).

Chapter 4

1. Ross D. Davis, quoted in SBA, *Stenographic Transcript*, Area Administrators and Regional Directors Meeting, 4 May 1966, SBA Records, National Archives (College Park), RG 309, box 285, folder "Meetings 3–1 (FY 66)", 48–49; Padriac Frucht, ibid., 69–70.

2. Randall L. Tyus, memorandum to Files, "Philadelphia 6X6 Loans in Liquidation and Delinquent," 8 December 1965, LBJPL, SBA Records, microfilm reel 2; Benjamin Goldstein, quoted in Monroe W. Karmin, "Negro Aid Muddle: Federal Programs to Help Businessmen at Cross Purposes," *Wall Street Journal*, 4 January 1966, 14; Charles Kriger [New York Regional Director], quoted in *Stenographic Transcript*, 6 May 1966, 163; Philip Zeidman [General Counsel], quoted in ibid., 316.

3. John W. Macy Jr., memorandum for the President, "SBA Administrator," 14 April 1966, LBJPL, WHCF, box 307, folder "FG 283A" [quote]; Marvin Watson to Lyndon B. Johnson, 4 May 1966, LBJPL, WHCF: FG 283, box 305, folder "2/17/66–11/28/66"; Schott and Hamilton, *People, Positions, and Power*, 119–21; "Boutin, Bernard L(ouis)"; Joe L. Evins, "Small Business Welcomes Bernard L. Boutin," *Congressional Record*, 23 May 1966, vol. 112, pt. 9:11216; Arch A. Moore Jr., "Appointment of Bernard Boutin," *Congressional Record*, 9 May 1966, vol. 112, pt. 8:10009. In January 1967, President Johnson proposed merging the Commerce and Labor Departments, the SBA, and other agencies into a "Department of Business and Labor." The Commerce Department was the main backer of the proposal; the agency had lost 80 percent of its budget to the newly created Department of Transportation and was "a department in search of a new role." Opposition from labor and small business advocates, however, resulted in the swift demise of this super-agency proposal. Redford and Blissett, *Organizing the Executive Branch*, 142–44, 150–56.

4. Bernard Boutin to W. Marvin Watson, 7 November 1966, LBJPL, WHCF: Confidential File, box 33, folder "FG 283: Small Business Administration (1965–66)"; Bernard L. Boutin to W. Marvin Watson, 1 September 1966, LBJPL, Bernard Boutin Papers, box 26, folder "Administrator's Chronological File: 9/1–9/15/66"; Bernard Boutin, interview with author, 21 October 1997.

5. Boutin to Watson, 7 November 1966; Bernard L. Boutin to Senior Staff, 23 May 1966, Boutin Papers, box 24, folder "May 1–May 31, 1966"; Boutin to Watson, 1 September 1966; Bernard Boutin to W. Marvin Watson, 25 July 1966, LBJPL, WHCF: FG 283, box 305, folder "2/17/66–11/28/66"; Bernard W. Boutin, memorandum for W. Marvin Watson, 30 September 1966, Boutin Papers, box 27, folder "Administrator's Chronological File: 9/1–9/30/66"; SBA, *1966 Annual Report*, 35; SBA, *1967 Annual Report*, 22.

6. SSBC, *Fifteenth Annual Report, S.* Rpt. 635, 89th Cong., 1st sess., 20 August 1965, 14; "A Freeze on Forming New SBICs," *Business Week*, 11 July 1964, 34, 36; "For SBICs, a New Flexibility," *Business Week*, 26 December 1964, 94; "SBICs Road Back," *Fortune* 74 (August 1966), 194, 196; HSBC, *Final Report, H.* Rpt. 2347, 89th Cong., 2d sess., 30 December 1966, 38; SSBC, *Seventeenth Annual Report, S.* Rpt. 345., 90th Cong.,

1st sess., 14 June 1967, 10–11; HSBC, *Final Report, H.* Rpt. 1985, 90th Cong., 2d sess., 31 December 1968, 26; SBA, *1966 Annual Report,* 25; Wharton, "Small Business Investment," 142.

7. "SBICs Road Back," 194, 196; "Agency Chief Promises Curb on 250 SBICs Called 'Unsatisfactory,'" *Wall Street Journal,* 18 July 1966, 3; Bernard Boutin to W. Marvin Watson, 25 July 1966 [quote]; "Mr. Boutin's Battle," *Wall Street Journal,* 19 April 1967, 18; Boutin interview.

8. "Mr. Boutin's Battle"; "SBICs Road Back"; Boutin, interview with author, 10 April 2000.

9. Boutin interviews, 21 October 1997 and 18 July 1998; Grogan Lord, testimony before HSBC, *Final Report,* 30 December 1966, 43; Lyndon B. Johnson, "Statement by the President Upon Signing the Small Business Investment Act Amendments, November 6, 1966," *Public Papers of the Presidents of the United States, Lyndon B. Johnson: 1966* (Washington, D.C.: GPO, 1967), 1342; "SBIC's Get the Pruning Treatment," *Business Week,* 10 June 1967, 84, 89, 92; Congressional Quarterly, *Congress and the Nation,* Vol. 2, 295–96; Parris, *Small Business Administration,* 33–35.

10. Mitchell and Simmons, *Beyond Politics,* 39 [quote]; Proxmire, *Can Small Business Survive?* 52.

11. Wright Patman, memorandum, 28 August 1958, in Wright Patman Papers, LBJPL, box 109C, folder 18]; "Small Business Investment Act of 1958," *Congressional Record,* 9 June 1958, vol. 104, pt. 8:10506, 10521 [quote]; Brown, *New Policies, New Politics,* 12, 45 [quote].

12. "SBIC's Get the Pruning," 84 [quote]; "The Dream That Failed," *Forbes,* 15 July 1967, 20–21; "This Year's Fever," *Forbes,* 15 January 1968, 30 [quote]; SSBC, *Nineteenth Annual Report, S.* Rpt. 627, 91st Cong., 1st sess., 20 December 1969, 6 [quote]; Noone and Rubel, *SBICs: Pioneers,* 109; Wharton, "Small Business Investment," 144, 147, 150.

13. Noone and Rubel, *SBICs,* 122; Reiner, "Transformation of Venture Capital," 281–82, 337–39.

14. Bernard L. Boutin, memorandum for Robert T. Cochran Jr., "Proposed White House Conference on Small Business," 25 May 1966, Boutin Papers, box 24, folder "May 1–May 31, 1966"; Bernard Boutin to Irving Maness, 28 July 1966, Boutin Papers, box 25, folder "Administrator's Chronological File: 7/1–7/15/65"; HSBC, *Status and Future of Small Business,* 46; SSBC, *Seventeenth Annual Report,* 4; Boutin interview, 21 October 1997; Bernard Boutin, memorandum for W. Marvin Watson, 1 August 1966, Boutin Papers, box 26, folder "Administrator's Chronological File: 8/1–8/24/66" [quote]; "Help for Not-So-Small," *Business Week,* 17 September 1966, 43; "How Big is Small? SBA's New List," *Newsweek,* 26 September 1966, 95; Boutin interview, 18 July 1998.

15. Peterson, Albaum, and Kozmetsky, "Public's Definition of Small Business," 65.

16. Opinion Research Corporation, *Big Business on the Spot,* A-12.

17. SSBC, *Fifteenth Annual Report,* 17; SBA, *Administrative History,* 1968, LBJPL, Administrative History of Small Business Administration, box 1, folder 2, p. 172; Parris, *Small Business Administration,* 55.

18. Bernard Boutin to the President, 27 June 1967, Boutin Papers, box 34, folder "Administrator's Chronological File 6/16–6/30/67."

19. Lyndon B. Johnson, "Statement by the President Announcing the Appointment of Robert C. Moot As Deputy Administrator, Small Business Administration, November 13, 1966," *Public Papers . . . 1966,* 1385; "Biographical Sketch of Robert C. Moot," U.S. Congress, Senate Committee on Banking and Currency, *Nomination of Rob-*

ert C. Moot, 6; SBA, *1967 Annual Report,* ii, 11; SBA, *1968 Annual Report,* 1–2, 13, 17; SBA, "20 Years' Loan Approvals," *1972 Annual Report,* 6; Elwyn A. Nellis, *A SCORE that Counts,* 30 [quote]; Harmon Tupper, "SCORE Spells Help for the Small Businessman," *Reader's Digest* (March 1967), 19–26.

20. Feagin and Hahn, *Ghetto Revolts,* 102–7; Thernstrom and Thernstrom, *America in Black and White,* 160.

21. Banfield, "Rioting," 211–33. See also, Ernest Van den Haag, "How Not to Prevent Civil Disorders," *National Review,* 26 March 1968, 284–86; James Burnham, "The Right to Riot," *National Review,* 8 October 1968, 1000; Methvin, *The Riot Makers*; Decter, "Looting and Liberal Racism," 48–54; Bray, "Reading America," 32–36.

22. Feagin and Hahn, *Ghetto Revolts,* 44 [quote], 47 [quote]; Skolnick, *Politics of Protest*; Fogelson, *Violence as Protest*; Hayden, *Rebellion in Newark*; Sears and Tomlinson, "Riot Ideology," 485–503; Sears and McConahay, *Politics of Violence,* 171–73, 181; Siegel, "Riot Ideology," 1–13; Browne, "Constellation of Politics," 44–55 [quotes on 46].

23. Feagin and Hahn, *Ghetto Revolts,* 21–22, 27, 244, 253; Gale, *Understanding Urban Unrest,* 205, 59–85; Jacoby, *Someone Else's House,* 138; Lyndon B. Johnson, "Remarks in Kansas City, Missouri, at the Meeting of the International Association of Chiefs of Police" (14 September 1967), *Public Papers of the Presidents of the United States, Lyndon B. Johnson: 1967* (Washington, D.C.: GPO, 1968), 831–36 [quote on 836]; Button, *Black Violence,* 158; Singer and Osborn, *Black Rioters,* 35; Weir, *Politics and Jobs,* 83–88. Michael Flamm discusses the liberal response to the riots in "'Law and Order.'" For statistics on the redirection of antipoverty spending to riot cities, see Skrentny, *Ironies of Affirmative Action,* 89; Weir, *Politics and Jobs,* 83–88; and Button, *Black Violence,* passim.

24. Belz, *Equality Transformed,* 65 [quote]; Skrentny, "Crisis Management through Affirmative Action," chap. 4 in *Ironies of Affirmative Action,* 67–110; George H. Gallup, "Race Relations (May 2–7, 1968)," *The Gallup Poll,* vol. 3, 2128. For more on public attitudes toward the riots, see Erskine, "The Polls: Demonstrations and Riots."

25. Boutin interview, 21 October 1997 [quote]; Burt Schorr, "Antipoverty Setback," *Wall Street Journal,* 17 July 1967, 1, 10; "Charitable Lending," *Wall Street Journal,* 6 December 1966, 18 [quote]; Mark Levy, "Putting the Poor Out of Business," *Nation,* 12 June 1967, inserted in U.S. Congress, Senate Committee on Labor and Public Welfare, *Examination of the War on Poverty,* 3036–40 [quote on 3037]; Parris, *Small Business Administration,* 116. See also, Shirley Scheibla, "You've Got to Expect Losses: Anti-Poverty Has Given the Small Business Administration a Blank Check," *Barron's,* 4 July 1966, 5, 12–14.

26. Bernard Boutin to Padriac Frucht, 7 July 1966, Boutin Papers, box 25, folder "Administrator's Chronological File: 7/1–7/15/65"; Bernard Boutin, Opening Remarks, Area Administrators and Regional Directors Conference (Silver Spring, Md.), 26 April 1967, RG 309, box 298, folder "Meetings 3–1."

27. "Helping the Poor to Be Boss: SBA's Loans," *Time,* 16 December 1966, 90 [quote]; Levy, "Putting the Poor," 3040; Carmichael and Hamilton, *Black Power,* 22 [quote from Kenneth Clark].

28. On Washington's philosophy and the early history of the National Negro Business League, see Washington, *Up from Slavery*; Washington, *Negro in Business*; Burrows, *Necessity of Myth.* As late as 1960, Berkeley Burrell, then-president of the D.C. Chamber of Commerce, had urged African American entrepreneurs to "stress business rather than race." Burrell, "Washington, D.C., Inaugural," *League Notes* (January 1960), 3–5.

29. Berkeley Burrell, testimony before HSBC, *Organization and Operation of the Small Business Administration (SBA's Role—Present and Future),* 19 July 1966, 220 [quotes];

Burrell, quoted in "Negro Aid Muddle," 14; Boutin, testimony before U.S. Congress, Senate Committee on Labor and Public Welfare, *Examination of the War on Poverty,* 3028–29, 3035 [quote on 3029]. Previously dependent on membership dues, the NBL now relied upon government grants to fund its programs. Joel Dreyfus, "Rowboating in the Economic Mainstream," *Black Enterprise* 5, no. 6 (January 1975), 43–45; Henderson and Ledebur, "Programs," 28–32.

30. Foley, *Achieving Ghetto,* 3–5, 11 [quote], 143 [quote], 147 [quote], 38–47, 103–23.

31. U.S. Riot Commission, *Report,* 1 [quote], 560; Graham, "On Riots and Riot Commissions," 17 [quote]. The Kerner report, like many other contemporary riot studies, was based on a flawed, ideological reading of the riot data. See Miller and Halligan, "New Urban Blacks," 338–67; and Bean, "Burn, Baby, Burn."

32. Jesse Jackson, quoted in Mary Smith, "Big Boost for Small Business: Loans to Negro Businesses," *Ebony* (September 1968), 87; Katz, *Undeserving Poor,* 60–61. See, e.g., Carmichael and Hamilton, *Black Power,* 17, 20; Bluestone, "Black Capitalism," 36–55; Julian Bond, foreword to *Black Business Enterprise,* ed. Ronald Bailey, x; Zweig, "Dialectics of Black Capitalism," 25–37.

33. See, e.g., Percy Sutton, testimony before SSBC, *Economic Development Opportunity,* 17 June 1968, 62–63; and "Fuller, S.B.," in Ingham and Feldman, *African-American Business Leaders.*

34. See, e.g., Courtney Weeks, testimony before SSBC, *Economic Development Opportunity,* 24 May 1968, 50; Preston Lambert, testimony before ibid., 17 June 1968, 105.

35. Bernetta Howell, quoted in Smith, "Big Boost," 79; George Kelsey, testimony before SSBC, *Economic Development Opportunity,* 24 May 1968, 26; Charles H. Kriger and Bruce Llewellyn, testimony before SSBC, ibid., 17 June 1968, 143–44, 151; P. Bernard Nortman, ibid. hearing, 24 May 1968, 4 [quote].

36. Doctors and Huff, *Minority Enterprise,* 45 [quote]; Stans, "Richard Nixon," 179; Nixon, "Let a New Day Dawn," 94. Nixon also ran a television commercial entitled "Black Capitalism," characterizing the new program as a response to the riots. Blaustein and Faux, *Star-Spangled Hustle,* 16.

37. Blaustein and Faux, *Star-Spangled Hustle,* 21–24, 13 [quote]; Bluestone, "Black Capitalism"; "Rustin Scores Separatism As Old Tribalism," *Washington Post,* 23 February 1969, A6; AFL-CIO executive council, quoted in William F. Buckley Jr., "On Black Capitalism," *National Review,* 25 March 1969, 298; Skrentny, *Ironies of Affirmative Action,* 182, 193; Nixon, quoted in Doctors and Huff, *Minority Enterprise,* 45; National Election Studies, "Table 9A1.2: Presidential Vote: 2 Major Parties 1952–1996," http://www.umich.edu/~nes/nesguide/2ndtable/t9a_1_2.htm; "Black Capitalism: What Is It?" *U.S. News and World Report,* 30 September 1968, 64–65.

38. Moreno, *From Direct Action,* 180–87 [quote on 187]; Jones, "Origins of Affirmative Action," 383–419; Staros, "Affirmative Action." On Nixon's early civil rights record, see Ambrose, *Nixon: The Education of a Politician,* 308, 396, 434–35, 538; Nixon, "Civil Rights."

39. Nixon, *RN,* 435–38 [quotes on 435]; Stans, "Nixon's Economic Policy"; Ambrose, *Nixon: Triumph of a Politician,* 154. In March 1969, Nixon told Secretary of Commerce Maurice Stans, "I don't think this is a good political move; it won't get us any votes. But we'll do it because it's the right thing to do." Kotlowski, "Nixon's Southern Strategy," 222.

40. Robert C. Moot to Hubert Humphrey, 26 March 1968, LBJPL, Office Files of James Gaither, box 21, folder "Gaither: Minority Entrepreneurship (3)"; "Summary of a National Program for Promoting Minority Entrepreneurs" (attachment), ibid.; "Black Capitalism: What Is It?"

41. Howard J. Samuels, "Address by Howard J. Samuels . . . Before National Business League Conference . . . Cleveland, Ohio," 5 September 1968, LBJPL, SBA Records, box 1, folder "SBA Statements, 8–12/68," 4; Antoinette (Sharkey) Samuels, phone interview with author, 16 October 1997; Walter Stults, interview with author, 16 December 1999; George H. Robinson, interview with author, 30 September 1998; Paul Lodato, interview with author, 15 October 1998; "Biographical Sketch of Howard J. Samuels," in U.S. Senate Committee on Banking and Currency, *Nomination of Howard J. Samuels* hearing, 90th Cong., 2d sess., 16 July 1968, 1–2; William D. Carey, memorandum for Mr. Nimetz, "Commerce Minority Entrepreneurship Proposal," 20 June 1968, LBJPL, Office Files of James Gaither, box 21, folder "Gaither: Minority Entrepreneurship (2)"; Howard J. Samuels, memorandum for the President, "Proposed Response to the Poor People's Campaign," 21 June 1968, ibid.; Howard J. Samuels to John W. Macy Jr., 24 June 1968, LBJPL, WHCF: FG 283, box 305, folder "11/18/67–6/30/68"; John W. Macy Jr., memorandum for the President, "Appointment of Robert C. Moot as Assistant Secretary of Defense Comptroller and Howard Samuels as Administrator of Small Business Administration," 24 June 1968, LBJPL, WHCF, box 307, folder "FG 283A"; SBA, *Administrative History*, 266 [quote].

42. Howard J. Samuels, "Transcript of News Conference Announcing Project OWN . . . August 13, 1968," LBJPL, SBA Records, box 1, folder "SBA Statements, 8–12/68"; Howard J. Samuels, "Address by Howard J. Samuels . . . Before National Business League," ibid., 1 [quote], 7 [quote].

43. Samuels, "Project OWN"; Howard J. Samuels, testimony before HSBC, *Organization and Operation . . . 1969*, 23 July 1969, 178; Samuels, "Transcript of News Conference," 1; Howard J. Samuels, "Remarks of Small Business Administrator Howard J. Samuels Before the 1968 Democratic Platform Committee, Washington, D.C., Wednesday, August 21, 1968," LBJPL, SBA Records, box 1, folder "SBA Statements, 8–12/68."

44. Samuels, "How to Even the Odds"; "Black Capitalism: What is It?" 64; "'Black Capitalism:' Whites Help"; Samuels, "Transcript of News Conference," 3, 10.

45. Samuels, "Transcript of News Conference," 4; "'Black Capitalism:' Whites Help Negroes Buy Ghetto Firms"; "Aiding Black Capitalism: SBA Programs for Black Enterprise," *Business Week*, 17 August 1968, 32; Lodato interview; Howard J. Samuels to Joe L. Evins, 10 August 1968, Joe L. Evins Papers (Cookeville, Tenn.), box 563, folder 7 ("Small Business—Correspondence"); HSBC, *Final Report*, 31 December 1968, 32–33.

46. Howard Samuels to Lyndon B. Johnson, 22 July 1968, LBPL, Office Files of James Gaither, box 21, folder "Gaither: Minority Entrepreneurship (2)"; Joe Califano memorandum for the President, 24 July 1968, LBJPL, WHCF: FG 283, box 306, folder "7/1/68– "; Samuels, "Transcript of News Conference," 14; "Black Capitalism: SBA Project OWN," *Newsweek*, 26 August 1968, 71; "Small Business Administration, Economic Opportunity Loan Approvals," data provided to author by SBA.

47. Samuels, "How to Even the Odds," 24–25 [quote]; Samuel E. Harris, et al., "Compensatory Capitalism: A Description and Evaluation of Project OWN," in *Organization and Operation . . . 1969*, hearings, 22–25 July 1969, A16–17, A14; Antoinette Samuels, 16 October 1997; SBA, *1968 Annual Report*, 35, 37; Samuels, "Address by Howard J. Samuels . . . Before National Business League," 6 [quote].

48. Wilfred J. Garvin, "Fostering Minority Business Ownership," chap. 21 in *The Vital Majority*, ed. Deane Carson, 413; King, "Relationships," 130–31; Lodato interview; Anonymous, memorandum for Stanley H. Ruttenberg, "FY 1969 Recommendations on Minority Entrepreneurship Programs" [1968], LBJPL, Presidential Task Forces (Gaither), box 21, folder

"Gaither: Minority Entrepreneurship (3)"; HSBC, *Final Report*, 31 December 1968, 18; SBA, *Administrative History*, 151–52 [quote on 151]; Theophilos, "Government Procurement."

49. V.L. Broussalian, memorandum for Mr. [William D.] Carey, "Survey of Measures to Foster Negro Entrepreneurship—Progress Report," 9 August 1968. LBJ Library, Presidential Task Forces (Gaither), box 21, folder "Gaither: Minority Entrepreneurship (2)."

50. Bob Weinberg, memorandum for Matt Nimetz, "Minority Entrepreneurship."

51. Samuel E. Harris, et al., "Compensatory Capitalism," A2–A3; "Birth Pangs of Black Capitalism," *Time*, 18 October 1968, 98–99 [quote on 99]; Bob Weinberg, memorandum for Matt Nimetz.

52. Burton and Corman, in HSBC, *Final Report*, 31 December 1968, 34–38; Howard Samuels, ibid., 34; Corman in HSBC, *Organization and Operation . . . 1969*, 169 [quote]; William T. Gennetti [Acting General Counsel] to the Administrator, "Authority for Project OWN," 22 October 1968, ibid., 71–72.

53. "Table 17—Percentage of Total Financial Assistance to Minority Enterprises by Loan Program: Fiscal Years 1968–72," in SSBC, *Twenty-Third Annual Report*, S. Rpt. 357., 93d Cong., 1st sess., 27 July 1973, 47; SBA, "Small Business Administration General Business Loan Approvals," data provided to author.

54. SBA, "Small Business Administration General Business Loan Approvals," data provided to author.

55. Nellis, *A SCORE That Counts*, 28–31; Moon, "An Evaluation"; SSBC, *Twenty-third Annual Report*, 22; Brudney, "SBA and SCORE," 57–67.

56. Higgs, *Crisis and Leviathan*.

57. Button, *Black Violence*, 171. Button surveyed fifty-eight officials in OEO, HUD, HEW, and the Justice Department.

58. Bates, *Black Capitalism*, 127; Bates and Bradford, *Financing Black Economic Development*, 164.

59. Sowell, "Economics and Black People," 3–21 [quote on 15]. See also, Henderson, "Government Incentives," 202–21; Allen, "Making Capitalism."

60. Bates, *Race, Upward Mobility, and Self-Employment*, 9–12, 143–44.

61. Sowell, *Vision of the Anointed*. This was a common criticism of Great Society liberalism. See, e.g., Banfield, *The Unheavenly City Revisited*, 273–78; Pressman and Wildavsky, *Implementation*, 126–36.

62. For more on the riots, their impact on small business and the SBA's feeble response, see Bean, "Burn, Baby, Burn." Crime was also a growing problem for small business. See SSBC, *Crime Against Small Business*. Urban renewal had a dual destructive effect on inner-city businesses: first, by moving their customers, and second, by physically destroying their buildings. Congress authorized the SBA to make loans to displaced firms, but the agency helped very few. Kinnard and Malinowski, *Impact of Dislocation*; Zimmer, *Rebuilding Cities*; Anderson, *Federal Bulldozer*; HSBC, Subcommittee No. 5, *Small Business Problems in Urban Areas*, H. Rpt. 2343, 29 December 1966.

63. L. Patrick Finch, quoted in Hoff, *Nixon Reconsidered*, 80.

Chapter 5

1. Hoff, *Nixon Reconsidered*, 3, 19; Whitaker, "Nixon's Domestic Policy," 131; Ambrose, *Nixon: The Triumph of a Politician*, 431, 435 [quote]; Parmet, *Richard Nixon*, 600 [Ehrlichman quote, "zigs" and "zags"]; Hamby, *Liberalism and Its Challengers*, 356; Matusow, *Nixon's Economy*, 1, 3.

2. Stein, *Presidential Economics*, 135–38; Silk, *Nixonomics*, 205 [quote].

3. Stein, *Presidential Economics*, 136 [quote]; Herbert Stein, interviewed in Hargrove and Morley, *The President and the Council of Economic Advisers*, 366; Hamby, *Liberalism and Its Challengers*, 283; Kotlowski, "Black Power—Nixon Style," 416–17; Matusow, *Nixon's Economy*, 2; Silk, *Nixonomics*, 23; Hugh W. Sloan Jr. memorandum for the President, 15 July 1970, NPM, WHCF, Subject Files: BE, box 34, folder "EX BE 4–3 Small Business [4 of 5]" [quote]. Nixon reminisces about his father's business in "Special Message to the Congress on Small Business, March 20, 1970," *Public Papers of the Presidents of the United States, Richard Nixon: 1970* (Washington, D.C.: GPO, 1971), 288.

4. Blaustein and Faux, *Star-Spangled Hustle*, 138; John Tower, "Appointment of Hilary Sandoval Jr. as Administrator of Small Business Administration," *Congressional Record*, 3 April 1969, vol. 115, pt. 7:8652; U.S. Congress, Senate Committee on Banking and Currency, *Nominations of Lawrence M. Cox and Hilary J. Sandoval Jr.*, 23.

5. Leonard Garment to Peter Flanigan, 17 January 1969, NPM, WHCF, Staff Member and Office Files, Leonard Garment, box 147, folder "(SBA) Small Business Administration [CFOA 10180]" [quotes]; Jan Dykman, "SBA File" [January 1969], ibid.; Mike Brewer, memorandum for Len Garment, "Hilary Sandoval," 14 January 1969, ibid.; Mike Brewer, memorandum for Leonard Garment, "Hilary Sandoval," 15 January 1969, ibid.; Robert J. Brown, memorandum for Secretary of Commerce, "Possible Black Reaction to Proposed Appointment of Mr. Hillary Sandoval as SBA Administrator," 17 February 1969, NPM, WHCF, Subject Files: FG 217, box 1, folder "FG 217 Small Business Administration, Begin—7/31/69"; Paul Lodato, interview with author, 15 October 1998.

6. Dwyer, *Small Business Administration*, 58–59 [quote on 58]; Lodato interview.

7. Lodato interview [quote]; "Sandoval Stands Siege at the SBA," *Business Week*, 18 July 1970, 244–45, inserted in HSBC, *Organization and Operation of the Small Business Administration (1970)*, 22 July 1970, 244–45; Jerome R. Gulan [NFIB Legislative Director], testimony before ibid., 295; Executive Committee, AFGE Local 3134 (SBA) to Jerome R. Gulan, 29 December 1970, in National Archives, Record Group 46, SSBC, Group 10, box 5, folder "Association 1 Small Business Administration, 92d Cong. [3 of 3]"; SSBC, *Twenty-First Annual Report, S.* Rpt. 535, 91st Cong., 2d sess., 2 December 1971, 16; HSBC, *Final Report (1969–1970)* H. Rpt. 1795, 91st Cong., 2d sess., 28 December 1970, 24–25.

8. Blaustein and Faux, *Star-Spangled Hustle*, 127; Stans, *Terrors of Justice*, 102–5; Stans, "Richard Nixon," 179–80; Richard M. Nixon, "Statement About a National Program for Minority Business Enterprise, March 5, 1969," *Public Papers of the Presidents of the United States, Richard Nixon: 1969* (Washington, D.C.: GPO, 1971), 197–98; Graham, *Civil Rights Era*, 314; Graham, "Incoherence," 166.

9. Alan Bible, "Small Business Programs at the Crossroads," *Congressional Record*, 20 March 1969, vol. 115, pt. 6:6974–87; HSBC, *Organization and Operation of the Small Business Administration (1971)* H. Rpt. 1006, 92d Cong., 2d sess., 19 April 1972, 41 [quote]; Arthur F. Burns, memorandum for the President, 18 March 1969, NPM, WHCF, Subject Files: FG 217, box 1, folder "FG 217 Small Business Administration, Begin—7/31/69"; Thomas S. Kleppe, interview with author, 21 October 1997.

10. Rowland Evans and Robert Novak, "Government Innovations Stifled by Representative Rooney" (March 1969), inserted in SSBC, *Review of Small Business Administration's Programs*, 15 October 1969, 669–70; Eugene Foley, interview with author, 14 December 1997; Bernard Boutin, interview with author, 21 October 1997; Antoinette (Sharkey) Samuels, interview with author, 16 October 1997; Lodato interview; Hilary Sandoval,

"Sandoval Press Conference" transcript, 30 June 1969, in RG 46, SSBC, Group 7, box 3, folder "Associations 1—Small Business Administration—1969," 30–31.

11. Dan Thomasson, "SBA Aware of Gang Ties," *Washington Daily News*, 28 March 1969, 2; Rowland Evans and Robert Novak, "SBA Policy Appears to Favor Mafia Over Ghetto," *Washington Post*, 19 March 1969, A19 [quote]; Rowland Evans and Robert Novak, "SBA Loans to Mafia-Based Firm Continued Even After FBI Report," *Washington Post*, 26 March 1969, A27 [quote]; Bernard Boutin, interview with author, 21 October 1997; "Boutin, Bernard L(ouis)."

12. Anonymous, "Fact Sheet: SBA Performance, March 1969–January 1970, [1970]," NPM, WHCF, Subject Files: FG 217, box 1, folder "FG 217 Small Business Administration 1/1/70–5/31/70"; SBA, *1969 Annual Report,* v, 29; "Firm Returns 2 SBA Loans After Mafia Link Is Alleged," *Wall Street Journal,* 19 January 1970, 23; "SBA Investigation of Louisiana Dealings Details Loan to an Underworld Figure," *Wall Street Journal,* 18 February 1970:, 4; HSBC, *Organization and Operation . . . 1970,* hearing, 66–67; Al Knight and Richard O'Reilly, "SBA Moves to Fire Jack Biggs," *Denver Rocky Mountain News,* 25 September 1971, 1, 5; Paul Delaney, "Mafia Links to U.S. Business Unit Found," *New York Times,* 28 February 1974, 24.

13. Henry B. Gonzalez, "Scandal at SBA—IV," *Congressional Record,* 29 April 1969, vol. 115, pt. 8:11512; Henry B. Gonzalez, "Scandal at SBA—VI," *Congressional Record,* 19 May 1969, vol. 115, pt. 10:12944–45; Henry B. Gonzalez, "Scandal at SBA—VIII," 21 May 1969, ibid., 13286; Wright Patman, "Small Business Administrator Attempting to Cover Up Fuentes Affair," 20 May 1969, ibid., 13145–47; Henry B Gonzalez, "Scandal at SBA—XI," *Congressional Record,* 20 December 1969, vol. 115, pt. 30:40468.

14. John Price, memorandum for Daniel P. Moynihan, "SBA National Advisory Council for Black Economic Development," 29 January 1969, NPM, WHCF, Subject Files: FG 217, box 1, folder "FG 217 Small Business Administration, Begin—7/31/69"; Daniel P. Moynihan, memorandum for John Ehrlichman, "Minority Business Enterprise," 16 May 1969, NPM, WHCF, Subject Files: BE, box 34, folder "EX BE 4–3 Small Business [1969–1970] [1 of 5]" [Sandoval quote]; "GOP Study of SBA Raps Sandoval," *Congressional Record,* 10 June 1969, vol. 115, pt. 11:15357; William L. Claiborne, "SBA Snubs Negroes, Unit Says," *Washington Post,* 28 May 1969, A34 [Buress quote]; "Sandoval Press Conference," 14–15, 25; Lodato interview.

15. Robert C. Maynard, "'Black Capitalism' Chief Quits, Hits Nixon," *Washington Post,* 12 July 1969, inserted in SSBC, *Review of Small Business Administration's Programs,* 15 October 1969, 680–81 [Pruitt quote on 680]; Ken Harnett, "Nixon Blasted as Key Negro in SBA Quits," *Washington Star,* 17 July 1969, ibid., 684–85 [Evers quote on 684]; "High-Ranking Negro Quits SBA, Charging Nixon Hasn't Kept Black Capitalism Vow," *Wall Street Journal,* 14 July 1969, ibid., 682; John Ehrlichman to Peter Flanigan, 24 July 1969, NPM, White House Special Files, WHCF: Subject Files, Confidential Files, box 24, folder "FG 217 Small Business Administration [1969–70]"; Evans and Novak, *Nixon in the White House,* 151; Lodato interview.

16. Peter Flanigan, memorandum for the President's File, 1 July 1969, NPM, White House Special Files, WHCF: Subject Files, Confidential Files, box 24, folder "FG 217 Small Business Administration [1969–70]"; Peter Flanigan to Dwight Chapin, 2 June 1969, ibid.; Peter M. Flanigan, memorandum for the President, 8 August 1969, ibid.; H.R. Haldeman, memorandum for Mr. Flanigan, 2 September 1969, ibid.; John Ehrlichman to Peter Flanigan, 15 October 1969, ibid.; Peter M. Flanigan to the President, 17 October 1969, ibid.; Peter Flanigan, memorandum for John Ehrlichman, "Your Meet-

ing with Hilary Sandoval on Monday, February 9, 4 P.M.," 9 February 1970, ibid.; Hilary Sandoval Jr. to Peter M. Flanigan, 9 February 1970, NPM, WHCF, Subject Files: FG 217, box 1, folder "FG 217 Small Business Administration 1/1/70–5/31/70"; Peter Flanigan to John Ehrlichman, 27 February 1970, ibid. ["atomic explosion" quote]; W.D. Brewer "Memorandum for the Record," 6 March 1970, ibid.; Lodato interview.

17. "Sandoval Stands Siege" [Brewer quote]; "SBA Chief Hilary Sandoval Wins Battle for Undisputed Control of His Agency," *Wall Street Journal*, 27 February 1970, 1; Brewer, "Memorandum for the Record."

18. Tod R. Hullin, memorandum for John Ehrlichman, "Telephone Call to Secretary Stans Regarding Firing of Hilary Sandoval," 13 November 1970, NPM, WHCF, Subject Files: FG 217, box 3, folder "FG 217/A Small Business Administration [1969–1970]" [quotes]; U.S. Department of Justice, Federal Bureau of Investigation, "Hilary Sandoval Jr.," file 161–6042, 1969. Unfortunately, it is impossible to confirm or deny these allegations. Under director J. Edgar Hoover, senior FBI officials placed sensitive documents in a "Do Not File" file. These memoranda were periodically destroyed. "The 'Do Not File' File."

19. Harry S. Flemming [Special Assistant to the President] to John D. Ehrlichman, 20 November 1970, NPM, White House Special Files, WHCF: Subject Files, Confidential Files, box 24, folder "FG 217 Small Business Administration [1969–70]"; Hilary J. Sandoval Jr. to Richard Nixon, 18 November 1970, NPM, WHCF, Subject Files: FG 217, box 3, folder "FG 217/A Small Business Administration [1969–1970]"; "SBA Head to Resign Jan. 1," *Wall Street Journal*, 20 November 1970, 27; "Hilary J. Sandoval Jr. is Dead; Headed Small Business Bureau," *New York Times Biographical Edition* (New York: Arno Press, 1973).

20. SBA, *1970 Annual Report*, 6; SBA, *1971 Annual Report*, 5; SBA, "20 Years' Loan Approvals," *1972 Annual Report*, 6; SSBC, *Twenty-First Annual Report*, 4–7.

21. Hilary Sandoval, testimony before SSBC, *Review of Small Business Administration's Programs*, 10 June 1969, 8–9, 15; Richard M. Nixon, "Memorandum Requesting Support for the Minority Business Enterprise Program, December 5, 1969," *Public Papers . . . 1969*, 994–95; "Table 16—SBA Financial Assistance to Minority Enterprises—Number and Amount of Loans Approved, By Loan Program: Fiscal Years 1968–1972," SSBC, *Twenty-Third Annual Report, S*. Rpt. 357, 93d Cong., 1st sess., 27 July 1973, 47; "Table 17—Percentage of Total Financial Assistance to Minority Enterprises by Loan Program: Fiscal Years 1968–72," ibid.; SBA, "Small Business Administration General Business Loan Approvals," data provided to author by SBA.

22. SBA, *1969 Annual Report*, 9; SSBC, *Twenty-First Annual Report*, 3–4; Burke, "Role," 20. The MESBIC program was the brainchild of Republican businessman Robert Dehlendorf. See Karuna-Karan and Smith, "A Constructive Look at MESBICs," 82; Blaustein and Faux, *Star Spangled Hustle*, 189.

23. Kotlowski, "Black Power—Nixon Style," 430–32, 432n (note 132); SSBC, *Twenty-Fourth Annual Report, S*. Rpt. 931, 93d Cong., 2d sess., 13 June 1974, 38–39; King, "Relationships," 142; Leonard Garment to Ken Cole, "Minority Business Enterprise," 20 April 1970, NPM, WHCF, Subject Files: BE, box 34, folder "EX BE 4–3 Small Business [2 of 5] January–April 1970."

24. Kotlowski, "Black Power—Nixon Style," 417, 435 [quote]; U.S. Chamber of Commerce, "Action for the '70s on: Minority Enterprise," HSBC, *Organization and Operation of the Small Business Administration (1969)*, A68–69; Joel Dreyfus, "Rowboating in the Economic Mainstream," *Black Enterprise* (January 1975), 43–45 [quote on 44]; Ronald E. Kisner, "Black Businesses Map Strategies to Meet Economic Challenges," *Jet*, 27 Sep-

tember 1973, 46; "The National Business League," *Black Business Digest* (December 1972), 31; "The National Business League," *Black Enterprise* (June 1972), 37–41; "Chamber of Commerce for Blacks Is Proposed at Maryland Meeting," *Jet*, 24 February 1972, 27.

25. Seder and Burrell, *Getting It Together*, 232–33 [Burrell quote on 232]; Burrell quoted in Ofari, *Myth of Black Capitalism*, 79; Berkeley Burrell, testimony before SSBC, *Review of Small Business Administration's Programs*, 20 June 1969, 326–29; Berkeley Burrell, testimony before HSBC, *Organization and Operation . . . 1969*, hearing, 25 July 1969, 455–57; Jackie Robinson, testimony before U.S. Congress, Senate Committee on Banking and Currency, Subcommittee on Small Business, *Federal Minority Enterprise Program*, 144–53 [quote on 153]; William Clay, quoted in "Negro Solon Raps SBA," *Jacksonville (Florida) Times-Union*, 29 April 1969, inserted in SSBC, *Review of Small Business Administration's Programs*, 15 October 1969, 671; William Clay, "How Long, Mr. President, Before You Reply?" *Congressional Record*, 29 July 1970, vol. 116, pt. 19:26464–65; "Black Capitalism: Still a Promise," *Newsweek*, 4 August 1969, 75; "Black Capitalism: a Study in Frustration," *Newsweek*, 28 September 1970, 70–72.

26. Leonard Garment to Ken Cole, "Minority Business Enterprise," 20 April 1970, NPM, WHCF, Subject Files: BE, box 34, folder "EX BE 4–3 Small Business [2 of 5] January–April 1970" [quote]; Leonard S. Zartman to Daniel P. Moynihan, 16 January 1970, ibid.; Stephen Bull, memorandum for Dwight L. Chapin, "100th MESBIC," 15 June 1970, ibid., folder "EX BE 4–3 Small Business [3 of 5]."

27. Stans, quoted in Kotlowski, "Black Power—Nixon Style," 422.

28. SSBC, *Nineteenth Annual Report*, S. Rpt. 627, 91st Cong., 1st sess., 20 December 1969, 9, 99–100; HSBC, *Final Report (1969–1970)*, 14–19, 33–35; SSBC, *Twenty-First Annual Report*, 12; "Sandoval Stands Siege," 244 [quote]; Jerome Gulan, testimony before HSBC, *Organization and Operation . . . 1970*, hearing, 22 July 1970, 296–98 [quote on 297]; William S. Bergman, testimony, ibid., 321–29; Ed Torrence, ibid., 329–30; Michael B. Rukin, ibid., 345–47; E. Alvin Foster to Richard Russell [Chairman, Senate Appropriations Committee], 24 February 1969, in RG 46, SSBC, Group 1, box 45, folder "Finance and Investment 8–3 Ghetto Business or Minority Entrepreneurship"; Ray A. Infantino to John Rousellot, 10 December 1970, RG 46, SSBC, Group 10, box 5, folder "Association 1 Small Business Administration, 92d Cong. [3 of 3]"; George S. Bullen [NFIB legislative director], testimony before SSBC, *Review of Small Business Administration's Programs*, 20 June 1969, 264 [quote]. See also, Rufus W. Gosnell [president, National Small Business Association], ibid., 341. In fiscal year 1970, minority businesses received 90 percent of direct 7(a) loan dollars and 80 percent of direct EOLs. "Table 19—Percentage of Total Business 7(a) and Total Economic Opportunity Loans by Type, Approved for Minority Enterprises: Fiscal years 1968–72," SSBC, *Twenty-Third Annual Report*, 49.

29. Hilary Sandoval, testimony before HSBC, *Organization and Operation . . . 1970*, hearing, 20 July 1970, 22; Sandoval, testimony, ibid., 21 July 1970, 153 [quote], 137 [quote]; "Exhibit H: 'National Directive Draft: Business Development Section 8(a) Program,'" ibid., A12–A13 [quotes].

30. "SBA Admits an Error, Sets Probe of Backing for Lou Brock's Loan," *Wall Street Journal*, 3 July 1969, 17; HSBC, *Organization and Operation . . . 1969*, 22 July 1969, 79–80.

31. Hilary Sandoval Jr., "Operation Mainstream," *Congressional Record*, 2 July 1969, vol. 115, pt. 14:18253 [quote]. See also, "Sandoval Press Conference," 9–10.

32. George H. Robinson [former director of EEO and Civil Rights Compliance], interview with author, 30 September 1998 [quote]; Marshall Parker [Associate Administrator for Procurement, Management Assistance, and 8(a)], interview with author, 31 August

1999. Between 1969 and 1970, the "Spanish American" share of the agency work force increased from 2.2 percent to 5.4 percent. SBA, *1970 Annual Report,* 55.

33. Skrentny, *Ironies of Affirmative Action,* 177, 192 [quote]; Belz, *Equality Transformed,* 95; HSBC, *Organization and Operation . . . 1971,* hearing, 21 September 1971, 11.

34. George Hornston [Area Civil Rights Director, Chicago], interview with author, 4 November 1998; George H. Robinson, "SBA's Share of the Actual Workload Performed in Equal Employment Opportunity in the Private Sector by the Federal Government," 1 July 1975, in possession of the author; "Table on Workload Factors in Monitoring of Equal Employment Opportunity in the Private Sector (Nonconstruction) by Federal Agencies," ibid.; Malcolm M. Hall [Acting Deputy Director for Compliance, Office of Equal Employment Opportunity and Compliance], memorandum for All Compliance Officers and Specialists, "Revised Guidelines for Negotiating the Setting of Minority Employment Goals and Timetables with SBA Recipients (Non-Construction)," 30 January 1973, in possession of the author; Malcolm M. Hall, memorandum for Senior Compliance Officers, "Revised Formats for Quarterly ME Progress Report Form and Goals & Timetables Plan (non-construction)," 17 July 1973, ibid. [quote]. The U.S. Commission on Civil Rights gave the agency high marks for its compliance procedures. U.S. Commission on Civil Rights, *Federal Civil Rights Enforcement,* 694.

35. HSBC, *Programs, Policies, and Operations,* hearing, 19 September 1973, 6; SBA, *1977 Annual Report,* 76, 78; SBA, *Annual Report FY 1980,* 71; Hornston interview.

36. Hornston interview. For current practices, EEO officials use an unofficial publication entitled *An Equal Opportunity Guide for Small Employers* [1995–], copy in author's possession.

Chapter 6

1. Fred Malek, memorandum for H.R. Haldeman, "Appropriate Swearing-In for Tom Kleppe," 22 February 1971, NPM, White House Special Files, WHCF: Subject Files, Confidential Files, box 24, folder "FG 217/A Small Business Administration [1971–74]" [quote]; Lee Byrd, "Kleppe to Chart New SBA Seas," *Tribune* (Bismarck, N. Dak.), 20 January 1971, 28 [quote]; "Biographical Sketch of Thomas S. Kleppe," in U.S. Congress, Senate Committee on Banking, Housing, and Urban Affairs, *Nomination of Thomas S. Kleppe,* 2; Dwyer, *Small Business Administration,* 60; Thomas Kleppe, phone interview with author, 21 October 1997.

2. SSBC, *Twenty-Second Annual Report,* S. Rpt. 1280, 92st Cong., 2d sess., 9 October 1972, 4 [quote]; HSBC] *Organization and Operation of the Small Business Administration (1971),* hearing, 21 September 1971, 5–13 [quote]; Karen DeWitt, "The Small Business Administration," *Black Enterprise* (January 1975), 27 [quote by former Deputy Administrator Anthony Chase].

3. Edward N. Rosa, "The Small Business Administration's Management Assistance Program," chap. 13 in *Vital Majority,* ed. Deane Carson, 264; Burr and Solomon, "SBI Program," 1–8; Dwyer, *Small Business Administration,* 62; Louis Laun, press release, "Address at Mountain Plains Management Conference, Boise State University, 15 October 1976," in author's possession.

4. SSBC, *Twenty-Second Annual Report,* 18; Nellis, *A SCORE That Counts,* 32, 34, 44–47, 55–56, 118.

5. "Success at a Discount," *Barron's,* 22 March 1971, 19; Wharton, "Small Business Investment," 167–68 [quote on 168], 78; "Table 20: 'Rate of Return on Capital for SBIC Industry (Including Capital Appreciation),'" ibid., 144; Kermit L. Culver, "Small

Business Investment Companies," chap. 4 in *Vital Majority*, ed. Deane Carson, 67; "Table B-3: Annual Percentage Rates of Return on Investment for SBICs and for Stocks in the Standard and Poors Stock Index," in Howat, "An Analysis," 87; HSBC, *Organization and Operation of the Small Business Administration (1971)* H. Rpt. 1006, 19 April 1972, 25–26; HSBC, *Programs, Policies, and Operations of the Small Business Administration (1973)* H. Rpt. 873, 4 March 1974, 19, 21.

6. HSBC, *Final Report (1971–1972)* H. Rpt. 1626, 92d Cong., 2d sess., 21 December 1972, 160–61; Clyde Bothmer, "The Small Business Administration Government Procurement Program," chap. 18 in *Vital Majority*, ed. Deane Carson, 345–63; SSBC, *Small Business Aspects*, 5–6; SSBC, *Twenty-Eighth Annual Report*, S. Rpt. 629, 95th Cong., 2d sess., 1 February 1978, 44; SBA, *Annual Report, FY 1983*, 97; HSBC, *Summary of Activities* H. Rpt. 1036, 99th Cong., 2d sess., 2 January 1987, 76–78.

7. Matusow, *Nixon's Economy*, 192–98, 187 [Stein quote]; Weatherford, "Interplay"; SBA, *1972 Annual Report*, 5–6; "Republican Party Platform" (1972), in Donald Bruce Johnson, comp., *National Party Platforms*, vol. 2, 863–64, 883. A later study found that SBA guaranteed loans increased during presidential elections for the period 1972–1992, though not quite as dramatically. Corder, "Politics of Credit Subsidy."

8. Matusow, *Nixon's Economy*, 216–19; SBA, "Small Business Administration: General Business Loan Approvals," data provided to author.

9. Aharoni, *No-Risk Society*, 93; Thomas S. Kleppe, interviewed by *U.S. News and World Report*, 1 October 1973, 74–76; David A. Wollard, "Small Business Administration Loan Programs," chap. 6 in *Vital Majority*, ed. Deane Carson, 117; Richard M. Nixon, "Veto of the Small Business Administration Loan Ceiling and Disaster Loan Amendments, September 22, 1973," *Public Papers of the Presidents of the United States, Richard Nixon: 1973* (Washington, D.C.: GPO, 1975), 818–19; SSBC, *Twenty-Fourth Annual Report*, S. Rpt. 931, 93d Cong., 2d sess., 13 June 1974, 16; "Disaster Relief," *Congress and the Nation*, vol. 4, 147–48.

10. HSBC, *Programs, Policies, and Operations*, H. Rpt. 873, 7; SSBC, *Twenty-Fourth Annual Report*, 16; Thomas S. Kleppe, "Fresh Plans," 74; Kleppe, "Administrator's Message," in SBA, *1973 Annual Report*, 5.

11. Lukas, *Nightmare*, 19–21; Parmet, *Richard Nixon*, 601–2; Kotlowski, "Black Power—Nixon Style," 440; "Minority SBA Contract Recipients Seen Pressured for Nixon Campaign," *Washington Post*, 14 March 1973, D16; Paul G. Edwards, "Watergate Probers Eye SBA," *Washington Post*, 2 December 1973, A2; Dwyer, *Small Business Administration*, 73; Thomas S. Kleppe, statement before House Subcommittee on Small Business, Committee on Banking and Currency, 4 December 1973, in possession of the author; Louis Laun, statement, n.d., ibid.; Kleppe interview; Marshall Parker, interview with author, 31 August 1999.

12. Paul Edwards, "Bid to Kill SBA Probe Told," *Washington Post*, 11 December 1973, A4; Robert J. Brown to Jon Rose, 6 November 1969, NPM, WHCF, Subject Files: FG 217, box 1, folder "FG 217 Small Business Administration, 11/6/69"; "Fuller, S.B.," *African-American Business Leaders: A Biographical Dictionary*, ed. Ingham and Feldman.

13. Martin Weil, "SBA Head Intervened for Firm," *Washington Post*, 10 December 1973, C1, 9; "Black Business Profile: Watts Mfg. Co. Aims at Discount Market," *Modern Retailer* (May 1970), 21, 25 [quote]; John Ehrlichman, memorandum for Staff Secretary, "Status of Watts Company," 25 March 1969, NPM, WHCF, Subject Files: BE, box 34, folder "EX BE 4–3 Small Business [1969–1970] [1 of 5]"; [Leonard] Story Zartman, memorandum for Daniel P. Moynihan, "Watts Manufacturing Company," 31 January

1969, ibid. [quote]; Alexander P. Butterfield, memorandum for Maurice Stans, 13 March 1969, ibid.; Melvin Laird to Robert Brown, 1 March 1969, ibid.; Robert J. Brown, memorandum for the President, "Status of Watts Company: Implication for Large Scale Corporate Involvement in Minority Entrepreneurship," 20 March 1969, ibid.; [Ken Cole?], memorandum for Robert Brown, "Progress Report on Watts Manufacturing Company," 16 April 1969, ibid.; SBA, *1970 Annual Report,* 219; "Watts Learns How to Run a Business," *Business Week,* 5 August 1972, 53; Richard Shane [retired 8(a) official], phone interview with author, 29 October 1997; Mark E. Rivers Jr. to Roger Smith, 22 July 1976, in author's possession.

14. Paul G. Edwards, "SBA Chief Says Aide Not in Conflict," *Washington Post,* 12 December 1973, A16; "Vesco, Robert L(ee)." The agency received more bad press when Washington *Post* columnist Jack Anderson reported that Senator Strom Thurmond (R-S.C.), a former segregationist, had placed three of his associates within the SBA's minority business division. Critics claimed that the "Thurmond Three" had undermined the minority enterprise program. However, it was not unusual to find Thurmond appointees employed within the executive branch; a later SBA administrator commented that, "wherever you turned over a rock, you would find a Strom Thurmond appointee." Other officials confirm that the placement of the "Thurmond Three" was innocuous. Nonetheless, it was ill advised; therefore, Kleppe promised to replace at least one of the officials with an African American. Jack Anderson, "Thurmond Proteges Run Aid to Blacks," *Washington Post,* 8 September 1973, D13; James C. Sanders, phone interview with author, 26 October 1997 [quote]; Laun interview; Shane interview; Kleppe interview.

15. Laun interview; Thomas S. Kleppe, testimony before the U.S. Congress, House Committee on Banking and Currency, Subcommittee on Small Business, *Oversight Investigation,* 333–41; Thomas S. Kleppe to Henry E. Petersen [Assistant Attorney General], 25 October 1973, in author's possession; Russell Hamilton to Louis Laun, attachment, ibid.

16. Paul G. Edwards, "SBA Probed for Corruption," *Washington Post,* 14 November 1973, A1, 10 [Hamilton quote]; Small Business Administration, Press release #1889, 12 July 1967, LBJPL, SBA Records, box 1, folder "SBA News Releases 1/64–3/68"; Bonnie Goldstein, "Abolish the SBA," *Washington Monthly* 11 (April 1979), 47–48 [quotes]; Paul G. Edwards, "SBA Official in Va. Denies Loan Conflict," *Washington Post,* 30 November 1973, A1, 12; Walter Shapiro, "How Not to Help Small Business," *Washington Monthly* 6 (October 1974), 31; U.S. Congress, House Committee on Banking and Currency, Subcommittee on Small Business, *SBA Investigation,* 53; Paul Delaney, "White House Pressure Alleged at Inquiry on S.B.A. Corruption," *New York Times,* 28 November 1973, 90.

17. Carl E. Grant [SBA Director of Personnel] to Russell Hamilton Jr., 20 December 1973, in possession of the author; Carl E. Grant to Thomas Regan, 20 December 1973, ibid.; Paul G. Edwards, "3 Officials Fired by the SBA," *Washington Post,* 23 December 1973, A1, 8; Laun interview; "Crime pays—but it shouldn't," *Philadelphia Inquirer,* 11 November 1976, A10; "Regan Gets 9-Year Term in SBA Fraud," *Washington Post,* 24 June 1976, C3; Paul Delaney, "White House Pressure Alleged at Inquiry on S.B.A. Corruption," *New York Times,* 28 November 1973, 90; "SBA Says Fourth of Its Offices Have 'Serious Problems,'" *New York Times,* 27 March 1974, 5; U.S. Congress, House Committee on Banking and Currency, Subcommittee on Small Business, *SBA Investigation Report,* 5 [Kleppe quote], 8 [reprimand]; 13; Paul G. Edwards, "Scandals Threaten Small Business Lending Program," *Washington Post,* 19 November 1973, A2; "Scandals: Numbers Game at SBA," *Newsweek,* 2 September 1974, 58–59.

18. Paul G. Edwards, "Scandals Threaten"; Goldstein, "Abolish the SBA," 46;

Shapiro, "How not to help," 31; Louis Laun to Bernard Layne, 4 June 1976, in author's possession; SBA, *1973 Annual Report*, 46.

19. "Interior: President's Nominee for Secretary Has His Problems," *Science*, 19 September 1975, 982; "Kleppe, Thomas S(avig)," *Current Biography: 1976*, 220; Bernard Rosen to Thomas S. Kleppe, 19 August 1974, in U.S. Congress, House Committee on Post Office and Civil Service, Subcommittee on Manpower and Civil Service, *Documents Related to Political Influence*, 4–5; Kleppe to Rosen, 7 October 1974, ibid., 42–44; U.S. Civil Service Commission, *A Report on Alleged Political Influence*, 6–41; Mike Causey, "House Probers to Call SBA Officials," *Washington Post*, 6 August 1975, B9.

20. Leonard Reed, "The Small Scandal Administration," *Inquiry Magazine*, 30 September 1979, 10–12; Joe L. Evins, "Irregularities in SBA's Loan Program," *Congressional Record*, 10 December 1973, vol. 119, pt. 31:40616; HSBC, *Programs, Policies, and Operations*, H. Rpt. 873, 20; Frank Annunzio, quoted in "Interior: President's Nominee," 983; Anglund, "American Core Values," 168–69 [Koch quote]; "Just a Short List," *Wall Street Journal*, 24 April 1974, 18 [quote]; Kleppe, quoted in "Scandals: Numbers Game," 59.

21. Anglund, "American Core Values," 169; Edwards, "SBA Probed," A10; Edwards, "Scandals threaten," A2; Szasz, "Process and Significance," 202–17; Kemp, "Accidents, Scandals," 401–27.

22. Dixon, "Minority Bank Growth," 8–10; SBA, *1972 Annual Report*, 27; SBA, *1973 Annual Report*, 36; "8(a) Procurement: FY 1969–1982," SSBC, *Federal Minority Business Development*, 31.

23. Browne, "Constellation of Politics," 50–53; Walter M. McMurty Jr., statement before HSBC, Subcommittee on Minority Enterprise, *Government Minority Small Business Programs*, 26 April 1972, 532 [quote]; Hudson, Leftwich & Davenport, untitled report, 6 March 1974, GFL, Domestic Council, Frederick Lynn May Files, box 32, f. "Minority Business Program"; DeWitt, "Small Business Administration," 25.

24. SSBC, *Twenty-First Annual Report, S.* Rpt. 535, 91st Cong., 2d sess., 2 December 1971, 17; HSBC, Subcommittee on Minority Small Business Enterprise, *Minority Small Business Enterprise* H. Rpt. 1615, 13–18; Minority report, HSBC, *Final Report (1971–1972)*, 216–20; HSBC, *Final Report (1969–1970)* H. Rpt. 1795, 91st Cong., 2d sess., 28 December 1970, 14–17; Kleppe, testimony before HSBC, Minority Enterprise Subcommittee, *Minority Enterprise and Allied Problems*, 135–36 [quote]; HSBC, *Final Report (1973–1974)* H. Rpt. 1651, 93d Cong., 2d sess., 30 December 1974, 251; HSBC, *Programs, Policies, and Operations*, H. Rpt. 873, 30–31.

25. Hilary Sandoval, testimony before HSBC, *Organization and Operation of the Small Business Administration (1970)*, hearing, 21 July 1970, 140; HSBC, *Programs, Policies, and Operations*, H. Rpt. 873, 16, 29–30; Shane interview; Laun interview; HSBC, Subcommittee on Minority Small Business, *Government Minority Enterprise Programs—Fiscal Year 1974*, 12 [quote], 19, 28–30; HSBC, Subcommittee on Minority Small Business, *Minority Small Business*, 14–16; Kotlowski, "Black Power—Nixon Style," 441 [quote].

26. Richard M. Nixon, "Special Message to the Congress on Minority Enterprise, March 19, 1972," *Public Papers of the Presidents of the United States, Richard Nixon: 1972* (Washington, D.C.: GPO, 1974), 446; Doctors and Huff, *Minority Enterprise*, 58 [quote]; 68–69 [quote]; SSBC, *Twenty-Second Annual Report*, 46; HSBC, *Organization and Operation . . . 1971*, H. Rpt. 1006, 10.

27. Kleppe, testimony, HSBC, *Organization and Operation . . . 1971*, hearing, 21 September 1971, 128, 153 [quote], 156; HSBC, Subcommittee on Minority Enterprise, *Government Minority Small Business Programs*, hearing, 27 July 1971, 18, 56 [quote]; Kleppe,

testimony, U.S. Congress, House Committee on Banking and Currency, Subcommittee on Small Business, *Minority Enterprise Small Business Investment*, 41, 52–61; SSBC, *Twenty-Fourth Annual Report*, 39; Theophilos, "Government Procurement."

28. John Evans, memorandum for Clark MacGregor, et al., "MESBIC Legislation," 8 May 1972, NPM, WHCF, Subject Files: BE, box 69, folder "EX BE 7 Small Business [3 of 6]"; HSBC, *Organization and Operation. . . (1971)*, H. Rpt. 1006, 25–28; Congressional Quarterly, *Congress and the Nation*, vol. 3, 186.

29. SSBC, *Twenty-Eighth Annual Report*, 113; Wharton, "Small Business Investment," 223–26; Bates, "Minority Enterprise"; "The Black and the Green," *Forbes*, 15 September 1972, 48; Bates, *Black Capitalism*, 127–29; Bates, "Financing Black Enterprise," 747–61 [quote on 755]; Bates and Osborne, "Perverse Effects"; Bates, "Black Entrepreneurship," 59–69. See also, Yancy, *Federal Government Policy*; Black, "An Evaluation," 35–36. Meanwhile, in the mainstream economy, minority firms were making progress without government assistance. Between 1972 and 1977, the number of minority businesses increased by 30 percent. Hispanic and Asian-owned businesses posted the largest gains, with African American firms trailing behind. The most successful black companies served integrated markets. Russell, "Minority Entrepreneur"; Bates, *Black Capitalism*, 30.

30. Michael Jett, "'An Asinine Sitution': New Job Safety Rules Perplex the Owners of Small Businesses," *Wall Street Journal*, 20 February 1973, 42 [quote]; Ronald G. Shafer, "Smaller Businesses Say Federal Red Tape Is Leading to Red Ink," *Wall Street Journal*, 28 June 1972, 1, 27; McConkey, "Will Ecology Kill Small Business?"; "Smothered in Paperwork, Businessmen Are Fed Up," *U.S. News and World Report*, 29 April 1974, 57–58; Michael L. Johnson, "Small Businessmen: More Rags Than Riches," *Industry Week*, 29 July 1974, 36–41; SSBC, *Twenty-First Annual Report*, 3; SSBC, *Twenty-Third Annual Report*, S. Rpt. 357, 93d Cong., 1st sess., 27 July 1973, 117–18; "Can SBA Rescue Small Firms Hurt by Federal Regulations?" *Industry Week*, 25 June 1973, 30–32; HSBC, *Final Report (1973–1974)*, 184–85.

31. Aimee L. Morner, "Junk Aid for Small Business," *Fortune* 96 (November 1977), 214; HSBC, *Final Report (1973–1974)*, 185–86; Calvin Walton [director, Independent Truckers League], testimony before HSBC, Subcommittee on Minority Enterprise, *Government Minority Small Business Programs*, 346–51; SSBC, *Twenty-Fifth Annual Report*, S. Rpt. 13, 94th Cong., 1st sess., 17 February 1975, 44–45; SBA, *1973 Annual Report*, [quote].

32. Harder was a conservative Republican who "hated Democrats" but cooperated with Congress to secure for small business an "equal voice in Washington." He began the NFIB in 1943 in the basement of his print shop, then hired hundreds of traveling salesmen to recruit members. By the 1960s, the Federation had 100 thousand dues-paying members, but turnover was high. The NFIB rank-and-file ostensibly determined the association's stance on issues by voting in the *Mandate*, a monthly opinion survey, but Harder set policy. During the 1950s and 1960s, Harder was primarily concerned with strengthening the antitrust laws and paid minimal attention to the SBA. Constance Burger, phone interview with author, 6 May 1998 [quote]; National Federation of Independent Business, *NFIB: A History*; Tom Hurley [former division Manager, NFIB], phone interview with author, 21 April 1998 [quote]; George Cates [former division manager, NFIB], phone interview with author, 5 May 1998. For a representative sampling of NFIB policy preferences, see *Legislative Victories*.

33. Hoff, *Nixon Reconsidered*, 17.

34. Whitaker, "Nixon's Domestic Policy," 132.

35. Zimmerman, *Curbing Unethical Behavior.*

36. Sergiovanni, "Cultural and Competing Perspectives," 531 [quote]; Smircich, "Organizations"; Schein, *Organizational Culture,* 4 [quote], 52 [quote]; Ott, *Organizational Culture*; Laun interview; Paul Lodato, interview with author, 17 December 1999; Walter Stults, interview with author, 16 December 1999.

37. Lodato interview, 13 January 2000; Grant Hornston, e-mail to author, 19 January 2000; James Gambardella, e-mail to author [quotes], 20 January 2000; Bernard Kulik, e-mail to author [quote], 3 February 2000.

Chapter 7

1. Greene, *Presidency,* 67–68.

2. Congressional Quarterly, *President Ford,* 27 [quote]; Sloan, "Economic Policymaking," 116–18; Greene, *Presidency,* 67–81.

3. Thomas S. Kleppe to Roy L. Ash, 25 November 1974, ibid.; F. Lynn May, memorandum for the President, "Meeting with Small Business Leaders October 14 1974," 11 October 1974, GFL, WHCF, Subject File: BE, box 97, folder "BE7 Small Business 8/9/74–12/31/74"; Roy L. Ash, memorandum for the President, "1976 Budget Decisions Small Business Administration [December 1974?],"GFL, Staff Secretary, Special Files, box 8, folder "FY 1976—12/6/74, Commerce, Treasury, SBA, Small Agencies"; Thomas S. Kleppe to Gerald Ford, 25 November 1974, ibid.; Thomas S. Kleppe to Donald Rumsfeld, 6 December 1974, GFL, WHCF, Subject File: FI 5–7, box 22, folder Small Business 8/9/74–12/31/74"; Thomas S. Kleppe to James M. Cannon, 30 July 1975, GFL, Domestic Council, James M. Cannon Files, box 33, folder "Small Business"; Jim Connor, memorandum for Dudley Chapman, "James Lynn's memo of 10/28/ 75 re Assistance to Small Business attaching Tom Kleppe's letter of recent date," 3 November 1975, GFL, WHCF, Subject File: BE, box 97, folder "BE7 7/1/75–12/31/75"; OMB, "1977 Presidential Review: Small Business Administration," n.d. GFL, Domestic Council, James M. Cannon Files, box 64, f. "FY 1977 Presidential Review—Small Business Administration"; OMB, "Small Business Administration: FY '78 Director's Review" [1976?], GFL, ibid., box 66, folder "FY 1978 Director's Review—SBA."

4. "Why Small Business May Find Federal Aid Harder to Get," *U.S. News and World Report,* 3 May 1976, 67–68; HSBC, *Summary of Activities* H. Rpt. 1791, 94th Cong., 2d sess., 3 January 1977, 12.

5. SSBC, *Twenty-Sixth Annual Report,* S. Rpt. 636, 94th Cong., 2d sess., 19 February 1976, 36, 39.

6. Gerald R. Ford, "Memorandum on the Minority Business Development Program, December 12, 1974," *Public Papers of the Presidents of the United States, Gerald R. Ford: 1974* (Washington, D.C.: GPO, 1975), 739 [quote]; "National Business League Seeking More U.S. Contracts for Blacks," *New York Amsterdam News* (October 1976), A-1, A-8; U.S. Comptroller General, General Accounting Office, *Questionable Effectiveness,* i [quote], 27–28, 51 [quote].

7. F. Lynn May, memorandum for James Cannon, "Small Business Policy," 25 April 1975, GFL, WHCF, Subject File: FG 217, box 173, folder "FG 217 1/1/75–6/30/75"; William F. Gorog, memorandum for the Economic Policy Board, "Progress Report Small Business Initiatives" [December 1975?], GFL, Domestic Council, James M. Cannon Files, box 54, folder "Economic Policy Board, 12/11/75"; Gerald R. Ford, "Statement on Small Business, February 12, 1976," *Public Papers of the Presidents of the United States, Gerald R.*

Ford: 1976 (Washington, D.C.: GPO, 1979), 252; SBA, *Fiscal Year 1975 Report*, 33 [quote]; Louis Laun, interview with author, 16 December 1999; Walter Stults, interview with author, 16 December 1999.

8. [Bill Keel],"Small Business Notes for President-Elect Carter's Advisors: Appendix A (President-Elect Carter's Small Business Commitments)," 8 December 1976, Jimmy Carter Library [hereafter JCL], Chief of Staff (Selig), box 163, folder "National Small Business Association, 12/6/76–2/25/77"; Philip Revzin, "A Friend in Washington?" *Wall Street Journal*, 27 January 1977, 38 [quote]; "A Pledge from Washington to Help Small Business," *Nation's Business* (July 1977), 31 [Weaver quote].

9. [Bill Keel], "Small Business Notes for President-Elect Carter's Advisors: SBA: It's Mission and Leadership," 6 December 1976, JCL, Chief of Staff (Selig), box 163, folder "National Small Business Association, 12/6/76–2/25/77", 3 [quote], 1 [quotes]; [Bill Keel], "Small Business Notes for President-Elect Carter's Advisors: The Presidency and Small Business: The First 100 Days," 8 December 1976, ibid., 4 [quotes], 7, 12; Juanita M. Kreps, memorandum for President Carter, "Small Business Administration," 25 January 1977. JCL, WHCF, Subject File, box FG-204, folder "FG 252: 1/20/77–12/31/77"; Stu Eizenstat memorandum for Rick Hutcheson, "Small Business Administration," 27 January 1977, ibid.; Jimmy Carter to Gaylord Nelson, 5 April 1978, in *Congressional Record*, 16 May 1979, vol. 125, pt. 9:11616.

10. SSBC, *Nomination of Arthur Vernon Weaver*, 3–8.

11. U.S. Comptroller General, General Accounting Office, *SBA's Pilot Programs*, i; James D. Snyder, "Suddenly, Small Is Big!" *Hotel and Motel Management* 194 (April 1979), 26; SBA, *Annual Report FY 1979*, 20–21; SBA, *Annual Report FY 1980*, 27 [quote]; Phillip K. Duncan, "Improved Guaranteed Lending Opportunities From the 'New' SBA," *Journal of Commercial Bank Lending* 62, no. 11 (July 1980):33–41.

12. "Congress Threatens the SBA: The Agency's Administrator Is Also Under Fire From Small-Business Advocates," *Business Week*, 12 February 1979, 105; James Martin (R-N.C.), "Questionable Actions of the Small Business Administration Involving Personnel," *Congressional Record*, 25 October 1979, vol. 125, pt. 23:29616; Timothy S. Robinson, "High SBA Deputy Should Be Fired, Merit Panel Says," *Washington Post*, 10 July 1980, A1, 14; Ron Kolgraf, "The Washington Connection–Part III: The Controversial, Troubled SBA," *Industrial Distribution* (June 1979), 55 [quote]; Richard Klein, "SBA's Business Loan Program," *Atlanta Economic Review* 28 (September–October 1978), 37, 35; SSBC, *Twenty-Ninth Annual Report*, 17; U.S. Comptroller General. General Accounting Office, *Efforts to Improve Management*; Hafer and Ambrose, "Fit or Misfit," 15–19; Nellis, *A SCORE That Counts*, 130 [quote].

13. HSBC, *Summary of Activities* H. Rpt. 1542, 96th Cong., 2d sess., 29 December 1980, 11; Bernard Kulik (Associate Administrator for Disaster Assistance), e-mail message, 26 April 1999.

14. SBA Office of Advocacy, "What is a Small Business?" in *The Study of Small Business*, 7 [quote]; U.S. Comptroller General, General Accounting Office, *What Is a Small Business?* 1–2; SSBC, *Twenty-Ninth Annual Report*, 17 [quote]; SSBC, *Thirty-First Annual Report*, S. Rpt. 1058, 96th Cong., 2d sess., 16 December 1980, 76–78.

15. Gary Jackson, interview with author, 28 July 1999. The 1984 rules for modifying size standards are set forth in SBA, *Report of the Size Policy Board* (unpublished report, 30 September 1985).

16. Joel Havemann, "Congress Opens Floodgates in the SBA's Disaster Loan Program," *National Journal*, 31 December 1977, 2001–3; Weaver, "Evaluating the SBA,"

190; "Get Your 3% Loans Right Here, Folks," *Forbes*, 11 December 1978, 56; "SBA No!," *Business Week*, 14 November 1977, 28, 33.

17. In 1972, women owned only 5 percent of U.S. businesses, but by the mid-1990s they owned nearly half and accounted for 25 percent of private employment. Furchtgott-Roth and Stolba, *Women's Figures*, 28; Brush and Hisrich, "Women-Owned Businesses," 111. The media published numerous books and articles on "female capitalism." See Schwartz, "Entrepreneurship"; Rich-McCoy, *Millionairess*; "Women Rise as Entrepreneurs," *Business Week*, 25 February 1980, 85–86, 91; C.R. Riggs, "The Rise of Women Entrepreneurs," *D&B Reports* (January–February 1981), 19–23; Charboneau, "Woman Entrepreneur," 21–23. For a general history of women business owners, see Kwolek-Folland, *Incorporating Women*.

18. Dorothy Rivers [National Women's Business Owners Association], testimony before SSBC, *Women and the Small Business Administration,* 102–4; Susan Hager [Association of Women Business Owners], testimony, ibid., 59; Louis Laun, testimony before ibid., 2–3; "Aid Urged to Women in Business," *Washington Post*, 11 June 1975, A16; David M. Bray, memorandum for Pat Lindh, "Agency Responses to Position Paper 'Women in Business,'" 29 August 1975, GFL, Public Liaison Office, Patricia Lindh Files, box 4, folder "Women and Business—March 3, 1976 [1 of 3]," 2, 16; SBA, *The Facts About Women As Users of SBA Services*; Mark Stevens, "SBA Forums Geared to Women Executives," *Newsday*, 8 November 1976, 31.

19. U.S. President's Interagency Task Force on Women Business Owners, *Bottom Line*, 3–5; Black, "An Evaluation," 90 [quote]; U.S. Department of Commerce, *Women and Business Ownership*, 30–31. Later studies found little or no evidence of credit discrimination against women. Buttner and Rosen, "Funding," 249–61; Riding and Swift, "Women Business Owners," 327–40; Brush, "Research on Women Business Owners," 15–16; "Businesswomen Enjoy Credit Access Similar to Men, Study Finds," *Wall Street Journal*, 17 October 1996, B2.

20. "National Women's Business Ownership Campaign," *Congressional Record*, 4 August 1977, vol. 123, pt. 22:27743–44; "Businesswomen Get a Champion at SBA," *Nation's Business* 65 (December 1977), 34–36; SBA, *Annual Report FY 1980*, 44; Jimmy Carter, "Women's Business Enterprise, Memorandum From the President, May 18, 1979," *Public Papers of the Presidents of the United States, Jimmy Carter: 1979* (Washington, D.C.: GPO, 1980), 894–95; "Cookie Concern Owner Pleads Guilty in Case Involving SBA Funds," *Wall Street Journal*, 30 August 1984, 31; Black, "Effectiveness," 21.

21. U.S. Comptroller General, General Accounting Office, *Most Borrowers*, ii–iii [quote on iii].

22. SSBC, *Small Business Administration 8(a)*, 13, 21–22, 37–38.

23. U.S. Congress, Senate Committee on Government Affairs, Subcommittee on Federal Spending Practices and Open Government, *Report Based on Hearings*, 7–8, 27 [quote]; 3 [quote], 16, 11–12, 19–23; Alex Poinsett, "SBA Scandals: Whites Bilk Black 'Fronts,'" *Ebony* (October 1977), 76 [quote]; Stephen Chapman, "Capitalism Without Tears: SBA Program for Black Businesses," *The New Republic*, 1 April 1978, 17 [quote].

24. Jimmy Carter, "Minority Business Enterprise: Statement by the President, September 12, 1977," *Public Papers of the Presidents of the United States, Jimmy Carter: 1977* (Washington, D.C.: GPO, 1977, 1978), 1579–80; Jimmy Carter, "National Conference on Fraud, Abuse and Error: Remarks . . . December 13, 1978," *Public Papers of the Presidents of the United States, Jimmy Carter: 1978* (Washington, D.C.: GPO, 1979), 2230; Black, "An Evaluation," 17.

25. SBA, *1978 Annual Report,* 19; Weaver, "Evaluating the SBA," 196; SBA, *The 8(a) Program: Management Issues and Recommendations,* 22 August 1980, JCL, Domestic Policy Staff (Farrow), box 22, folder "SBA—Minority Business, 8(a) Program", 5 [quote]; 2, 4, 23–25; Lawton Chiles, quoted in Donald Robinson, "Billion-Dollar Scandal at the SBA," *Reader's Digest* (June 1978), 131.

26. White, *America in Search of Itself,* 198; Jones, *Trusteeship Presidency;* Hargrove, *Jimmy Carter.*

27. William Proxmire, "Abolish the Small Business Administration," *Congressional Record,* 18 January 1979, vol. 125, pt. 1:488; Kolgraf, "Washington Connection," 58; "Abolition of SBA Raised As an Option by Senator," *Wall Street Journal,* 22 November 1978, 14 [quotes]; White House, "Option Paper" [January 1979], JCL, Chief of Staff (Selig), box 184, folder "Small Business Administration—Reorganization, 12/21/78–5/4/ 79 [O/A 605]"; Steve Selig, memorandum for Hamilton Jordan, "Reorganization for the Small Business Administration," 19 January 1979, ibid.

28. LaNoue and Sullivan, "Presumptions," 442; Chapman, "Capitalism without Tears," 16; Eastland, *Ending Affirmative Action,* 120.

29. James W. Singer, "Affirmative Action in the Wake of the Bakke Decision," *National Journal,* 5 August 1978, 1248–51; Parren J. Mitchell, press release, "President Carter Signs Major Legislation Affecting Minority Business Enterprise," 26 October 1978, JCL, Staff Offices Counsel (Lipshutz), box 45, folder "Small Business Administration 8–A Program, Investigation (NY, et al), 10/78–7/79 [CF, O/A 440]"; SSBC, *Twenty-Ninth Annual Report,* 27; Jackson-Park, "Minority Set-Aside Legislation," 184.

30. LaNoue and Sullivan, "Presumptions," 442–43.

31. Weaver, quoted in Samuel Ichiye Hayakawa (R-Calif.), "Rich Get Richer Using U.S. Aid to Minority Firms," *Congressional Record,* 25 September 1980, vol. 126, pt. 20:27340; A. Vernon Weaver to Regional Administrators, n.d. [1980], JCL, Domestic Policy Staff (Farrow), box 22, folder "SBA—Minority Business, 8(a) Program."

32. The self-employment income of British Americans was comparable to that of African Americans and less than Hispanic self-employment income. Polish and Russian Americans had twice the self-employment income of other "white" groups. Table: "Education and Income (By Ethnicity)," in Mayers, "In the Red," 165.

33. LaNoue and Sullivan, "Presumptions," 439–67.

34. William A. Clement Jr. to Daniel K. Inouye, 13 June 1979, JCL, WHCF, Subject File, box FG-204, folder "FG 252: 1/1/79–12/31/79"; Jack H. Watson Jr. to Suren G. Dutia, 23 July 1979, ibid.; Bates, "Changing Nature," 25–42; Chen and Cole, "Myths, Facts, and Theories," 111–23.

35. See, e.g., U.S. President's Interagency Task Force on Women Business Owners, *Bottom Line,* 8.

36. Steve Selig, memorandum for Margaret Costanza, "12/18/77 Meeting with Vernon Weaver," 19 December 1977, JCL, Chief of Staff (Selig), box 182, folder "Small Business Administration, 12/16/77–11/9/78"; Harold J. Logan, "Minorities, Women Battle Over SBA Program's Leftovers," *Washington Post,* 22 August 1978, A14 [quote]; Jack Anderson, "Women Seeking More U.S. Contracts," *Washington Post,* 5 May 1979, E47.

37. Jane Seaberry, "Hasidic Jews Seek SBA Assistance," *Washington Post,* 25 February 1980, D9; Jane Seaberry, "Hasidic Jews' Aid Plea Creates Furor," *Washington Post,* 6 March 1980, C3; Edward W. Norton, memorandum for Harry K. Schwartz, "Hasidic Application for Designation as a Socially Disadvantaged Group," 13 February 1980, JCL, WHCF, Subject File, box PQ-3, folder "PQ 2/1/80–2/29/80"; Bob Malson and Harry

Schwartz, memorandum for Stu Eizenstat, "Application of Hasidic Jews for Designation as a Socially Disadvantaged Group Entitled to Minority Procurement Set-Aside and Minority Subcontractor Benefits," 21 February 1980, ibid.; Bob Malson and Alan Heppel, memorandum for Stu Eizenstat, "SBA's decision on the certification of Hasidic Jews as a socially disadvantaged group for purposes of Section 8 a program," 1 April 1980, JCL, Domestic Policy Staff (Eizenstat), box 274, folder "Small Business [CF O/A 731] [2]."

38. Galbraith, *New Industrial State*.

39. Lipset and Schneider, *Confidence Gap*, 76, 83; McClosky and Zaller, *American Ethos*, 133–34; Gumpert, "Entrepreneurship"; Schumacher, *Small Is Beautiful*; Neal B. Freeman, "Small Is Beautiful," *National Review*, 17 April 1981, 408.

40. Omps, "Dynamic Small Business Sector," 52–56; Birch, *Job Generation Process*, 29; Birch, "Who Creates Jobs?"

41. Berney and Owens, "Table 14.4: Percentage Share of GNP by Firm Size: 1958, 1963, 1972, and 1977," in "Model," 217; Star, *Concentration*, 149; Table 2.14, "Share of Employment and Sales of Zero-Employee Firms, 1967, 1972 and 1977,"in U.S. President, *The State of Small Business: a Report of the President Transmitted to the Congress (March 1983)* (Washington, D.C.: GPO, 1983), 96; Chilton, "How the Feds Screw," 33.

42. HSBC, Subcommittee on Antitrust, *Future of Small Business in America*. See also, Gumpert, "Future."

43. "Billy Carter: Frustrations of the Small Businessman," *Nation's Business* 65 (May 1977), 28–32, 34, 36; Gary Allen, "We Could Be Losing the American Dream," *American Opinion* 20 (June 1977), 5, 72; Chilton, "How the Feds Screw," 33–36; John H. Sheridan. "Next Punch May K.O. Lead Producers," *Industry Week*, 13 November 1978, 23–24; "Endangered Species: Small Electroplaters," *Industry Week*, 15 October 1979, 46, 48; Susan J Duncan, "Regulation: It Makes Small Business Less Competitive," *Inc.* (June 1980), 51–54; Chilton and Weidenbaum, *Small Business*; Roberta Graham, "Small Business: Beset, Bothered, and Beleaguered . . . ," *Nation's Business* 68 (February 1980), 22–31.

44. Galbraith, "Government vs. Small Business," 42–44; Galbraith, "Perspective on Small Business."

45. Jerry Knight, "SBA Withheld Criticism of Labor Law Revisions," *Washington Post* (25 May 1978), inserted in *Congressional Record*, 25 May 1978, vol. 124, pt. 12:15486–87. The SBA's "economic injury" loans also failed to alleviate the regulatory burden: in a five-year period, the SBA approved 156 OSHA-compliance loans, reaching an infinitesimal percentage of the companies inspected by OSHA. Chilton and Weidenbaum, *Small Business*, 10–11; SSBC, *Twenty-Eighth Annual Report*, S. Rpt. 629, 95th Cong., 2d sess., 1 February 1978, 133.

46. Irving Kristol, "The New Forgotten Man," *Wall Street Journal*, 13 November 1975, 20; Vogel, *Fluctuating Fortunes*, 199; Ron Kolgraf, "Small Businessmen Take Washington by Storm," *Industrial Distribution* (September 1979), 59–61; Bill Mashaw, "It Seems to Me—Just Leave Us Alone—and No Hand-Outs, Please!" *Hardware Retailing* (April 1977), inserted in *Congressional Record*, 26 April 1977, vol. 123, pt. 10:12220; Allen, "Growing Resistance," 31–54 [quote on 37]; Lo, *Small Property Versus Big Government*; Richard Lamm, quoted in Levitt, "In Praise of Small Business,," 152; Ron Kolgraf, "The Washington Connection: A Guide to Political Action," *Industrial Distribution* (April 1979), 42 [quote].

47. National Federation of Independent Business, *NFIB: A History*, 11–18; "Small Business Lobby Plays Trick or Treat"; "Small Business Lobby," 113–19; Vogel, *Fluctuating Fortunes*, 205 [quote], 199; Richard E. Cohen, "Small Business Is Getting a Big Reception in Washington," *National Journal*, 11 June 1977, 896–99; Robert T. Gray, "Small Busi-

ness Shows Big Clout," *Nation's Business* (September 1978), 24–29; John Motley, interview with author, 11 August 1999.

48. "Antitrust and Small Business: Killing the Big-Is-Better Myth (II)," *Antitrust Law & Economics Review* 17, no. 3 (1985):45 [quote]; Harry Schwartz, memorandum for Stu Eizenstat, "Your remarks before the National Conference of the National Federation of Independent Businessmen," 13 June 1979, JCL, Domestic Policy Staff (Eizenstat), box 275, folder "Small Business [CF, O/A 731] [3]"; Vogel, *Fluctuating Fortunes*, 161; Kaufman, *Presidency*, 101–2; McQuaid, *Uneasy Partners*, 154–55; Ann M. Reilly, "Small Businesses' Big Clout," *Dun's Review* 115 (March 1980), 71 [quote].

49. Levitt, quoted in "The Verdict: More or Less a Success, but What's Next?" *Nation's Business* (March 1980), 70; U.S. White House Conference on Small Business and SBA, *The White House Conference*; Table A-5, "Federal Expenditures as a Percentage of Gross Domestic Product, Fiscal Years 1940–1992," in Stein, *Presidential Economics*, 460–61.

50. Jimmy Carter. "Regulation of Small Businesses and Organizations: Memorandum From the President, November 16, 1979." *Public Papers . . . 1979*, 2142; Len Strazewski, "Small Firms, OSHA Enter Detente," *Business Insurance*, 28 April 1980, 43.

51. Kuratko, "Small Business," 133.

52. SSBC, *Thirtieth Annual Report, S.* Rpt. 707, 96th Cong., 2d sess., 14 May 1980, 42–43.

53. Roberta Graham, "Small Business: Fighting to Stay Alive," *Nation's Business* (July 1980), 33–36; Jimmy Carter, "Small Business: Message to the Congress, January 14, 1980," *Public Papers . . . 1980–81*, 73–79; "Presidential Candidates: How They Stand on Small Business," *Industrial Distribution* 70 (June 1980), 65–66; Bill Brock to delegates of the White House Conference on Small Business, 5 September 1980, JCL, Domestic Policy Staff (Farrow), box 23, folder "Small Business Administration—White House Conference on Small Business, Follow Up, File No. 1"; Heller Institute for Small Business, *Small Business Assesses*, 4; "Lobbyists Buoyed by GOP Gains," *Wall Street Journal*, 17 November 1980, 31.

54. Leonard and Rhyne, "Federal Credit," 40–58; Aharoni, *No-Risk Society*, 120–21; Rhyne, *Small Business*, 18, 3.

55. SSBC, Table II: "8(a) Procurement," *Federal Minority Business Development Program*, 31.

56. Horowitz, *Beyond Left and Right.*

Chapter 8

1. Reagan, quoted in Ron Kolgraf, "Small Businessmen Take Washington by Storm," *Industrial Distribution* 69 (September 1979), 60.

2. Ronald Reagan, "Inaugural Address, January 20, 1981," *Public Papers of the Presidents of the United States, Ronald Reagan: 1981* (Washington, D.C.: GPO, 1982), 1; Stockman, "Social Pork Barrel."

3. Murray L. Weidenbaum, "Subsidies Business Does Not Need," *New York Times*, 31 March 1981, A19; Tom Richman, "Will the Real SBA Please Stand Up?" *Inc.* 6, no. 2 (February 1984), 90 [quote]; "Reagan Gets Advice," *Wall Street Journal*, 8 December 1980, 31 [quote].

4. "A Deep Cut in SBA's Loan Authority Is Called for Under Reagan Budget-Tightening," *Wall Street Journal*, 9 March 1981, 24; SBA, "Small Business Administration: General Business Loan Approvals," data provided to author; Andrews and Eisemann, *Who Finances Small Business*; Ronald Reagan, "Remarks at a White House Briefing on the State of Small Business," *Public Papers of the Presidents of the United States, Ronald Reagan:*

1982 (Washington, D.C.: GPO, 1983), 235–38; Jack F. Kemp, "NFIB Supports Reagan Tax Plan for Small Business," *Congressional Record*, 28 July 1981, vol. 127, pt. 13:17909.

5. HSBC, *Summary of Activities* H. Rpt. 993., 97th Cong., 2d sess., 30 December 1982, 51, 80; Thomas L. Amberg and Michael R. Montgomery, "SBA Loans: Fast Track to Failure (*St. Louis Globe-Democrat* Series, August 31–September 9, 1981)," in HSBC, Subcommittee on SBA, *Administration's Small*, A16–33 [quote on 20]; "Field Recommendations: National Meeting on Financial Assistance," in SSBC, *Small Business Administration's Direct Loan Programs*, 1, 32; SSBC, *Legislative and Oversight Activities*, 34.

6. Pendleton James, memorandum for Senior Staff, "Small Business Administration (SBA) Administrator," 17 February 1981, RRL, FG 252, ID# 000472; Ronald Reagan, "Nomination of Michael Cardenas to Be Administrator of the Small Business Administration, February 20, 1981," *Public Papers . . . 1981*, 145–46; SBA, *Annual Report: FY 1981*, 1; "Simply Delighted . . . . ," *Wall Street Journal*, 3 August 1981, 17; SBA, *Annual Report FY 1980*, 1; SSBC, *Nomination of Michael Cardenas*, 47–50.

7. "Speaking Strictly," *Wall Street Journal*, 17 April 1981, 1; "SBA Chief Discourages the Spread of Tales About 'Bermuda Triangle,'" *Wall Street Journal*, 29 December 1981, 23; James C. Sanders, interview with author, 26 October 1997; Frank Swain [Chief Counsel for Advocacy, 1981–1988], interview with author, 26 August 1999; Marshall Parker, interview with author, 31 August 1999; Richard Shane, interview with author, 29 October 1997; "Special Programs for Women Dying Away at Reagan's SBA," *Wall Street Journal*, 16 November 1981, 29 [quote]; Barbara Honegger, memorandum for Martin Anderson, "SBA 8(a) Program Discrimination against Women Business Owners Manifested as Discrimination against White Women and Proposed Correction," 3 November 1981, RRL, Martin Anderson Files, CFOA84, folder "Small Business Administration [3 of 4]"; Brooks Jackson, "Report Clears SBA's Chief of Misdeeds," *Wall Street Journal*, 24 November 1981, 35, 40; "Ex-SBA Chief Cardenas Is Cleared in U.S. Probe," *Wall Street Journal*, 26 February 1982, 18; "Reagan to Remove Cardenas As SBA Head Following Complaints on His Competence," *Wall Street Journal*, 1 February 1982, 6.

8. Ronald Reagan, "Nomination of James C. Sanders to Be Administrator of the Small Business Administration, February 4, 1982," *Public Papers . . . 1982* (Washington, D.C.: GPO, 1983), 114; SSBC, *Nomination of James C. Sanders*, 35 [quote]; Sanders interview; Myron Struck, "SBA Chief Boosts Morale," *Washington Post*, 4 July 1984, A17; Roger B. Porter, memorandum for Edwin Meese III, et al., "Mid-term Planning Session Small Business Administration (SBA)," 18 October 1982, RRL, Edwin Meese III Files, box OA6512, folder "Small Business Administration"; SBA, "Budget Review Board," 7 December 1983, ibid., box OA11835, folder "Budget FY '85 Small Business Administration"; Rector, "Agenda Deflection," 255–69.

9. Lloyd Bentsen (D-Tex.), "Senate Democratic Task Force on Small Business," *Congressional Record*, 19 May 1982, vol. 128, pt. 8:10556–60; Berkley Bedell (D-Iowa), "Small Business Programs Slashed in Time of Need," *Congressional Record* (20 July 1982), vol. 128, pt. 13:17138–39; Parren Mitchell (D-Md.), "Rebuilding the Road to Opportunity: Renewing the Entrepreneurial Spirit in America," *Congressional Record*, 13 September 1982, vol. 128, pt. 18:24841–46. See also, Easton, *Reagan's Squeeze on Small Business*.

10. James C. Sanders, memorandum for Craig L. Fuller [Deputy Assistant to the President], "Turnaround of Small Business Administration," 19 April 1982, National Archives (College Park, Md.), RG 309, Accession 86–006, Administrator's Organizational Files, 1982–83, box 6, folder "White House"; Elizabeth H. Dole, memorandum for James A. Baker III, "Big versus little: A Strategy for Small Business," 5 January 1982 [quotes],

ibid.; James C. Sanders to Elizabeth Dole, 29 July 1982, RRL, Elizabeth Dole Files, box OA6386, folder "Business (Small) 7–12/82 [2 of 2]"; James C. Sanders, memorandum for Craig L. Fuller, "Outline of Specific Proposals" [February 1983], RRL, BE006, I.D.# 124780CA; Elizabeth H. Dole, memorandum for Edwin Meese III et al., "Small Business Strategy," 28 June 1982, RRL, Elizabeth Dole Files, box OA6412, folder "Business—Small Business Strategy [1 of 2]"; Elizabeth H. Dole, memorandum for Edwin Meese III et al., "Proposed Action Plan for Small Business," 22 November 1982, RRL, Elizabeth Dole Files, box OA6386, folder "Business (Small) 7–12/82 [1 of 2]."

11. Cannon, *President Reagan*, 240; Sanders interview; Anonymous, memorandum, "Sanders Meeting," 19 March 1982, RRL, BE006, folder 086000–089299, no I.D.#.

12. Belz, *Equality Transformed*, 179–83, 196–201; Jacoby, *Someone Else's House*, 446–47; Detlefsen, *Civil Rights Under Reagan*, 151–56. For an excellent analysis of the internal administration debate over affirmative action, see Laham, *Reagan Presidency*.

13. In 1981, the GAO published yet another critical report. U.S. Comptroller General, General Accounting Office, *SBA 8(a) Procurement Program*.

14. A. Gorman Pinkston, [President, National Utility Contractors Association] to Ronald Reagan, 8 October 1981, RRL, FG 252, ID# 044604; "Talking Points: Minority Business Consolidation Proposal," n.d. [1982], RRL, Elizabeth Dole Files, box OA6390, folder "Minority Business Enterprise [4 of 5]"; Associated General Contractors of America to James W. Ciccooni [Special Assistant to the President], 10 October 1983, RRL, WHORM Subject File, BE006, ID# 199875; Kirk Fordice to Rep. Trent Lott, 19 June 1981, RRL, WHORM Subject File, BE006, ID# 045251; Kirk Fordice to Ronald Reagan, 19 June 1981, ibid.

15. Elizabeth H. Dole, memorandum for James A. Baker III, "Black Strategy," 9 February 1982, RRL, Diana Lozano Files, box OA7980, folder "Black Strategy" [quote]; Elizabeth H. Dole, memorandum for Edwin Meese III, James A. Baker III, and Michael Deaver, "Hispanic Strategy," 17 May 1982, ibid., folder "Hispanic Strategy"; White House, Office of Public Liaison, "Black Strategy" (draft), [1982], ibid., folder "Black Strategy" [quote]; White House Office of Public Liaison, "Hispanic Strategy Guidelines," [1982], ibid., folder "Hispanic Strategy."

16. Ronald Reagan, "Remarks on Signing a Statement on Minority Business Enterprise Development, December 17, 1982," *Public Papers . . . 1982*, 1613; Laham, *Reagan Presidency*, 105 [quote]; Isaiah J. Poole, "Are the Promises Being Kept?" *Black Enterprise* 14, no. 3 (October 1983), 117–22; Belz, *Equality Transformed*, 195–96; Ronald Reagan, "Remarks on Signing an Executive Order on Minority Business Enterprise Development, July 14, 1983," *Public Papers of the Presidents of the United States, Ronald Reagan: 1983* (Washington, D.C.: GPO, 1984, 1985), 1034 [quote]. The president also directed the SBA to increase the percentage of guaranteed loans awarded to minority business owners. Ronald Reagan, "Annual Report to the Congress on the State of Small Business, March 1, 1982" *Public Papers . . . 1982*, 247.

17. Ronald Reagan, "Remarks at Cinco De Mayo Ceremonies in San Antonio, Texas, May 5, 1983," *Public Papers . . . 1983*, 651; Ronald Reagan, "Remarks at the Annual Convention of the United States Hispanic Chamber of Commerce in Tampa, Florida, August 12, 1983," ibid., 1153 [quote]; Ronald Reagan, "Remarks at a White House Ceremony Marking the Observance of Minority Enterprise Development Week, October 3, 1983," ibid., 1399; Ronald Reagan, "Remarks to Members of the National Association of Minority Contractors, June 27, 1984," *Public Papers of the Presidents of the United States, Ronald Reagan: 1984* (Washington, D.C.: GPO, 1986, 1987), 921.

18. Howard Kurtz, "Civil Rights Commission Withdraws Its Report on Minority

Contracts: Chairman 'Upset' With White House Support of Set-Aside Programs [*Washington Post* article, 12 April 1986]," *Congressional Record*, 8 May 1986, vol. 132, pt. 7:10090 [quote]; Michael Oreskes, "The Set-Aside Scam," *The New Republic*, 24 December 1984, 17–20; "TRB," "Compassion, Reagan-Style," *The New Republic*, 21 October 1985, 4 [quotes], 42; Jeremy Rabkin, "Reagan's Secret Quotas," *The New Republic*, 5 August 1985, 15–18; "Set Set-Asides Aside," *The New Republic* (May 1986), 10–11.

19. SBA, *Annual Report FY 1983*, 78–79; SBA, *Annual Report FY 1984*, 63; SBA, *SBA Announces New Tough Policies for 8(a) Program*, 1 May 1981, RRL, WHORM Subject File, BE006, ID# 018576; Michael Thoryn, "New Administrator: "Serious Problems" at SBA," *Nation's Business* 69, no. 6 (June 1981), 44; HSBC, Subcommittee on SBA, *Administration's Small*, 5–6; Parren Mitchell, "In Response to the Administration's Tough New Policies for the 8(a) Program," *Congressional Record*, 7 May 1981, vol. 127, pt. 7:9021–23 [quote on 9022]; Parren Mitchell, in HSBC, *Small and Minority Business*, 3 [quote].

20. "The Boot Came Sooner Than Intended," *Wall Street Journal*, 12 July 1982, 21; Dan J. Smith, memorandum for Wendell Gunn, "Long-term Solution to 8(a)/GAO Problem," 30 July 1982, RRL, BE006, I.D.# 0934811; Elizabeth H. Dole, memorandum for Ed Harper, "Minority Business SBA 8(a) Grads," RRL, BE006, folder 101000–102999; Elizabeth H. Dole, memorandum for Ed Harper, "Minority Business: SBA 8(a) Grads," 28 December 1982, RRL, BE006, I.D.# 117839; Wendell W. Gunn, memorandum for Edwin L. Harper, "'Other than Small' 8(a) Contractors," 15 February 1983, RRL, BE006, folder 101000–102999; SSBC, *Legislative and Oversight Activities*, 122–23; Red Cavaney, memorandum for Dave Gergen, Craig Fuller, Helene von Damm, "8(a) Program Graduations," 9 February 1983, RRL, WHORM Subject File, BE006, ID# 124612; "The SBA Was Accused of 'Economic Genocide,'" *Wall Street Journal*, 11 February 1983, 1; James Sanders, interview with author, 3 June 1999.

21. Thompson, *Feeding the Beast*, 9–11 [quote on 11].

22. Ibid., 34–35 [quote on 35], 62, 152 [quote]; Traub, *Too Good*, 68–69; White House, Office of Public Liaison, "Hispanic Strategy Guidelines" [1982], RRL, Diana Lozano Files, box OA7980, folder "Hispanic Strategy."

23. Thompson, *Feeding the Beast*, 22–24 [quotes], 30 [quote], 180–83 [quote on 181]; George Lardner Jr., "White House Strongly Backed Wedtech Award, Congress Told," *Washington Post*, 10 September 1987, A1, 11; George Lardner Jr., "Wedtech Drew Quick Support," *Washington Post*, 11 September 1987, A3.

24. Mary Thornton, "Ex-SBA Head Cites White House Pressure," *Washington Post*, 26 May 1987, A5.

25. Lardner, "Wedtech"; Thompson, *Feeding the Beast*, 108, 115–17, 173; Traub, *Too Good*, 173 [quote], 223 [quote].

26. Thompson, *Feeding the Beast*, 200–4, 160, 192.

27. Ibid., 219–21, 233, 264–65; Traub, *Too Good*, 290–91.

28. Sternberg and Harrison, *Feeding Frenzy*, 298–303; Thompson, *Feeding the Beast*, 192; David C. Ruffin, "Parren Mitchell's Sixteen Years: a Legislative Legacy," *Black Enterprise* (June 1986), 59–60; McKay, et al., *Report of Independent Counsel*.; "Five Years of Troubles: A Chronology," *Boston Globe*, 6 July 1988: 8.

29. U.S. Congress, Senate Committee on Government Affairs, Subcommittee on Oversight of Government Management, *Wedtech*, 4–5; "Minority Business Development Program Reform Act," *Congressional Record*, 7 July 1988, vol. 134, pt. 12:17126–51; Congressional Quarterly, "SBA Minority Program Overhaul," *Congress and the Nation*, vol. 7, 401–3; Jeanne Sadler, "SBA Sets New Rules on Minority Program," *Wall Street Journal*, 16

August 1989, B2; Paul Starobin, "Revisal of SBA Minority Program Raises Questions on Many Sides," *Congressional Quarterly Weekly Report*, 15 October 1988:2984 [quote].

30. Patricia Forbes, [former SBA employee, Office of General Counsel], interview with author, 13 November 1997; Sanders interview [quote]; U.S. Comptroller General, General Accounting Office, *8(a) Is Vulnerable*; Eastland, *Ending Affirmative Action*, 139.

31. Peter de Leon cites Wedtech as an example of "systemic political corruption." De Leon, *Thinking About Political Corruption*, 107–10.

32. See, e.g., Amaker, *Civil Rights*.

33. Laham, *Reagan Presidency*, 105 [quote], 71 [quote].

34. Faucett, Skolnik, and Chmelynski, *Procurement Share*, vi; HSBC, *Summary of Activities* H. Rpt. 1036, 99th Cong., 2d sess., 2 January 1987, 79; Sanders interview; Hebert and Becker, "Preferential Treatment," 756–65; Paul N. McCloskey Jr. to Ronald Reagan, 23 June 1982, RRL, WHORM Subject Files, BE006, ID# 084957; William J. LaNouette, "Don't Do Us Any Favors." *National Journal*, 13 February 1982, 293; Bill Keller, "How Congress Spoils Small Business," *Washington Monthly* 14, no. 1 (1982):44–49; Wallsten, "Rethinking," 194–220; Wallsten, "Can Government-Industry R&D Programs Increase Private R&D?" unpublished paper [quote].

35. U.S. President, *The State of Small Business* (Washington, D.C.: GPO, 1988), xvi; SBA Office of Advocacy, *Small Business in the American Economy*, 41–43; "Small Is Beautiful Now in Manufacturing," *Business Week*, 22 October 1984, 152, 156; Piore and Sabel, *Second Industrial Divide*; Solomon, *Small Business USA*; Birch, *Job Creation*; Brock and Evans, "Small Business Economics"; Acs and Audretsch, "Innovation, Market Structure, and Firm Size"; Acs and Audretsch, *Innovation*; "The Rise and Rise of America's Small Firms," *Economist*, 21 January 1989, 73–74; Phillips, "Increasing Role"; "The Fall of Big Business," *The Economist*, 17 April 1993, 13–14. For opinion polls evaluating public attitudes toward small business, see Jackson, *American Entrepreneurial*; Geurtsen, "Attitudes"; Harrison, *Lean and Mean*, 38. This infatuation with small business was as unrealistic as the "big-is-better" myth of the 1960s. Further studies revealed methodological flaws in the pro–small business literature. Critics noted that small firms were generally less profitable, less productive, and less generous to their employees. Sympathetic analysts countered with their own studies of job creation, innovation, and worker job satisfaction, leaving the debate still very much alive in the 1990s. Harrison, *Lean and Mean*; Brown, Hamilton, and Medoff, *Employers Large and Small*; Lustgarten, "Firm Size"; Davis, Haltiwanger, and Schuh, "Small Business and Job Creation"; "Symposium on Harrison's *Lean and Mean*," *Small Business Economics* 7 (1995); Dennis, Phillips, and Starr, "Small Business Job Creation"; Acs, ed., *Are Small Firms Important?*

36. HSBC, *Summary of Activities* H. Rpt. 1830, 95d Cong., 2d sess., 2 January 1979, 162 [quote]; Ronald Reagan, "Remarks at a White House Briefing on the State of Small Business, March 1, 1982," *Public Papers . . . 1982* (Washington, D.C.: GPO, 1983), 236; Ronald Reagan, "Remarks at a White House Briefing for Members of the Small Business Community, October 29, 1987," *Public Papers of the Presidents of the United States, Ronald Reagan: 1987* (Washington, D.C.: GPO, 1989), 1248–49. See also, Ronald Reagan, "Radio Address to the Nation on Small Business, May 14, 1983," *Public Papers . . . 1983*, 705–6; Reagan, "Why This Is an Entrepreneurial Age."

37. Jonathan Rauch, "Small Business Agency Alive and Well Despite White House Attempt to Kill It," *National Journal*, 10 August 1985, 1848 [quote]; Stockman, *Triumph of Politics*, 420; Sanders interview; Myron Struck, "Chief Wages Quiet Battle for SBA Survival," *Washington Post*, 18 December 1984, A17; Robert D. Hershey Jr., "Small Busi-

ness Administration: Plans to Keep Agency From the Ax," *New York Times*, 31 January 1985, A20; "The Fact That White House Budget Director David Stockman Wants to Eliminate Their Agency Apparently Isn't Getting People Down at the Small Business Administration," *Wall Street Journal*, 17 December 1984, 37.

38. "'Rathole' and Rabbit Hole," *Wall Street Journal*, 28 February 1985, 28 [quote]; Stockman, testimony before SSBC, *S. 408*, 214–91 [quotes on 214, 219, 236, 241]; Kevin Farrell, "Does Selling the SBA Make Sense?" *Venture* 7 (March 1985), 120; Tom Nicholson, "David vs. the SBA Goliath," *Newsweek*, 4 March 1985, 44.

39. Gale, "Economic Effects"; Bosworth, Carron, and Rhyne, *Economics of Federal Credit*, 88–96; Rhyne, *Small Business, Banks, and SBA Loan Guarantees*; Haynes, "Qualitative Assessment." See also, Klein, "SBA's Business Loan Program." For a favorable appraisal of loan guarantees sponsored by the SBA, see Price Waterhouse, *Evaluation of the 7(a) Guaranteed Business Loan Program: Final Report* (Washington, D.C.: Price Waterhouse, 1992).

40. Ronald Reagan, "Remarks at a White House Meeting With the Deficit Reduction Coalition, April 16, 1985," *Public Papers of the Presidents of the United States, Ronald Reagan: 1985* (Washington, D.C.: GPO, 1988), 441; Ronald Reagan, "Address to the Nation on the Federal Budget and Deficit Reduction, April 24,1985," ibid., 496.

41. Sanders, testimony, *S. 408* hearing, 325–41; Howard Kurtz, "SBA Chief Says Stockman's Comments 'Slander' Agency," *Washington Post*, 16 February 1985, A4 [quote]; Sanders, quoted in Rector, "Agenda Deflection," 264.

42. Lorette, Walton, and Dianich, "Proposal for Restructuring the SBA," 23; "NAM Small Manufacturers: Abolish SBA Loans to Help Reduce Deficit," 23 April 1985, inserted in David Dreier, "Abolish SBA Loans to Help Reduce Deficit," *Congressional Record*, 1 May 1985, vol. 131, pt. 8:10187; Fred Barnes, "Free Lunch Fans," *The New Republic*, 30 June 1986, 8, 10; Jay Finegan, "Washington: Cleaning House," *Inc.* 8, no. 6 (June 1986), 34 [quote].

43. *NFIB Mandate,* no. 455, June 1984:5, 1; NFIB, *Small Business Evaluates SBA*; NFIB, press release, "SBA: The 'Great Unknown' to Small Business" [1984], RG 309, Accession 86–013 (Administrators Personal Files, 1983–84), box 1, folder "NFIB"; "Poll of Some Small Business Owners on SBA Shows Unexpected Responses," *Wall Street Journal*, 25 June 1984, 29; Frank Swain, interview with author, 26 August 1999; Rauch, "Small Business Agency," 1847; John Sloan Jr. [President, NFIB] to Donald T. Regan [White House Chief of Staff], 19 December 1985, RRL, FG 252, ID# 367708.

44. Gary Slutsker, "Rest in Peace?" *Forbes*, 11 February 1985, 74; Harold Bergan, "The Maverick Moneylender," *The New Republic*, 10 February 1982, 21–23; Thomas E. Bennett Jr., "What If . . . There Were No SBA?" *Journal of Commercial Bank Lending* 67, no. 9 (May 1985):28–32; Andrea Green, "Banking's Big Supporters of Small Business," *Bankers Monthly* 106, no. 10 (October 1989):35–43; Martha E. Mangelsdorf, "Banker's Delight," *Inc.* (June 1991), 24, 28.

45. Howard Kurtz, "SBA Entrenched As Petty Cash Drawer," *Washington Post*, 11 February 1985, A12; William Proxmire, "Don Lambro's 10 Worst Boondoggles," *Congressional Record*, 15 May 1985, vol. 131, pt. 9:12016–17; David Dreier, "We Can No Longer Afford the SBA," *Congressional Record*, 26 February 1985, vol. 131, pt. 3:3507; David Dreier, "In Debate on SBA's Survival Some Say It Deserves to Die," *Congressional Record*, 14 May 1985, vol. 131, pt. 9:11913–14; Barnes, "Free Lunch," 8; Lowell Weicker, "Hearings on S. 408," *Congressional Record*, 7 March 1985, vol. 131, pt. 4:4944–46; HSBC, Subcommittee on SBA, *Small Business Administration Program Review*; "Senate Votes to Preserve SBA," *Washington Post*, 17 July 1985, A4; "Small-Business Agency Cut Assailed," *New York Times*, 25 April 1985, D13 [quote]; Rauch, "Small Business Agency," 1845–48 [quotes on 1845].

46. "Administrator of Embattled SBA to Resign," *Washington Post*, 28 January 1986, A15; Steven P. Galante, "White House Choice at SBA May Rouse Agency's Backers." *Wall Street Journal*, 31 March 1986, 21; Maria E. Recio, "Reagan's Hit Man at the SBA," *Business Week*, 26 May 1986, 90, 92 [quotes]; Heatherly, ed., *Mandate for Leadership*, 1086 [quote]; "SBA Head Fires Five Regional Chiefs Who Oppose Plan to Close Down Agency," *Wall Street Journal*, 2 April 1986, 50; SBA, *Future of SBA*.

47. "SBA Head Opens Fire on Critics," *Philadelphia Inquirer* 16 April 1986, inserted in SSBC, *Implementation*, 47 [quote]; Weicker, ibid., 1 [quote], Robert Kasten Jr. (R-Wis.), ibid., 66 [quote]; Heatherly testimony, ibid., 17 [quote]; "Heated Debate Over the SBA," *Nation's Business* (June 1986), 18 [quote]; Alfred Kingon, memorandum for Donald T. Regan, "SBA Transfer," 2 June 1986, RRL, FG 252, ID# 406573; Alfred H. Kingon, memorandum for Donald T. Regan, "SBA," 25 June 1986, RRL, FG 252, ID# 406751; Ronald Reagan, "Remarks to State Chairpersons of the National White House Conference on Small Business, August 15, 1986." *Public Papers of the Presidents of the United States, Ronald Reagan: 1986* (Washington, D.C.: GPO, 1989), 1111; Paul Thiel, "SBA Gets Mixed Support at Conference," *Washington Post*, 22 August 1986, C1, 10; Ronald Reagan, "Remarks on Receiving the Report of the National White House Conference on Small Business, December 23, 1986," ibid., 1643; "Can James Abdnor Revive SBA?" *ABA Banking Journal* 79, no. 6 (June 1987):52–53.

48. "SBICs Seek to Sever Congressional Ties," *Wall Street Journal*, 10 October 1983, 31; Lee Kravitz. "Why SBICs Want to Break From the SBA," *Venture* (October 1984), 64; Mary-Margaret Wantuck, "Investment Firms Want to Go Private," *Nation's Business* (September 1985), 20; Kevin Farrell and Michele H. Fleischer, "The SBIC 100: Slower Growth Looms . . . ," *Venture* (October 1985), 46–54; Sabin Russell, "1986 Was a Sad Time for SBICs," *Venture* 9 (1987), 103–4, 106; Ellen L. James, "Desperate for Dollars," *Venture* (May 1988), 57–58, 60; James Abdnor, testimony, SSBC, *S. 1929*, 251–53 [quote on 253].

49. "Can James Abdnor," 52–53 [quote on 53]; Richard Behar and Christie Brown, "It's Alive! Alive!" *Forbes*, 17 April 1989, 169–70; "Small Business Administration General Business Loan Approvals."

50. Finegan, "Washington," 33 [quote]; Rauch, "Small Business Agency," 1848 [quote], 1845 [Domenici quote]. See, e.g., Niskanen, "Reflections on Reaganomics" and Stockman, *Triumph of Politics*. For an excellent analysis of the pessimism in conservative ranks, see Frum, *Dead Right*.

51. Roberts, *Supply-Side Revolution*, 254; Heatherly, "Policy, Ideology, and Pragmatism." See also, Rector, "Agenda Deflection."

52. Barnes, "Free Lunch," 8; Stockman, *Triumph of Politics*, 454.

53. Daniel Seligman, "The Iron Triangle Strikes Again," *Fortune*, 29 September 1986, 148.

54. Michael Thoryn, "Carrying the Ball for Small Business," *Nation's Business* (March 1981), 76 [quote].

55. Frum, *Dead Right*, 45 [quote], 187, 13 [Barnes quote]; Barnes, "Free Lunch," 10 [quote]; Stein, *Presidential Economics*, 312–13.

56. George Bush, quoted in Bennett and Bennett, *Living With Leviathan*, 143–44; U.S. Office of Management and Budget, "Table 3.1: Outlays by Superfunction and Function: 1940–2003," in *Historical Tables*, 48; "Small Business Administration General Business Loan Approvals"; "Small Business Administration '504' Certified Development Co. Loan Approvals," ibid.; O'Hara, *SBA Loans*, 44–46.

57. Bill Hogan, "The Swamp at the SBA," *D&B Reports* 39, no. 5 (September–

October 1991):50–51; SBA, *Financing Entrepreneurial Business*; Brewer, "Performance and Access"; Jane Applegate, "Revamped SBA Program Thriving," *Chicago Sun-Times*, 27 September 1995, 66; Sougata Mukherjee, "Congress Warms to Venture Capital Program, " *South Florida Business Journal*, 4 April 1997, 1.

58. SBA, *1994 Annual Report*, 4; "Administration Wants More Funds for Small Business," *America's Community Banker* 8, no. 4 (April 1999):10. The agency economized actual outlays by lowering guarantee percentages and raising borrower fees.

59. For statistics and analysis of the minority business boom, see O'Hare, "Reaching for the Dream"; Palmaffy, "El Millonario."

60. Davis, "Perceived Effects," 90; Kevin D. Thompson, "Is the 8(A) Process Worth All the Trouble?" *Black Enterprise* (August 1992), 64–74; Rochelle Sharpe, "Who Benefits: Asian-Americans Gain Sharply in Big Program of Affirmative Action," *Wall Street Journal*, 9 September 1997, A1, 8.

61. O'Connor, "Set-Asides," 237–44; Rice, "Justifying"; LaNoue, "Social Science"; LaNoue and Sullivan, "'But for' Discrimination"; Zelnick, *Backfire*, 304–6; Lawrence B. Lindsey, "Why Whites Are Never 'Disadvantaged,'" *Wall Street Journal*, 8 October 1997, A22.

62. Ruth Marcus, "Dole Pursued Set-Aside for Ex-Aide," *Washington Post*, 23 March 1995, A9; John R. Emshwiller and Bruce Ingersoll, "Loans for Disadvantaged Go to the Advantaged," *Wall Street Journal*, 5 November 1993, B1, 2; Susan Schmidt, "Aides Say SBA Shared Data on Clinton Foe," *Washington Post*, 29 November 1995, A1; "Whitewater Oozes Out Once More," *Economist*, 1 June 1996, 23–24. See also, U.S. Comptroller General, General Accounting Office, *Small Business Administration: Inadequate Oversight*. Corruption was also rampant at the local level. See Jacoby, *Someone Else's House*, chap. 12–17; "Fat White Wallets," *The Economist*, 27 November 1993, 29–30; Bates and Williams, "Preferential Procurement," 2, 7, 15.

63. Shanahan, "Regulating the Regulators"; Weidenbaum, "Government Regulation"; Reiland, "Small Business"; Jack Faris [NFIB president], *Small Business Under Siege*; Lesher [President, U.S. Chamber of Commerce], *Meltdown on Main Street*; Byron York, "Twisting Erskine Bowles," *American Spectator* (January 1997), 20–24; Richard I. Kirkland Jr., "Today's GOP: The Party's Over for Big Business," *Fortune*, 6 February 1995, 50–62; Samuels, "Tinkers, Dreamers, and Madmen," 38–39; Jeffrey H. Birnbaum and Eric Pooley, "New Party Bosses," *Time*, 8 April 1996, 28–32; Jeffrey H. Birnbaum, "Washington's Power 25," *Fortune*, 8 December 1997, 145–52; David Hosansky, "Hills Feels the Big Clout of Small Business," *Congressional Quarterly*, 10 January 1998:55–60. The NFIB remained distant from the SBA. In 1997, the federation testified at a SBA-related hearing for the first time in almost ten years! Susan Eckerly, testimony before SSBC, *Oversight of SBA's Non-Credit Programs*, 136.

Conclusion

1. Garson, *Group Theories*; Lowi, *End of Liberalism*, 51 [quote]; Lustig, "Pluralism," 910–21 [quote on 916]; McConnell, "Lobbies and Pressure Groups"; Loomis and Cigler, "Introduction: The Changing Nature of Interest-Group Politics"; Cigler and Loomis, "Contemporary Interest Group Politics."

2. Other state, federal, and foreign agencies have likewise failed to devise consistent definitions of smallness. Nappi and Vora, "Small Business Eligibility"; Hertz, *In Search of a Small Business Definition*. For an economic analysis of "small" business definitions, see Lippitt and Oliver, "Productive Efficiency."

3. Proxmire, *Can Small Business Survive?* 52; Carl S. Shoup, foreword to Phillips, *Little Business*, v.

4. Between 1958 and 1996, very small businesses (0–19 employees) saw their share of total receipts decline from 31 percent to 16.8 percent. Table 2.13, "Distribution of Sales and Employment by Employment Size of Firm, 1958–77," U.S. President, *The State of Small Business: A Report of the President Transmitted to the Congress* (Washington, D.C.: GPO, 1982), 92; SBA, Office of Advocacy, "Employer Firms, Establishments, Employment, Annual Payroll and Estimated Receipts by Firm Size, 1988–1996," http://www.sba.gov/ADVO/stats/us88_96.pdf; Star, *Concentration*. See also, Table 2.14, "Share of Employment and Sales of Zero-Employee Firms, 1967, 1972 and 1977," U.S. President, *The State of Small Business: A Report of the President Transmitted to the Congress* (Washington, D.C.: GPO, 1983), 96.

5. Hamilton, "Politics."

6. "Small Business and the Future of SBA," inserted in SSBC, *Oversight of SBA's Non-Credit Programs*, 142–45; Walstad, *Entrepreneurship and Small Business*, "Table 34: Sample Characteristics."

7. Anthony Chase, quoted in Karen DeWitt, "The Small Business Administration," *Black Enterprise* (January 1975), 27.

8. Sniderman and Piazza, *Scar of Race*, 134.

9. See Clint Bolick, "The Republican Abdication," chap. 8 in *Affirmative Action Fraud*.

10. Jennifer Roback makes this point in her essay, "Separation of Race and State."

11. Corder, "Politics of Credit Subsidy," 166–86; Wilson, *Bureaucracy*, 227. See also, Jameson W. Doig and Erwin C. Hargrove, "'Leadership' and Political Analysis," chap. in *Leadership and Innovation*, ed. Doig and Hargrove; and Lewis, *Public Entrepreneurship*.

12. Wilson, *Bureaucracy*, 189.

13. Ibid., 190–91.

14. Rauch, *Demosclerosis*; Rauch, "Eternal Life, "17–21; Samuelson, *Good Life and Its Discontents*, 171–90.

15. See, e.g., Anderson and Hill, *Birth*, 93–94.

16. Will, *Restoration*, 199.

17. Rauch, "Policy Forum," 8 [quote]; Brown, *New Policies, New Politics*.

18. Hughes, *Governmental Habit*, 215. See also, Drucker, *"Really* Reinventing Government."

19. Kelman, *Making Public Policy*; Osborne and Gaebler, *Reinventing Government*.

20. Schultze, *Public Use of Private Interest*.

21. David Vogel characterizes business as the only interest group with "an underlying suspicion and distrust of government." He notes the "remarkable consistency of business attitudes toward government over the last one hundred and twenty-five years." Vogel, "Why Businessmen Distrust," 45–46. See also, Gibson, "Political Attitudes."

22. Ninety-eight percent favored "cutting or slowing the growth of federal spending." Eighty-two percent supported greater deregulation. Kirkland, "Today's GOP," 53. In an earlier survey, 87 percent of the CEOs described themselves as "somewhat" or "strongly" conservative on economic issues. Susan Caminiti, "A Bright Future for Conservatism," *Fortune*, 2 July 1990, 92. See also, Thomas Moore, "The New Libertarians Make Waves," *Fortune*, 5 August 1985, 74–78.

23. Lesher, *Meltdown on Main Street*.

24. Hofstadter, "What Happened," 88.

BIBLIOGRAPHY

Manuscript Collections

Presidential Papers

Dwight D. Eisenhower Presidential Library (Abilene, Kans.)
John F. Kennedy Presidential Library (Boston, Mass.)
Lyndon B. Johnson Presidential Library (Austin, Tex.)
Nixon Presidential Materials. National Archives (College Park, Md.)
Gerald Ford Library (Ann Arbor, Mich.)
Jimmy Carter Library (Atlanta, Ga.)
Ronald Reagan Library (Simi Valley, Calif.)

Personal Papers

Boutin, Bernard. Lyndon B. Johnson Presidential Library
Butler, Paul M. Lyndon B. Johnson Presidential Library
Evins, Joe L. Tennessee Technological University (Cookeville, Tenn.)
Hamlin, John H. Dwight D. Eisenhower Presidential Library
Horne, John E. John F. Kennedy Presidential Library
Patman, Wright. Lyndon B. Johnson Presidential Library
Sprecher, Drexel. John F. Kennedy Presidential Library
Taft, Robert A. Library of Congress (Washington, D.C.)
Yates, Sidney R. Harry S. Truman Presidential Library (Independence, Mo.)

National Archives (Washington, D.C., and College Park, Md.)

Record Group 46: U.S., Congress, Senate; Banking and Currency Committee; Small Business Committee
Record Group 309: Small Business Administration

Small Business Administration (Washington, D.C.)

Personal Interviews and Correspondence

Boutin, Bernard. Phone interviews with author. 21 October 1997; 18 July 1998; 10 April 2000
Burger, Constance. Phone interview with author. 6 May 1998.
Cates, George. Phone interview with author. 5 May 1998.
Dockett, Alfred. Phone interview with author. 24 October 1997.
Foley, Eugene. Phone interviews with author. 14 December 1997 and 30 June 1998.
Forbes, Patricia. Phone interview with author. 13 November 1997.
Gambardella, James A. E-mail correspondence. 5 October 1998
Hornston, George. Phone interview with author. 4 November 1998.
Hurley, Tom. Phone interview with author. 21 April 1998.
Kleppe, Thomas S. Phone interview with author. 21 October 1997.
Jackson, Gary. Phone interview with author. 28 July 1999.
Jehle, Philip. Phone interview with author. 19 February 1998.
Kulik, Bernard. E-mail correspondence. 26 April 1999; 18 June 1999.
Laun, Louis. Phone interview with author. 6 and 8 January 1998, 16 December 1999.
Lodato, Paul. Phone interviews with author. 15 October 1998, 17 December 1999, 13 January 2000
Morris, Thomas. Phone interview with author. 20 October 1997.
Motley, John. Phone interview with author. 11 August 1999.
Parker, Marshall. Phone interview with author. 31 August 1999.
Robinson, George H. Phone interviews with author. 30 September and 29 October 1998.
Samuels, Antoinette (Sharkey). Phone interview with author. 16 October 1997.
Sanders, James C. Phone interviews with author. 26 October 1997 and 3 June 1999.
Shane, Richard. Phone interview with author. 29 October 1997.
Stults, Walter. Phone interviews with author. 5 February 1998 and 16 December 1999.
Swain, Frank. Phone interview with author. 26 August 1999.
Stanton, Dean. Phone interview with author. 16 October 1997.
Wallace, Juanita. Phone interview with author. 16 October 1997.
Weaver, A. Vernon. E-mail interview. 24 February 1998.

Newspapers and Periodicals

ABA Banking Journal
America's Community Banker
American Druggist
Bismarck Tribune
Black Business Digest
Black Enterprise
Bankers Monthly
Barron's
Business Week
Chicago Sun-Times
Congressional Digest
Congressional Quarterly Almanac
Congressional Quarterly Weekly Report
Current Biography

Denver Rocky Mountain News
D&B Reports
Dun's Review
Ebony
Economist
Forbes
Fortune
Harper's Magazine
Hotel and Motel Management, Inc.
Industrial Distribution
Industry Week
Jet
Journal of Commercial Bank Lending
Journal of Purchasing
League Notes (National Business League)
Life
Modern Retailer
Nation
Nation's Business
National Journal
National Review
New Republic
Garden City, N.Y. Newsday
Newsweek
New York Amsterdam News
New York Times
Philadelphia Inquirer
Purchasing
Reader's Digest
Science
St. Louis Globe-Democrat
South Florida Business Journal
Time
U.S. News and World Report
Venture
Wall Street Journal
Washington, D.C. Daily News
Washington, D.C. Evening Star
Washington Post

Books, Articles, and Government Documents

Acs, Zoltan and David B. Audretsch. "Innovation and Firm Size in Manufacturing." *Technovation* 7, no. 3 (July 1988):197–210.
———. "Innovation, Market Structure, and Firm Size." *Review of Economics and Statistics* 69 (November 1987):567–74.
———. *Innovation and Small Firms.* Cambridge: MIT Press, 1990.
Acs, Zoltan J. *Are Small Firms Important? Their Role and Impact.* Boston: Kluwer, 1999.

———. "Flexible Specialization Technologies, Innovation, and Small Business." In *Small Business in a Regulated Economy: Issues and Policy Implications*, ed. Richard J. Judd, William T. Greenwood, and Fred W. Becker, chap. 2. New York: Quorum, 1988.

Adams, Walter. "The Regulatory Commissions and Small Business." *Law and Contemporary Problems* 24, no. 1 (winter 1959):147–68.

Aharoni, Yair. *The No-Risk Society*. Chatham, N.J.: Chatham House, 1981.

Allen, Gary. "Growing Resistance by Small Business." *American Opinion* 20 (May 1977):31–54.

———. "We Could Be Losing the American Dream." *American Opinion* 20 (June 1977):1–7, 71–88.

Allen, Louis L. "Making Capitalism Work in the Ghettos." *Harvard Business Review* 47 (May–June 1969):83–92.

Amaker, Norman C. *Civil Rights and the Reagan Administration*. Washington, D.C.: Urban Institute Press, 1988.

Ambrose, Stephen E. *Nixon: The Education of a Politician, 1913–1962*. New York: Simon and Schuster, 1987.

———. *Nixon: The Triumph of a Politician, 1962–1972*. New York: Simon and Schuster, 1989.

Anderson, James E. and Jared E. Hazleton. *Managing Macroeconomic Policy: the Johnson Presidency*. Austin: University of Texas Press, 1986.

Anderson, Martin. *The Federal Bulldozer*. New York: McGraw-Hill, 1964; rpt. 1967.

Anderson, Terry L. and Peter J. Hill. *The Birth of a Transfer Society*. Stanford, Calif.: Hoover Institution Press, 1980.

Andrews, Victor L. and Peter C. Eisemann. *Who Finances Small Business Circa 1980?* Washington, D.C. Interagency Task Force on Small Business Finance, 1981.

Anglund, Sandra Mary. "How American Core Values Influence Public Policy: Problem Definitions in Federal Aid to Small Business, 1953–1993." Ph.D. diss., University of Connecticut, 1997.

Ban, Carolyn. *How Do Public Managers Manage? Bureaucratic Constraints, Organizational Culture, and the Potential for Reform*. San Francisco: Jossey-Bass, 1995.

Banfield, Edward C. "Rioting Mainly for Fun and Profit." Chap. 9 in *The Unheavenly City Revisited*. Boston: Little, Brown, and Company, 1974.

Bates, Timothy. *Black Capitalism: A Quantitative Analysis*. New York: Praeger, 1973.

———. "Black Entrepreneurship and Government Programs." *Journal of Contemporary Studies* 4 (fall 1981):59–69.

———. "The Changing Nature of Minority Business: A Comparative Analysis of Asian, Nonminority, and Black-Owned Businesses." *Review of Black Political Economy* 18, no. 2 (1989):25–42.

———. "Financing Black Enterprise." *Journal of Finance* 29, no. 3 (June 1974):747–61.

———. "The Minority Enterprise Small Business Investment Company Program: Institutionalizing a Nonviable Minority Business Assistance Infrastructure." *Urban Affairs Review* 32, no. 5 (May 1997):683–703.

———. *Race, Upward Mobility, and Self-Employment: Illusive American Dream*. Baltimore: Johns Hopkins University Press, 1997.

Bates, Timothy and William Bradford. *Financing Black Economic Development*. New York: Academic Press, 1979.

Bates, Timothy and Alfred E. Osborne Jr. "Perverse Effects of SBA Loans to Minority Wholesalers." *Urban Affairs Quarterly* 15 (September 1979):87–97.

Bates, Timothy and Darrell Williams. "Preferential Procurement Programs and Minority-Owned Businesses." *Journal of Urban Affairs* 17, no. 1 (1995):1–17.

Bean, Jonathan J. *Beyond the Broker State: Federal Policies Toward Small Business, 1936–1961* Chapel Hill: University of North Carolina Press, 1996.

———. "'Burn, Baby, Burn': Small Business in the Urban Riots of the 1960s." *The Independent Review: A Journal of Political Economy* 5, no. 2(fall 2000):165–88.

Belz, Herman. *Equality Transformed: A Quarter-Century of Affirmative Action.* New Brunswick, N.J.: Transaction, 1991.

Bennett, Linda L.M. and Stephen Earl Bennett. *Living With Leviathan: Americans Coming to Terms With Big Government.* Lawrence: University Press of Kansas, 1990.

Bergmann, Barbara R. *In Defense of Affirmative Action.* New York: Basic Books, 1996.

Berney, Robert E. and Ed Owens. "A Model for Contemporary Small Business Policy Issues." In *Small Business in a Regulated Economy: Issues and Policy Implications,* ed. Richard J. Judd, William T. Greenwood, and Fred W. Becker, chap. 14. New York: Quorum Books, 1988.

———. "Small Business Policy: Subsidization, Neutrality, or Discrimination." *Journal of Small Business Management* 22, no. 3 (July 1984):49–58.

Berry, William D. and David Lowery. *Understanding United States Government Growth: An Empirical Analysis of the Postwar Era.* New York: Praeger, 1987.

Berson, Lenora E. *The Case Study of a Riot: The Philadelphia Story.* New York: Institute of Human Relations Press, 1966.

Birch, David L. *Job Creation in America: How Our Smallest Companies Put the Most People to Work.* New York: Free Press, 1987.

———. *The Job Generation Process.* Washington, D.C.: Economic Development Administration, 1979.

———. "Who Creates Jobs?" *Public Interest,* no. 65 (1981):3–14.

Black, Dennis Eugene. "Effectiveness of the Women-Owned Business Set-Aside Contracting Goals: A Regression Analysis." *Policy Studies Review* 5, no. 1 (1985): 21-32.

———. "An Evaluation of Federal Contract Set-Aside Goals in Reducing Socioeconomic Discrimination." Ph.D. diss., The American University, 1986.

Blackford, Mansel G. *A History of Small Business in America.* New York: Twayne, 1991.

Blaustein, Arthur I. and Geoffrey Faux. *The Star-Spangled Hustle.* Garden City, N.Y.: Doubleday, 1972.

Bluestone, Barry. "Black Capitalism: The Path to Liberation?" *Review of Radical Political Economics* 1 (May 1969):36–55.

Bolick, Clint. *The Affirmative Action Fraud: Can We Restore the American Civil Rights Vision?* Washington, D.C.: Cato Institute, 1996.

Borcherding, Thomas E. *Budgets and Bureaucrats: The Sources of Government Growth.* Durham, N.C.: Duke University Press, 1977.

Bosworth, Barry, Andrew S. Carron, and Elisabeth Rhyne. *The Economics of Federal Credit Programs.* Washington, D.C.: The Brookings Institution, 1987.

"Boutin, Bernard L(ouis)." *Political Profiles: The Johnson Years,* ed. Nelson Lichtenstein. New York: Facts on File, 1976.

Bradford, Amory. *Oakland's Not for Burning.* New York: David McKay Company, 1968.

Branch, Taylor. *Parting the Waters: America in the King Years, 1954–1963.* New York: Simon and Schuster, 1988.

Brauer, Carl M. *John F. Kennedy and the Second Reconstruction.* New York: Columbia University Press, 1977.

Bray, Thomas J. "Reading America the Riot Act: The Kerner Report and Its Culture of Violence." *Policy Review* (winter 1988):32–36.

Brewer, Elijah, III, et al. "Performance and Access to Government Guarantees: The Case of Small Business Investment Companies." *Economic Perspectives* 20, no. 5 (September–October 1996):16–32.

Brimmer, Andrew F. and Henry S. Terrell. "The Economic Potential of Black Capitalism." *Public Policy* 19, no. 2 (spring 1971):289–308.

Brock, William and David S. Evans. "Small Business Economics." *Small Business Economics* 1 (1989):7–20.

Brown, Charles, James Hamilton, and James Medoff. *Employers Large and Small*. Cambridge: Harvard University Press, 1990.

Brown, Gilbert T., et al. "Availability and Cost of External Equity Capital for Small Business Ventures." In *Financing Small Business: Surveys of Credit and Capital Sources*, pt. II, vol. 2, chap. 7. Washington, D.C. Federal Reserve System, [1958].

Brown, Lawrence D. and Brookings Institution. *New Policies, New Politics: Government's Response to Government's Growth*. Washington, D.C.: The Brookings Institution, 1983.

Browne, Robert S. "The Constellation of Politics and Economics: A Dynamic Duo in the Black Economy." *Review of Black Political Economy* 2 (fall 1971):44–55.

Brownstein, Ronald and Nina Easton. "Small Business Administration: James Sanders." In *Reagan's Ruling Class: Portraits of the Presidents Top 100 Officials*, 87–93. Introduction by Ralph Nader. Washington, D.C.: Presidential Accountability Group, 1983.

Brudney, Jeffrey L. "The SBA and SCORE: Coproducing Management Assistance Services." *Public Productivity Review* 10, no. 2 (winter 1986):57–67.

Brush, Candida G. "Research on Women Business Owners: Past Trends, a New Perspective and Future Directions." *Entrepreneurship Theory and Practice* 16, no. 4 (summer 1992):5–30.

Brush, Candida and Robert D. Hisrich. "Women-Owned Businesses: Why Do They Matter?" In *Are Small Firms Important? Their Role and Impact*, ed. Zoltan J. Acs, chap. 7. Boston: Kluwer, 1999.

Bunzel, John H. *The American Small Businessman*. New York: Alfred A. Knopf, 1962.

———. "The General Ideology of American Small Business." *Political Science Quarterly* 70 (1955):87–102

Burke, Dermott Brandon. "The Role of the Small Business Administration in Assisting Minority Businesses." M.B.A. thesis, New York Institute of Technology, 1976.

Burner, David and Oscar Handlin. *John F. Kennedy and a New Generation*. Boston: Little, Brown, 1988.

Burr, Pat L. and George T. Solomon. "The SBI Program—Four Years Down the Academic Road." *Journal of Small Business Management* 15, no. 2 (April 1977):1–8.

Burrows, John H. *The Necessity of Myth: A History of the National Negro Business League, 1900–1945*. Auburn, Ala.: Hickory Hill Press, 1988.

Buttner, E. Holly and Benson Rosen. "Funding New Business Ventures: Are Decision Makers Biased Against Women Entrepreneurs?" *Journal of Business Venturing* 4 (1989):249–61.

Button, James W. *Black Violence: Political Impact of the 1960s Riots*. Princeton, N.J.: Princeton University Press, 1978.

Califano, Joseph A. Jr. *The Triumph and Tragedy of Lyndon Johnson*. New York: Simon and Schuster, 1991.

Campbell, Ballard. *The Growth of American Government: Governance From the Cleveland Era to the Present*. Bloomington: Indiana University Press, 1995.

Cannon, Lou. *President Reagan: The Role of a Lifetime*. New York: Touchstone, 1991.

Canterbery, E. Ray. *Economics on a New Frontier.* Belmont, Calif.: Wadsworth, 1968.

Carmichael, Stokely and Charles V. Hamilton. *Black Power: The Politics of Liberation in America.* New York: Random House, 1967.

Carson, Deane, ed. In *The Vital Majority: Small Business in the American Economy.* Washington, D.C.: GPO, 1973.

Carter, Jimmy. *Public Papers of the Presidents of the United States, Jimmy Carter.* Washington, D.C.: GPO, 1977–1981.

Chamber of Commerce of the United States. *Small Business: Its Role and Its Problems.* Washington, D.C.: Chamber of Commerce, 1962.

Chamberlain, John. *The American Stakes.* New York: Carrick and Evans, 1940.

Charboneau, F. Jill. "The Woman Entrepreneur." *American Demographics* 3, no. 6 (June 1981):21–23.

Chen, Gavin M. and John A. Cole. "The Myths, Facts, and Theories of Ethnic, Small-Scale Enterprise Financing." *Review of Black Political Economy* 16, no. 4 (1988):111–23.

Chilton, Kenneth W. "How the Feds Screw Small Business." *Reason* 10, no. 5 (1978):33–36.

Chilton, Kenneth W. and Murray L. Weidenbaum. *Small Business Performance in the Regulated Economy.* St. Louis: Center for the Study of American Business, 1980.

Cho, Hyo Won. "The Evolution of the Functions of the Reconstruction Finance Corporation: A Study of the Growth and Death of a Federal Lending Agency." Ph.D. diss., The Ohio State University, 1953.

Cigler, Allan J. and Burdett A. Loomis. "Contemporary Interest Group Politics: More Than 'More of the Same.'" In *Interest-Group Politics,* ed. Allan J. Cigler and Burdett A. Loomis, chap. 18. Washington, D.C.: CQ Press, 1995.

Cohen, Nathan. *The Los Angeles Riots: A Socio-Psychological Study.* New York: Praeger, 1970.

Collins, Robert M. *The Business Response to Keynes, 1929–1964.* New York: Columbia University Press, 1981.

———. "Growth Liberalism in the Sixties." In *The Sixties: From Memory to History,* ed. David Farber, chap. 1. Chapel Hill: University of North Carolina Press, 1994.

Congressional Quarterly. *Congress and the Nation: A Review of Government and Politics.* 9 vol. Washington, D.C., Congressional Quarterly Service, 1965–1998.

———. *President Ford: The Man and His Record.* Washington, D.C., Congressional Quarterly Service, 1974.

Corder, J. Kevin. "The Politics of Credit Subsidy: Small Business Administration 7(a) Loan Guarantees." *American Review of Public Administration* 28, no. 2 (June 1998):166–86.

Coulter, Ann H. *High Crimes and Misdemeanors: The Case Against Bill Clinton.* Washington, D.C.: Regnery, 1988.

Daughters, Charles G. *Relationship of Small Business and Democracy,* confidential report, 27 December 1942. In J.P. Seiberling Papers, Ohio Historical Society (Columbus), box 11, folder 62.

Davis, Joseph William. "Perceived Effects of Federal Procurement Legislation on Small Disadvantaged Businesses." D.B.A. diss., U.S. International University, 1990.

Davis, Steven J., John Haltiwanger, and Scott Schuh. "Small Business and Job Creation: Dissecting the Myth and Reassessing the Facts." NBER Working Paper No. 4492. October, 1993.

de Leon, Peter. *Thinking About Political Corruption,* Peter de Leon. Armonk, N.Y.: M.E. Sharpe, 1993.

Decter, Midge. "Looting and Liberal Racism." *Commentary* (September 1977):48–54.

Dennis, William J. Jr., Bruce D. Phillips, and Edward Starr. "Small Business Job Creation: The Findings and Their Critics." *Business Economics* (July 1994):23–30.

Detlefsen, Robert R. *Civil Rights Under Reagan.* San Francisco: ICS Press, 1991.

Dickerson, O.D. and Michael Kawaja. "The Failure Rates of Business." In *The Financing of Small Business: A Current Assessment,* ed. Irving Pfeffer. New York: Macmillan, 1967.

Dixon, George H. "Minority Bank Growth Is Stimulated by Deposit Program." *Treasury Papers* 2, no. 4 (October 1976):8–10.

Doctors, Samuel I. and Anne Sigismund Huff. *Minority Enterprise and the President's Council.* Cambridge, Mass.: Ballinger, 1973.

Doig, Jameson W. and Erwin C. Hargrove, ed. *Leadership and Innovation: A Biographical Perspective on Entrepreneurs in Government.* Baltimore: Johns Hopkins University Press, 1987.

Donham, Paul. "Whither Small Business?" *Harvard Business Review* (March–April 1957):73–81.

Drucker, Peter F. "*Really* Reinventing Government." *Atlantic Monthly* (February 1995), 49–61.

Dwyer, Christopher. *The Small Business Administration.* New York: Chelsea House, 1991.

Eastland, Terry. *Ending Affirmative Action: The Case for Colorblind Justice.* New York: Basic Books, 1996.

Easton, Nina. *Reagan's Squeeze on Small Business: How the Administration Plan Will Increase Economic Concentration.* Washington, D.C. Presidential Accountability Group, 1981.

Eisenhower, Dwight D. *Public Papers of the Presidents of the United States: Dwight D. Eisenhower.* Washington, D.C.: GPO, 1953–1961.

Erskine, Hazel. "The Polls: Demonstrations and Riots." *Public Opinion Quarterly* 31 (1967):655–77.

Evans, Rowland Jr. and Robert D. Novak. *Nixon in the White House: The Frustration of Power.* New York: Random House, 1971.

Fairlie, Henry. *The Kennedy Promise: the Politics of Expectation.* Garden City, N.Y.: Doubleday, 1973.

Faris, Jack. *Small Business Under Siege: How Government Is Threatening Your Business. What You Can Do to Fight Back and Win.* Nashville, Tenn.: Hammock, 1994.

Faucett, Jack, Jonathan Skolnik, and Harry J. Chmelynski. *Procurement Share vs. Industry Share.* Washington, D.C.: SBA, 1986.

Feagin, Joe R. and Harlan Hahn. *Ghetto Revolts: The Politics of Violence in American Cities.* New York: Macmillan, 1973.

Flamm, Michael William. "'Law and Order': Street Crime, Civil Disorder, and the Crisis of Liberalism." Ph.D. diss., Columbia University, 1998.

Fogelson, Robert M. *Violence As Protest: A Study of Riots and Ghettos.* Garden City, N.Y.: Doubleday, 1971.

Foley, Eugene P. *The Achieving Ghetto.* Washington, D.C.: The National Press, 1968.

———. "The Negro Businessman: In Search of a Tradition." *Daedalus* (winter 1966), 107–44.

Ford, Gerald R. *Public Papers of the Presidents of the United States, Gerald R. Ford.* Washington, D.C.: GPO, 1974–1977.

Frazier, E. Franklin. *Black Bourgeoisie: The Rise of a New Middle Class.* New York: Free Press, 1957.

Frum, David. *Dead Right.* New York: Basic Books, 1994.

Furchtgott-Roth, Diana and Christine Stolba. *Women's Figures: The Economic Progress of Women in America.* Washington, D.C.: American Enterprise Institute, 1996.

Galbraith, John Kenneth. *The Affluent Society*. Boston: Mentor, 1958.

———. "Government vs. Small Business." *Washington Monthly* 10 (September 1978):42–44.

———. *The New Industrial State*. 2d ed. Boston: Houghton-Mifflin, 1971.

———. "Perspective on Small Business: Galbraith." Interviewed by Greg Miller and Ron Kolgraf. *Industrial Distribution* 70 (November 1980):54–56, 59.

Gale, Dennis E. *Understanding Urban Unrest: From Reverend King to Rodney King*. Thousand Oaks, Calif.: Sage, 1996.

Gale, William G. "Economic Effects of Federal Credit Programs." *American Economic Review* 81, no. 1 (March 1991): 133–52.

Gallup, George H. *The Gallup Poll: Public Opinion: 1935–1971*. 3 vol. New York: Random House, 1972.

Garson, G. David. *Group Theories of Politics*. Beverly Hills, Calif.: Sage, 1978.

Geurtsen, M. "Attitudes Towards Small Business in the U.S.A. and Europe: Can We Learn From an American Example?" In *Small and Medium-Sized Enterprises: Keystone for a Free and Prosperous Europe*, ed. Harry Roose, et al., 159–98. The Netherlands: Tilburg University Press, 1986.

Gibson, Donald. *Battling Wall Street: The Kennedy Presidency*. Lanham, Md.: Sheridan Square, 1994.

Glazer, Nathan. *Affirmative Discrimination: Ethnic Inequality and Public Policy*. New York: Basic Books, 1975.

Goldstein, Bonnie. "Abolish the SBA." *Washington Monthly* 11 (April 1979):44–48, 50–51.

Gompers, Paul A. "The Rise and Fall of Venture Capital." *Business and Economic History* 23, no. 2 (winter 1994):1–26.

Graham, Hugh D. "The Incoherence of the Civil Rights Policy in the Nixon Administration." In *Richard M. Nixon: Politician, President, Administrator*, ed. William F. Levantrosser and Leon. Friedman. New York: Greenwood Press, 1991.

———. *The Civil Rights Era: Origins and Development of National Policy, 1960–1972*. New York: Oxford University Press, 1990.

———. "On Riots and Riot Commissions: Civil Disorders in the 1960s." *The Public Historian* 2, no. 4 (summer 1980):7–27.

———. "The Stunted Career of Policy History: A Critique and An Agenda," *The Public Historian* 15, no. 2 (spring 1993):15–37.

Green, George Earl. "The Small Business Administration: A Study in Public Policy and Organization." Ph.D. diss., University of Colorado, 1965.

Greene, John Robert. *The Presidency of Gerald R. Ford*. Lawrence: University Press of Kansas, 1995.

Gumpert, David E. "Entrepreneurship: A New Literature Begins." *Harvard Business Review* 60 (March–April 1982):50–52, 54, 58, 60.

———. "Future of Small Business May Be Brighter Than Portrayed." *Harvard Business Review* 57 (July–August 1979):170–76, 188.

Hafer, J.C and D.M Ambrose. "Fit or Misfit: Restructuring SCORE for Effectiveness in Managerial Assistance." *Journal of Small Business Management* 19, no. 4 (October 1981):15–19.

Hamby, Alonzo L. *Liberalism and Its Challengers: From F.D.R. to Bush*. 2nd ed. New York: Oxford University Press, 1992.

Hamilton, Richard. "The Politics of Independent Business." In *Restraining Myths: Critical Studies of U.S. Social Structure and Politics*, chap. 2. New York: Sage, 1975.

Harden, Victoria. "What Do Federal Historians Do?" *Perspectives* 37, no. 5 (May 1999):19–24.

Hargrove, Erwin C. *Jimmy Carter As President: Leadership and the Politics of the Public Good*. Baton Rouge: Louisiana State University Press, 1988.

Hargrove, Erwin C. and Samuel A. Morley. *The President and the Council of Economic Advisers: Interviews With CEA Chairmen*. Boulder, Colo.: Westview, 1984.

Harrington, Michael. *The Other America: Poverty in the United States*. New York: Macmillan, 1962.

Harris, Seymour Edwin. *The Economics of the Political Parties, With Special Attention to Presidents Eisenhower and Kennedy*. New York: Macmillan, 1962.

Harrison, Bennett. *Lean and Mean: The Changing Landscape of Corporate Power in the Age of Flexibility*. New York: Basic Books, 1994.

Hawley, Ellis W. *The New Deal and the Problem of Monopoly: A Study in Economic Ambivalence*. Princeton, N.J.: Princeton University Press, 1966.

Hayden, Tom. *Rebellion in Newark: Official Violence and Ghetto Response*. New York: Vintage, 1967.

Hayes, Samuel L. and Donald H. Woods. "Are SBICs Doing Their Job?" *Harvard Business Review* 41 (March 1963–April 1963):6–8+.

Haynes, George Walser. "A Qualitative Assessment of the Small Business Administration Loan Guarantee Program's Influence on the Effects of Financial Market Concentration." Ph.D. diss., Cornell University, 1993.

Heath, Jim F. *John F. Kennedy and the Business Community*. Chicago: University of Chicago Press, 1969.

Heatherly, Charles. *Mandate for Leadership: Policy Management in a Conservative Administration*. Washington, D.C.: The Heritage Foundation, 1981.

———. "Policy, Ideology, and Pragmatism in the Reagan Revolution." *The Heritage Lectures* 104 (1987).

Hebert, F. Ted and Fred W. Becker. "Preferential Treatment for Small Businesses in Federal Contract Awards." *Policy Studies Journal* 13, no. 4 (1985):756–65.

Heckman, James J. "The Impact of Government on the Economic Status of Black Americans." In *The Question of Discrimination: Racial Inequality in the U.S. Labor Market*, ed. Steven Schulman and William Darity Jr., chap. 3. Middletown, Conn.: Wesleyan University Press, 1989.

Heimlich, Judith Ann. "The Business of Poverty: the Small Business Administration, the Economic Opportunity Act, and the Problem of Political Innovation." Ph.D. diss., Columbia University, 1967.

Heller Institute for Small Business. *Small Business Assesses the Reagan Administration*. Chicago: W.E. Heller International Corporation, 1981.

Henderson, William L. "Government Incentives and Black Economic Development." *Review of Social Economy* (September 1969):202–21.

Henderson, William L. and Larry C. Ledebur. "Programs for the Economic Development of the American Negro Community: the Moderate Approach." *American Journal of Economics and Sociology* 30 (January 1971):27–45.

Hertz, Leah. *In Search of a Small Business Definition: An Exploration of the Small-Business Definitions of the U.S., the U.K., Israel and the People's Republic of China*. Washington, D.C.: University Press of America, 1982.

Higgs, Robert. *Crisis and Leviathan: Critical Episodes in the Growth of American Government*. New York: Oxford University Press, 1987.

———. ed., *Arms, Politics, and the Economy: Historical and Contemporary Perspectives*. New York: Holmes & Meier, 1990.

Hodges, Luther H. Interviewed by Dan B. Jacobs. Oral History Collection. John F. Kennedy Presidential Library. 21 March 1964.

Hoff, Joan. *Nixon Reconsidered*. New York: Basic Books, 1994.

Hofstadter, Richard. "What Happened to the Antitrust Movement?" In *The Paranoid Style in American Politics and Other Essays*. New York: Alfred A. Knopf, 1966.

Hooper, Carolyn Nell. "Public Policy Toward Small Business: Implications for Efficient Utilization of Resources." Ph.D. diss., University of Texas at Austin, 1968.

Horne, John E. Interviewed by John F. Stewart. Oral History Collection, John F. Kennedy Presidential Library. 3 May 1967.

———. Interview. Oral History Collection, Lyndon B. Johnson Presidential Library, 22 July 1969.

Horowitz, David A. *Beyond Left and Right: Insurgency and the Establishment*. Urbana: University of Illinois Press, 1997.

Howard University. Graduate School. Division of the Social Sciences. *The Post-War Outlook for Negroes in Small Business, the Engineering Professions, and the Technical Vocations: Papers and Proceedings of the Ninth Annual Conference, April 9–11, 1946*. ed. H. Naylor Fitzhugh. Washington, D.C.: Howard University Press, 1946.

Howat, John Donald. "An Analysis of the Investments of Small Business Investment Companies." Ph.D. diss., University Of Illinois At Urbana-Champaign, 1978.

Hughes, Jonathan R. T. *The Governmental Habit Redux: Economic Controls From Colonial Times to the Present*. Princeton, N.J.: Princeton University Press, 1991.

Humphrey, Hubert H. *Bridging the Gap in Our Inner Cities*. Washington, D.C.: SBA, 1968.

———. *War on Poverty*. New York: McGraw-Hill, 1964.

Hunter, William C. "Insurance, Incentives, and Efficiency in Small Business Lending." *Southern Economic Journal* 50, no. 4 (April 1984):1171–84.

Ingham, John N. and Lynne B. Feldman, ed. *African-American Business Leaders: A Biographical Dictionary*. Westport, Conn.: Greenwood Press, 1994.

Jackson, John E. *The American Entrepreneurial and Small Business Culture*. n.p.: Institute for Enterprise Advancement, 1986.

Jackson-Park, Betty Jean. "Minority Set-Aside Legislation: an Exploratory Case Study of Policy Legislation, Implementation and Performance." Ph.D. diss., University Of Pittsburgh, 1984.

Jacoby, Tamar. *Someone Else's House: America's Unfinished Struggle for Integration*. New York: Free Press, 1998.

Johnson, Donald Bruce, comp. *National Party Platforms*. Rev. ed., vol. 2 (1960–1976). Urbana: University of Illinois Press, 1978.

Johnson, Lyndon B. *Public Papers of the Presidents of the United States, Lyndon B. Johnson* (Washington, D.C.: GPO, 1964–1969).

Jones, Charles O. *The Trusteeship Presidency: Jimmy Carter and the United States Congress*. Baton Rouge: Louisiana State University Press, 1988.

Jones, James E. Jr. "The Origins of Affirmative Action." *U.C. Davis Law Review* 21 (1988):383–419.

Judkins, C.J. "Do Associations Represent the Small Business Firm?" *Domestic Commerce* (July 1946):15–20.

Karuna-karan, Arthur and Earl R.I. Smith. "A Constructive Look at MESBICS." *California Management Review* 14, no. 3 (spring 1972).

Katz, Michael B. *The Undeserving Poor: From the War on Poverty to the War on Welfare*. New York: Pantheon, 1989.

Kaufman, Burton Ira. *The Presidency of James Earl Carter Jr.* Lawrence: University Press of Kansas, 1993.

Kaufman, Herbert. *Are Government Organizations Immortal?* Washington, D.C.: The Brookings Institution, 1976.

Keith, E. Gordon. "The Impact of Taxation on Small Business." *Law and Contemporary Problems* 24, no. 1 (winter 1959):98–117.

Keller, Bill. "How Congress Spoils Small Business." *Washington Monthly* 14, no. 1 (1982):44–49.

Kelman, Steven. *Making Public Policy: A Hopeful View of American Government.* New York: Basic Books, 1987.

Kemp, Kathleen A. "Accidents, Scandals, and Political Support for Regulatory Agencies." *Journal of Politics* 46, no. 2 (May 1984):401–27.

Kennedy, John F. *Compilation of Statements, Pledges and Actions by John F. Kennedy Concerning Small Business, the Small Business Administration and Related Organizations, Made As a Member of the U.S. Senate (1954–60), As Candidate for President (1960), and As President (1961–).* John F. Kennedy Library (Boston), SBA Records, Box 1, No Folder.

———. *John Fitzgerald Kennedy: A Compilation of Statements and Speeches Made During His Service in the United States Senate and House of Representatives.* Washington, D.C.: GPO, 1964.

———. *Public Papers of the Presidents of the United States, John F. Kennedy.* Washington, D.C.: GPO, 1962–1964.

King, Arthur Thomas. "The Relationships Between Socioeconomic Programs and the Department of the Air Force Budget: Section 8(a) of the Small Business Act—the Economic Development and Public Finance Aspects of a Public Policy Program." Ph.D. diss., University Of Colorado At Boulder, 1977.

King, Martin Luther Jr. *Why We Can't Wait.* New York: Harper and Row, 1964.

Kinnard, William N. Jr. and Zenon S. Malinowski. *The Impact of Dislocation From Urban Renewal Areas on Small Business.* Storrs: University of Connecticut, 1960.

Kirkland, Richard I. Jr. "Today's GOP: The Party's Over for Big Business." *Fortune*, 6 February 1995, 50–62.

Klein, Richard H. "SBA's Business Loan Program." *Atlanta Economic Review* 28 (September–October 1978):28–37.

Kotlowski, Dean. "Black Power—Nixon Style: The Nixon Administration and Minority Business Enterprise." *Business History Review* 72 (autumn 1998):409–45.

———. "Nixon's Southern Strategy Revisited." *Journal of Policy History* 10, no. 2 (1998):207–38.

Kull, Andrew. *The Color-Blind Constitution.* Cambridge: Harvard University Press, 1992.

Kuratko, Donald F. "Small Business Challenging Contemporary Public Policy: A Coalition for Action." In *Small Business in a Regulated Economy: Issues and Policy Implications*, ed. Richard J. Judd, William T. Greenwood, and Fred W. Becker. New York: Quorum Books, 1988.

Kwolek-Folland, Angel. *Incorporating Women: A History of Women and Business in the United States.* New York: Twayne, 1998.

Laham, Nicholas. *The Reagan Presidency and the Politics of Race: In Pursuit of Colorblind Justice and Limited Government.* Westport, Conn.: Praeger, 1998.

LaNoue, George R. "Social Science and Minority 'Set-Asides.'" *Public Interest*, no. 110 (winter 1993):49–62.

LaNoue, George R. and John Sullivan. "'But for' Discrimination: How Many Minority-

Owned Businesses Would There Be?" *Columbia Human Rights Law Review* 24, no. 1 (winter 1992–1993):93–133.

———. "Presumptions for Preferences: The Small Business Administration's Decisions on Groups Entitled to Affirmative Action." *Journal of Policy History* 6, no. 4 (1994):439–67.

Larkey, Patrick D., Chandler Stolp, and Mark Winer. "Theorizing About the Growth of Government: A Research Assessment." *Journal of Public Policy* 1 (1981):157–220.

LeLoup, Lance T. and Steven A. Shull. *Congress and the President: The Policy Connection.* Belmont, Calif.: Wadsworth Publishing, 1993

Leonard, Herman B. and Elisabeth H. Rhyne. "Federal Credit and the 'Shadow Budget.'" *Public Interest* 65 (fall 1981):40–58.

Lesher, Richard. *Meltdown on Main Street: Why Small Business Is Leading the Revolution Against Big Government.* Foreword by Newt Gingrich. New York: Dutton, 1996.

Levitt, Arthur Jr. "In Praise of Small Business." *New York Times Magazine*, 6 December 1981, 136–152.

Levitt, Theodore. "Why Business Always Loses." *Harvard Business Review* (March–April 1968):81–89.

Lewis, Eugene. *Public Entrepreneurship: Toward a Theory of Bureaucratic Political Power: The Organizational Lives of Hyman Rickover, J. Edgar Hoover, and Robert Moses.* Bloomington: Indiana University Press, 1980.

Lippitt, Jeffrey W. and Bruce L. Oliver. "The Productive Efficiency and Employment Implications of the SBA's Definition of 'Small.'" *American Journal of Small Business* 8, no. 3 (winter 1984):46–48.

Lipset, Seymour Martin. "The Sources of the 'Radical Right.'" In *The New American Right*, ed. Daniel Bell, chap. 7. New York: Criterion, 1955.

Lipset, Seymour Martin and William Schneider. *The Confidence Gap: Business, Labor, and Government in the Public Mind.* New York: Free Press, 1983.

Lo, Clarence Y.H. *Small Property versus Big Government: Social Origins of the Property Tax Revolt.* Berkeley: University of California Press, 1990.

Loomis, Burdett A. and Allan J. Cigler. "Introduction: The Changing Nature of Interest-Group Politics." In *Interest-Group Politics,* 4th ed., ed. Allan J. Cigler and Burdett A. Loomis, chap. 1. Washington, D.C.: CQ Press, 1995.

Lorette, Richard J., H. Charles Walton, and David F. Dianich. "A Proposal for Restructuring the SBA: Reducing Its Contracting Role and Providing High Technology Assistance to Small Business." *National Contract Management Journal* 19, no. 1 (summer 1985):21–32.

Lowi, Theodore J. *The End of Liberalism: The Second Republic of the United States.* 2d ed. New York: Norton, 1979.

Lukas, J. Anthony. *Nightmare: The Underside of the Nixon Years.* New York: Penguin, 1976.

Lumer, Wilfred. *Small Business at the CrossRoads: A Study of the Small Business Retreat of 1953–1955.* Washington, D.C.: Public Affairs Institute, 1956.

Lustgarten, Steven A. "Firm Size and Productivity Growth in Manufacturing Industries." In *Small Business in a Regulated Economy: Issues and Policy Implications*, ed. Richard J. Judd, William T. Greenwood, and Fred W. Becker, chap. 9. New York: Quorum Books, 1988.

Lustig, Jeffrey R. "Pluralism." In *Encyclopedia of American Political History: Studies of the Principal Movements and Ideas*, 910–21. ed. Jack P. Greene. Vol. 2. New York: Scribner, 1984.

Mansfield, Harvey C. "The Congress and Economic Policy." In *The Congress and America's Future.* 2d ed., ed. David B. Truman, chap. 6. Englewood Cliffs, N.J.: Prentice-Hall, 1973.

Marchum, R.E. and E.O. Boshell. "Financing the Small and Medium-Size Business: Where's the Money Coming From?" *Management Review* 52 (January 1963):4–12.

Marcus, Sumner. "The Small Business Act of 1953: A Case Study of the Development of Public Policy Affecting Business." D.B.A. diss., University of Washington, 1958.

Matusow, Allen J. *Nixon's Economy: Booms, Busts, Dollars, and Votes.* Lawrence: University Press of Kansas, 1998.

———. *The Unraveling of America: A History of Liberalism in the 1960s.* New York: Harper & Row, 1984.

Mayers, Kenneth Elsas. "In the Red in Black and White: A Policy Analysis of 'Black Capitalism' in the Light of White Small Business." Ph.D. diss., University of California, Berkeley, 1978.

McClosky, Herbert and John Zaller. *The American Ethos: Public Attitudes Toward Capitalism and Democracy.* Cambridge: Harvard University Press, 1984.

McConkey, Dale D. "Will Ecology Kill Small Business?" *Business Horizons* 15 (April 1972):61–69.

McConnell, Grant. "Lobbies and Pressure Groups." In *Encyclopedia of American Political History: Studies of the Principal Movements and Ideas*, 764–76. ed. Jack P. Greene. Vol. 2. New York: Scribner, 1984.

McDougal, Jim and Curtis Wilkie. *Arkansas Mischief: The Making of a National Scandal.* New York: John Macrae, 1998.

McKay, James C., et al. *Report of Independent Counsel In Re Edwin Meese III.* Submitted to United States Court of Appeals for the District of Columbia Circuit, 5 July 1988.

McQuaid, Kim. *Big Business and Presidential Power: From FDR to Reagan.* New York: Morrow, 1982.

———. *Uneasy Partners: Big Business in American Politics, 1945–1990.* Baltimore: Johns Hopkins University Press, 1994.

Meltzer, Allan H. and Scott F. Richard. "Why Government Grows (and Grows) in a Democracy." *The Public Interest* (summer 1978):111–18.

Methvin, Eugene H. *The Riot Makers: The Technology of Social Demolition.* New Rochelle, N.Y.: Arlington House, 1970.

Miller, Abraham H. and Mark R. Halligan. "The New Urban Blacks." *Ethnicity* 3 (1976):338–67.

Miller, Warren E. and Santa Traugott. *American National Election Studies Data Sourcebook, 1952–1986.* Cambridge: Harvard University Press, 1989.

Miroff, Bruce. *Pragmatic Illusions: The Presidential Politics of John F. Kennedy.* New York: McKay, 1976.

Mitchell, William C. and Randy T. Simmons. *Beyond Politics: Markets, Welfare, and the Failure of Bureaucracy.* Boulder, Colo.: Westview Press, 1994.

Moon, Grant C. "An Evaluation of Selected Management Aspects of the SBA SCORE Program." Ph.D. diss., George Washington University, 1966.

Moreno, Paul D. *From Direct Action to Affirmative Action: Fair Employment Policy and Policy in America, 1933–1972.* Baton Rouge: Louisiana State University Press, 1997.

Moynihan, Daniel P. "The Negro Family: The Case for National Action." In *The Essential Neoconservative Reader*, ed. Mark Gerson, 23–37. Foreword by James Q. Wilson. Reading, Mass.: Addison-Wesley, 1996.

Murray, Charles. *Losing Ground: American Social Policy, 1950–1980*. New York: Basic Books, 1984.

Nappi, Andrew T. and Jay Vora. "Small Business Eligibility: A Definitional Issue." *Journal of Small Business Management* 18, no. 4 (October 1980):22–27.

National Election Studies, "Table 9A1.2: Presidential Vote: 2 Major Parties 1952–1996." http://www.umich.edu/~nes/nesguide/2ndtable/t9a_1_2.htm

National Federation of Independent Business. *Attitudes of Independent Business Proprietors Toward Antitrust Laws, 1943 to 1963*. San Mateo, Calif.: NFIB, n.d.

———. *Mandate*, nos. 385, 392, 455.

———. *Legislative Victories Accomplished Through Your Mandate Votes*. NFIB, [1969].

———. *NFIB: A History, 1943–1985*. n.p.: NFIB, n.d.

———. *Small Business Evaluates SBA*. n.p.:NFIB, 1984.

Nellis, Elwyn A. *A SCORE That Counts: The Story of the Service Corps of Retired Executives*. Washington, D.C.: Service Corps of Retired Executives Association, 1989.

Niskanen, William A. "Reflections on Reaganomics." In *Assessing the Reagan Years*, ed. David Boaz, chap. 1. Washington, D.C.: Cato Institute, c1988.

Nixon, Richard M. "Civil Rights." *The Challenges We Face: Edited and Compiled From the Speeches and Papers of Richard M. Nixon*. New York: McGraw-Hill, 1960.

———. "Let a New Day Dawn for the U.S.A.!" *Reader's Digest* (October 1968), 89–95.

———. *Public Papers of the Presidents of the United States, Richard Nixon*. Washington, D.C.: GPO, 1969–1975.

———. *RN: The Memoirs of Richard Nixon*. New York: Grosset & Dunlap, 1978.

Noone, Charles M. and Stanley M. Rubel. *SBICs: Pioneers in Organized Venture Capital*. Chicago: Capital Publishing, 1970.

Nossiter, Bernard D. *The Mythmakers: an Essay on Power and Wealth*. Boston: Houghton Mifflin, 1964.

O'Connor, Sandra Day. "Set-Asides Violate the Equal Protection Clause [*Croson* Opinion]." In *Racial Preference and Racial Justice: The New Affirmative Action Controversy*, ed. Russell Nieli, chap. 19. Washington, D.C.: Ethics and Public Policy Center, 1991.

O'Hara, Patrick D. *SBA Loans: A Step-by-Step Guide*. 2d ed. New York: John Wiley, 1994.

O'Hare, William. "Reaching for the Dream." *American Demographics* 14, no. 1 (January 1992):32–36.

Ofari, Earl. *The Myth of Black Capitalism*. New York: Monthly Review Press, 1970.

Olson, Mancur Jr. *The Logic of Collective Action: Public Goods and the Theory of Groups*. Cambridge: Harvard University Press, 1965.

Omps, James R. "Dynamic Small Business Sector As a Solution for Stagflation." *Journal of Small Business Management* 15 (January 1977):52–56.

Opinion Research Corporation. *Big Business on the Spot: A Report of the Public Opinion Index for Industry*. Princeton, N.J.: Opinion Research Corporation, August 1948.

———. *Free Market vs. Socialistic Thinking—1955*. Princeton, N.J.: Opinion Research Corporation, 1955.

———. *Socialistic Thinking in America—1953*. Princeton, N.J.: Opinion Research Corporation, 1953.

———. *What People Are Saying About Big Business Today*. Princeton, N.J.: Opinion Research Corporation, 1955.

Osborne, David and Ted Gaebler. *Reinventing Government: How the Entrepreneurial Spirit is Transforming the Public Sector*. Reading, Mass.: Addison-Wesley, 1992.

Ott, J. Steven. *The Organizational Culture Perspective*. Chicago: Dorsey Press, 1989.

Palmaffy, Tyce. "El Millonario Next Door: The Untold Story of Hispanic Entrepreneurship." *Policy Review* (July–August 1998):30–35.

Parmet, Herbert S. *Richard Nixon and His America*. Boston: Little, Brown, 1990.

Parris, Addison. *The Small Business Administration*. New York: Praeger, 1968.

Patterson, James T. *America's Struggle Against Poverty, 1900–1985*. Rev. ed. Cambridge: Harvard University Press, 1986.

Peterson, Robert A., Gerald Albaum, and George Kozmetsky. "The Public's Definition of Small Business." *Journal of Small Business Management* 24, no. 3 (July 1986):63–68.

Phillips, Bruce D. "The Increasing Role of Small Firms in the High-Technology Sector: Evidence From the 1980s." *Business Economics* 26, no. 1 (January 1991):40–47.

Phillips, Joseph D. *Little Business in the American Economy*. Urbana: University of Illinois Press, 1958.

Piore, Michael J. and Charles F. Sabel. *The Second Industrial Divide: Possibilities for Prosperity*. New York: Basic Books, 1984.

Pressman, Jeffrey L. and Aaron Wildavsky. *Implementation: How Great Expectations in Washington Are Dashed in Oakland; Or, Why It's Amazing That Federal Programs Work at All*. Rev. ed. Berkeley: University of California Press, 1979.

Price Waterhouse. *Evaluation of the 7(a) Guaranteed Business Loan Program: Final Report*. Washington, D.C.: Price Waterhouse, 1992.

Proxmire, William. *Can Small Business Survive?* Chicago: Regnery, 1964.

Rauch, Jonathan. *Demosclerosis: The Silent Killer of American Government*. New York: Times Books, 1994, 1995.

———. "Eternal Life: Why Government Programs Won't Die." *Reason* (August–September 1996):17–21.

———. "Policy Forum: Can Government Change?" *Cato Policy Report* (March–April 1997): 8.

Reagan, Ronald. *Public Papers of the Presidents of the United States, Ronald Reagan*. Washington, D.C.: GPO, 1982–1989.

———. "Why This is an Entrepreneurial Age." *Journal of Business Venturing* 1, no. 1 (winter 1985):1–4.

Rector, Robert. "Agenda Deflection: James Sanders and the Small Business Administration." In *Steering the Elephant: How Washington Works*, ed. Robert Rector and Michael Sanera, chap. 22. New York: Universe Books, 1987.

Redford, Emmette S. and Marlan Blissett. *Organizing the Executive Branch: The Johnson Presidency*. Chicago: University of Chicago Press, 1981.

Reeves, Richard. *President Kennedy: Profile of Power*. New York: Simon & Schuster, 1993.

Reiland, Ralph. "Small Business, Big Government & American Prosperity." *The American Enterprise* (July–August 1997), 46–48.

Reiner, Martha Louise. "The Transformation of Venture Capital: A History of Venture Capital Organizations in the United States." Ph.D. diss., University Of California, Berkeley, 1989.

Rhyne, Elisabeth Holmes. *Small Business, Banks, and SBA Loan Guarantees: Subsidizing the Weak or Bridging a Credit Gap?* New York: Quorum Books, 1988.

Rice, Mitchell F. "Justifying State and Local Government Set-Aside Programs Through Disparity Studies in the Post-Croson Era." *Public Administration Review* 52, no. 5 (September–October 1992):482–90.

Rich-McCoy, Lois. *Millionairess: Self-Made Women of America*. New York: Harper and Row, 1978.

Riding, Allan L. and Catherine S. Swift. "Women Business Owners and Terms of Credit:

Some Empirical Findings of the Canadian Experience." *Journal of Business Venturing* 5 (1990):327–40.

Roback, Jennifer. "The Separation of Race and State." *Harvard Journal of Law and Public Policy* 14 (1991):58–64.

Roberts, Paul Craig. *The Supply-Side Revolution: An Insider's Account of Policymaking in Washington.* Cambridge: Harvard University Press, 1984.

Roberts, Paul Craig and Lawrence M. Stratton. *The New Color Line: How Quotas and Privilege Destroy Democracy.* Washington, D.C.: Regnery, 1995.

Robinson, Roland I. "The Financing of Small Business in the United States." In *Small Business in American Life*, ed. Stuart W. Bruchey, 280–304. New York: Columbia University Press, 1980.

Rowen, Hobart. *The Free Enterprisers: Kennedy, Johnson, and the Business Establishment.* New York: Putnam, 1964.

Russell, Cheryl. "The Minority Entrepreneur." *American Demographics* 3, no. 6 (June 1981):18–20.

Ryan, William. *Blaming the Victim.* New York: Pantheon, 1971.

Samuels, David. "Tinkers, Dreamers, and Madmen: The New History According to Newt." *Lingua Franca* (January–February 1995), 32–39.

Samuels, Howard. "How to Even the Odds." *Saturday Review*, 23 August 1969, 22–25.

———. "Project Own: Compensatory Capitalism." *Vital Speeches* 35 (February 1969): 250–253.

Samuelson, Robert J. *The Good Life and Its Discontents: The American Dream in the Age of Entitlement, 1945–1995.* New York: Times Books, 1995.

Schein, Edgar H. *Organizational Culture and Leadership.* San Francisco: Jossey-Bass, 1985.

Schott, Richard L. and Dagmar S. Hamilton. *People, Positions, and Power: the Political Appointments of Lyndon Johnson.* Chicago: University of Chicago Press, 1983.

Schrieber, Albert N. "Small Business and Government Procurement." *Law and Contemporary Problems* 29 (spring 1964):390–417.

Schrieber, Albert N., et al., *Defense Procurement and Small Business: A Survey of Practices and Opinions of Small Business Firms Selling to Defense Programs.* Seattle: University of Washington Press, 1961.

Schultze, Charles L. *The Public Use of Private Interest.* Washington, D.C.: The Brookings Institution, 1977.

Schumacher, E.F. *Small Is Beautiful: Economics As If People Mattered.* New York: Harper and Row, 1973.

Schwartz, E.B. "Entrepreneurship: A New Female Frontier." *Journal of Contemporary Business* 5 (winter 1976):47–76

Schweiger, Irving. "Adequacy of Financing for Small Business Since World War II." *Journal of Finance* 13, no. 3 (September 1958):323–47.

Scott, Daryl Michael. "The Politics of Pathology: The Ideological Origins of the Moynihan Controversy." *Journal of Policy History* 8, no. 1 (1996):81–105.

Sears, David O. and John B. McConahay. *The Politics of Violence: The New Urban Blacks and the Watts Riot.* Boston: Houghton Mifflin, 1973.

Sears, David O. and T.M. Tomlinson. "Riot Ideology in Los Angeles: A Study of Negro Attitudes." *Social Science Quarterly* 49 (1968):485–503.

Sergiovanni, Thomas J. "Cultural and Competing Perspectives in Administrative Theory and Practice." Article 47 in *Classics of Organization Theory*, ed. Jay M. Shafritz and J. Steven Ott, 3d. ed. Pacific Grove, Calif.: Brooks/Cole Publishing, 1992.

Shanahan, John. "Regulating the Regulators: Regulatory Process Reform in the 104th Congress." *Regulation* (winter 1997): 27–32.

Shapiro, Fred C. and James W. Sullivan. *Race Riots: New York 1964.* New York: Thomas Y. Crowell, 1964.

Shapiro, Walter. "How Not to Help Small Business." *Washington Monthly* 6 (October 1974): 29–34.

Siegel, Fred. "The Riot Ideology." In *The Future Once Happened Here: New York, D.C., L.A., and the Fate of America's Big Cities*, chap. 1. New York: Free Press, 1997.

Silberman, Charles E. "The City and the Negro." *Fortune* 65, no. 3 (March 1962), 88–91, 139–54.

———. *Crisis in Black and White.* New York: Random House, 1964.

Silk, Leonard Solomon. *Nixonomics: How the Dismal Science of Free Enterprise Became the Black Art of Controls.* New York: Praeger, 1972.

Singer, Benjamin D. and Richard W. Osborn. *Black Rioters.* Lexington, Mass: Heath Lexington, 1970.

Skolnick, Jerome H. *The Politics of Protest.* New York: Simon and Schuster, 1969.

Skrentny, John David. *The Ironies of Affirmative Action: Politics, Culture, and Justice in America.* Chicago: University of Chicago, 1996.

Sloan, John. "Economic Policymaking in the Johnson and Ford Administrations." *Presidential Studies Quarterly* 20 (winter 1990):111–25.

———. *Eisenhower and the Management of Prosperity.* Lawrence: University of Kansas Press, 1991.

"Small Business Lobby." In *The Washington Lobby*, ed. Nancy Lammers, 113–19. 4th. ed. Washington, D.C.: Congressional Quarterly, 1982.

"Small Business Lobby Plays Trick or Treat." In *The Washington Lobby*, ed. Nancy Lammers, 79. 4th ed. Washington, D.C.: Congressional Quarterly, 1982.

Smircich, Linda. "Organizations As Shared Meanings." Article 46 in *Classics of Organization Theory*, ed. Jay M. Shafritz and J. Steven Ott, 3d. ed. Pacific Grove, Calif.: Brooks/Cole Publishing, 1992.

Sniderman, Paul and Thomas Piazza. *The Scar of Race.* Cambridge: Belknap Press, 1993.

Solomon, Steven. *Small Business USA: The Role of Small Companies in Sparking America's Economic Transformation.* New York: Crown, 1986.

Sowell, Thomas. "Economics and Black People." *Review of Black Political Economy* (winter 1971–spring 1972): 3–21.

———. *Vision of the Anointed: Self-Congratulation as a Basis for Social Policy.* New York: Basic Books, 1995.

Sprecher, Drexel A. Interviewed by Larry J. Hackman. 17 August 1972. John F. Kennedy Presidential Library.

Stans, Maurice H. "Nixon's Economic Policy Toward Minorities." In *Richard M. Nixon: Politician, President, Administrator*, ed. William F. Levantrosser and Leon Friedman, chap. 14. New York: Greenwood Press, 1991.

———. "Richard Nixon and His Bridges to Human Dignity." *Presidential Studies Quarterly* 26, no. 1 (winter 1996):179–83.

———. *The Terrors of Justice.* New York: Everest House, 1978.

Star, Alvin D. *Concentration in Retail Trade and Services.* Washington, D.C.: SBA, 1982.

Staros, James. "Affirmative Action: Progression of Policy through the President's Committee on Government Contracts." Unpublished paper in author's possession.

Stebenne, David L. *Arthur J. Goldberg: New Deal Liberal.* New York: Oxford University Press, 1996.

Stein, Herbert. *Presidential Economics: The Making of Economic Policy From Roosevelt to Clinton.* 3d ed. Washington, D.C.: American Enterprise Institute, 1994.

Sterling, Warren S. "SBA and the 'Iron Law of Small Business': More Means Less." *Antitrust Law & Economics Review* 11, no. 3 (1979):73–85.

Sternberg, William and Matthew C. Harrison Jr. *Feeding Frenzy.* New York: Henry Holt, 1989.

Stewart, James B. *Blood Sport: The President and His Adversaries.* New York: Simon and Schuster, 1996.

Stillman, Richard, II, *The American Bureaucracy: The Core of Modern Government* 2d ed. Chicago: Nelson-Hall, 1996.

———. *Preface to Public Administration: A Search for Themes and Directions.* New York: St. Martin's Press, 1991.

Stockman, David. "The Social Pork Barrel." *Public Interest* 39 (spring 1975):1–30.

———. *The Triumph of Politics: The Inside Story of the Reagan Revolution.* New York: Avon, 1987.

Storey, David J. "Symposium on Harrison's 'Lean and Mean': A Job Generation Perspective." *Small Business Economics* 7 (1995):337–40.

Sundquist, James L. *Politics and Policy: The Eisenhower, Kennedy, and Johnson Years.* Washington, D.C.: The Brookings Institution, 1968.

Suss, Fredric T. "Set-Asides and Certificates of Competency: Positive Programs for Small Business in Government Procurement." *Law and Contemporary Problems* 29 (spring 1964):418–37.

Sutton, Francis X. *The American Business Creed.* Cambridge: Harvard University Press, 1956.

Sykes, Jay G. *Proxmire.* Washington, D.C.: Robert B. Luce, 1972.

Szasz, Andrew. "The Process and Significance of Political Scandals: A Comparison of Watergate and the 'Sewergate' Episode at the Environmental Protection Agency." *Social Problems* 33, no. 3 (February 1986):202–17.

Theophilos, Anthony. "Government Procurement and the Small Business Act of 1958: The Judicial Challenge to 8(a) Contracts." *American University Law Review* 22, no. 4 (summer 1973):735–65.

Thernstrom, Stephan and Abigail Thernstrom. *America in Black and White: One Nation, Indivisible.* New York: Simon and Schuster, 1997.

Thompson, Marilyn W. *Feeding the Beast: How Wedtech Became the Most Corrupt Little Company in America.* New York: Charles Scribner's Sons, 1990.

Thomson, Charles A.H. and Frances M. Shattuck. *The 1956 Presidential Campaign.* Washington, D.C.: The Brookings Institution, 1960.

Traub, James. *Too Good to Be True: The Outlandish Story of Wedtech.* New York: Doubleday, 1990.

Trow, Martin. "Small Businessmen, Political Tolerance, and Support for McCarthy." *American Journal of Sociology* (November 1958):270–281.

University Publications of America. "The 'Do Not File' File." *University Publications of America, Research Collections 1991.* Bethesda, Md.: University Publications of America, 1990, 36.

U.S. Civil Service Commission. *A Report on Alleged Political Influence in Personnel Actions at the Small Business Administration.* Washington, D.C.: GPO, 1974.

U.S. Commission on Civil Rights. *Federal Civil Rights Enforcement Effort.* Washington, D.C.: GPO, 1970.

U.S. Commission on Organization of the Executive Branch of Government. Task Force on Lending Agencies. *Report on Lending Agencies,* February 1955.

U.S. Comptroller General. General Accounting Office. *8(a) Is Vulnerable to Program and Contractor Abuse.* Washington, D.C.: GAO, 1995.

———. *Efforts to Improve Management of the Small Business Administration Have Been Unsatisfactory—More Aggressive Action Needed.* Washington, D.C.: GAO, 1979.

———. *Most Borrowers of Economic Opportunity Loans Have Not Succeeded in Business: Report to the Congress.* Washington, D.C.: GAO, 1980.

———. *Questionable Effectiveness of the 8(a) Procurement Program.* Washington, D.C.: GAO, 1975.

———. *The SBA 8(a) Procurement Program: A Promise Unfulfilled: Report to the Congress.* Washington, D.C.: GAO, 1981.

———. *SBA's Pilot Programs to Improve Guaranty Loan Procedures Need Further Development.* Washington, D.C.: GAO, 1981.

———. *SBA's 7(a) Loan Guarantee Program: An Assessment of Its Role in the Financial Market.* Washington, D.C.: GAO, 1983.

———. *Small Business Administration: Inadequate Oversight of Capital Management Services, Inc.—an SSBIC.* Washington, D.C.: GAO, 1994.

———. *What Is a Small Business? The Small Business Administration Needs to Reexamine Its Answer.* Washington, D.C.: GAO, 1978.

U.S. Congress. *Congressional Record*

U.S. Congress. House. Committee on Banking and Currency. *Creation of Small Business Administration.* Hearings, 83d Cong., 1ˢᵗ sess., 14–18 May 1953.

———. Subcommittee on Small Business. *Minority Enterprise Small Business Investment Company Act of 1972.* Hearing, 92d Cong., 2d sess., 22 June 1972.

———. *Oversight Investigation of the Small Business Administration.* Hearing, 93d Cong., 1st sess., 4 December 1973

———. *The SBA Investigation Report.* Hearing, 93th Cong., 2d sess., 9 April 1974.

U.S. Congress. House. Committee on Education and Labor. *Economic Opportunity Act of 1964.* Hearing, 88th Cong., 2d sess., 8 April 1964.

U.S. Congress. House. Committee on Lobbying Activities, *Conference of American Small Business Organizations,* 81st Cong., 2d sess., 1950, H. Rpt. 3232.

U.S. Congress. House. Committee on Post Office and Civil Service. Subcommittee on Manpower and Civil Service. *Documents Related to Political Influence in Personnel Actions at the Small Business Administration.* Committee Print, 94th Cong., 1st sess., July 1975.

U.S. Congress. House. Small Business Committee. *Final Report* (various titles), 1953–1989.

———. *Organization and Operation of the Small Business Administration—1966.* H. Rpt. 2339, 89th Cong., 2d sess., 29 December 1966.

———. *Organization and Operation of the Small Business Administration (1969).* Hearings, 91st Cong., 1st sess., 22–25 July 1969.

———. *Organization and Operation of the Small Business Administration (1970).* Hearings, 91st Cong., 2d sess., 20–22 July 1970.

———. *Organization and Operation of the Small Business Administration (1971).* Hearings, 92d Cong., 1st sess., 21–22 September 1971.

———. *Organization and Operation of the Small Business Administration (1971).* H. Rpt. 1006, 92d Cong., 2d sess., 19 April 1972.

———. *Organization and Operation of the Small Business Administration (Reorganization, Curtailed Loan Program, New Small Loan Programs).* Hearings, 89th Cong., 1st sess., 7–8 April 1965.

———. *Organization and Operation of the Small Business Administration (SBA's Role— Present and Future)*. Hearings, 89th Cong., 2d sess., 18–20 July 1966.

———. *Programs, Policies, and Operations of the Small Business Administration (1973)*. Hearings, 93d Cong., 1st sess., 19 September 1973.

———. *Programs, Policies, and Operations of the Small Business Administration (1973)*. H. Rpt. 873, 93d Cong., 2d sess., 4 March 1974.

———. *Small and Minority Business in the Decade of the '80s*. Hearing (Los Angeles), pt. 1, 97th Cong., 1st sess., 7 July 1981.

———. *Small Business Organizations: Four Case Studies of Organizations Purporting to Represent Small Business*, H. Rpt. 1675, 81st Cong., 2d sess., 21 February 1950.

———. *Status and Future of Small Business*. Hearings, 90th Cong., 1st sess., 1 March 1967.

———. Subcommittee on Antitrust, Consumers, and Employment. *Future of Small Business in America*. H. Rpt. 1810, 95th Cong., 2d sess., 9 November 1978.

———. Subcommittee on Minority Enterprise. *Government Minority Small Business Programs*. Hearings, 2 vol., 92d Cong., 1st sess., 27 July 1971 and 25–26 April 1972.

———. Subcommittee on Minority Small Business Enterprise. *Minority Small Business Enterprise*. H. Rpt. 1615, 92d Cong., 2d sess., 18 October 1972.

———. Subcommittee on Minority Enterprise and General Oversight. *8(a) Program Moratorium and Small Business Administration Personnel Practices*. Hearing, 95th Cong., 1st sess., 19 October 1977.

———. Subcommittee on Minority Small Business Enterprise and Franchising. *Government Minority Enterprise Programs—Fiscal Year 1974*. Hearing, pt. 1, 93d Cong., 1st sess., 3 October 1973.

———. Subcommittee No. 2. *Definition of "Small Business" Within Meaning of Small Business Act of 1953, As Amended*. Hearings, 85th Cong., 2d sess., 27 May and 3–25 June 1958.

———. Subcommittee No. 5. *Small Business Problems in Urban Areas*. Hearings, 89th Cong., 1st sess., 7–12 June 1965.

———. Subcommittee No. 5. *Small Business Problems in Urban Areas*. H. Rpt. 2343, 89th Cong., 2d sess., 29 December 1966.

———. Subcommittee on SBA and SBIC Authority, Minority Enterprise and General Small Business Problems. *Administration's Small and Minority Enterprise Development Programs*. Hearing, 97th Cong., 2d sess., 16 June 1982.

———. Subcommittee on SBA and SBIC Authority, Minority Enterprise and General Small Business Problems. *Small Business Administration Program Review*. Hearing (Fresno, Calif.), pt. 1, 99th Cong., 1st sess., 22 March 1985.

———. Subcommittee on SBA Oversight and Minority Enterprise. *Minority Enterprise and Allied Problems of Small Business*. Hearing, 94th Cong., 1st sess., 9 July 1975.

U.S. Congress. Senate. Committee on Banking and Currency. *Financing Small Business*. Hearing, 85th Cong., 2d sess., 30 April 1958.

———. *Government Lending Agencies*. Hearing, 83d Cong., 1st sess., 21 May 1953.

———. *Nomination of Howard J. Samuels*. Hearing, 90th Cong., 2d sess., 16 July 1968.

———. *Nomination of John E. Horne*. Hearing, 87th Cong., 1st. sess., 31 January 1961.

———. *Nomination of John E. Horne and Eugene P. Foley*. Hearing, 88th Cong., 1st sess., 30 July 1963.

———. *Nomination of Philip McCallum*. Hearing, 86th Cong., 2d sess., 15 January 1960.

———. *Nomination of Robert C. Moot*. Hearing, 90th Cong., 1st sess., 13 July 1967.

————. *Nominations of Lawrence M. Cox, and Hilary J. Sandoval Jr.* Hearing, 91st Cong., 1st sess., 26 February 1969.

————. Subcommittee on Small Business. *Conflict of Interest Problems in SBICs.* Hearing on S. 298, 88th Cong., 1st sess., 5 September 1963.

————. Subcommittee on Small Business. *Credit Needs of Small Business.* Hearing, 85th Cong., 1st sess., 11 June 1957.

————. Subcommittee on Small Business. *Federal Minority Enterprise Program.* Hearing, 91st Cong., 1st sess., 11 December 1969.

U.S. Congress. Senate. Committee on Banking, Housing, and Urban Affairs. *Nomination of Thomas S. Kleppe.* Hearing, 92d Cong., 1st sess., 9 February 1971.

U.S. Congress. Senate. Committee on Government Affairs. Subcommittee on Federal Spending Practices and Open Government. *Report Based on Hearings and Inquiries Conducted on the Small Business Administration Involving Abuses in the 8(a) Program and Irregularities Concerning Minority Businesses.* Committee Print, 95th Cong., 2d sess., February 1978.

————. Subcommittee on Oversight of Government Management. *Wedtech: A Review of Federal Procurement Decisions.* S. Prt. 108, 100th Cong., 2d sess., May 1988.

U.S. Congress. Senate. Committee on Labor and Public Welfare. *Examination of the War on Poverty.* Hearings, 90th Cong., 1st sess., 10 July 1967.

U.S. Congress. Senate. Small Business Committee. *Annual Reports* (various titles), 1953–1989.

————. *Crime Against Small Business.* S. Doc. 91–14, 91st Cong., 1st sess., 3 April 1969.

————. *Economic Development Opportunity.* Hearings, 90th Cong., 2d sess., 24 May 1968 and 17 June 1968.

————. *Federal Minority Business Development Program.* Hearing, 98th Cong., 1st sess., 24 March 1983.

————. *Impact of Current Tax Proposals on Small Business.* S. Rpt. 397, 88th Cong., 1st sess., 15 August 1963.

————. *Implementation of Title XVIII of Public Law 99–272, The Reconciliation Act.* Hearing, 99th Cong., 2d sess., 28 April 1986.

————. *Legislative and Oversight Activities During the 97th Congress.* S. Rpt. 9, 98th Cong., 1st sess., 23 February 1983.

————. *Nomination of Arthur Vernon Weaver Jr., of Arkansas, to Be Small Business Administrator.* Hearing, 95th Cong., 1st sess., 31 March 1977.

————. *Nomination of James C. Sanders to Be an Administrator of the Small Business Administration.* Hearing, 97th Cong., 2d sess., 9 March 1982.

————. *Nomination of Michael Cardenas to Be Administrator of the Small Business Administration.* Hearing, 97th Cong., 1st sess., 23 March 1981.

————. *Operations of Small Business Investment Companies.* S. Rpt. 161, 88th Cong., 1st sess. 25 April 1963.

————. *Oversight of SBA's Non-Credit Programs.* Hearing, 105th Cong., 1st. sess., 24 April 1997.

————. *Review of Small Business Administration Activities, 1959–1960.* S. Rpt. 30. Committee Print, 87th Cong., 1st sess., 2 February 1961.

————. *Review of Small Business Administration's Programs and Policies—1969.* Hearings, 91st Cong., 1st sess., 10 and 20 June 1969; and 15 October 1969.

————. *S. 1929, a Bill to Create the Corporation for Small Business Investment.* Hearing, 100th Cong., 2d sess., 31 March 1988.

———. *S. 408, a Bill to Authorize and Provide Program Levels for the Small Business Administration for Fiscal Years 1986, 1987, and 1988.* Hearing, 99th Cong., 1st sess., 28 February 1985.

———. *SBA's Financial Assistance Programs.* Hearing, 90th Cong., 1st sess., 25 August 1967.

———. *Small Business Administration: Title II of Small Business Act of 1953.* Committee Print 83d Cong., 1st sess., 10 August 1953.

———. *Small Business Administration—1961.* Hearing, 87th Cong., 1st sess., 21 June 1961.

———. *Small Business Administration—1961.* S. Rpt. 1117, 87th Cong., 2d sess., 15 January 1962.

———. *Small Business Administration—1963.* Hearing, 88th Cong., 1st sess., 2 December 1963.

———. *Small Business Administration 8(a) Contract Procurement Program.* S. Prt., 95th Cong., 1st sess., 16 February 1977.

———. *Small Business Administration's Direct Loan Programs.* Hearing, 97th Cong., 1st. sess., 27 October 1981.

———. *Small Business Aspects of Selected Recommendations of the Commission on Government Procurement.* S. Rpt. 760, 93d Cong., 2d. sess., 28 March 1974.

———. *The Small Business Competitiveness Demonstration Program Act of 1988.* Hearing, 100th Cong., 2d sess., 14 April 1988.

———. *Small Business Investment Act of 1958,* S. Rpt. 1652, 85th Cong., 2d sess., 4 June 1958.

———. *Women and the Small Business Administration.* Hearing, 94th Cong., 2d sess., 24 February 1976.

———. Subcommittee on Government Procurement. *Government Small Business Procurement Practices and Programs.* Hearing, 88th Cong., 2d sess., 29 July 1964.

———. Subcommittee on Taxes. *Impact of Current Tax Proposals on Small Business.* Hearing, 88th Cong., 1st sess., 29 April 1963.

U.S. Department of Commerce. *Problems and Opportunities Confronting Negroes in the Field of Business: Report on the National Conference on Small Business* [Washington, D.C., 30 November–2 December 1961], ed. H. Naylor Fitzhugh. Washington, D.C.: GPO, 1962.

———. *Women and Business Ownership: An Annotated Bibliography.* Washington, D.C.: GPO, 1986.

U.S. Department of Justice. Federal Bureau of Investigation. "Hilary Sandoval Jr.," file 161–6042. 1969.

U.S. Office of Management and Budget. *Historical Tables: Budget of the United States Government (Fiscal Year 1999).* H. Doc. 105–177.

U.S. President. *The State of Small Business: A Report of the President Transmitted to the Congress.* Washington, D.C.: GPO, 1982–1996.

U.S. President. Committee on Government Contracts. *Five Years of Progress, 1953–1958.* Washington, D.C.: GPO, 1958.

U.S. President. Interagency Task Force on Women Business Owners. *The Bottom Line: UnEqual Enterprise in America.* Washington, D.C.: GPO, 1978.

U.S. Riot Commission. *Report of the National Advisory Commission on Civil Disorders.* Special Introduction by Tom Wicker. New York: Bantam Books, 1968.

U.S. Small Business Administration. *An Equal Opportunity Guide for Small Employers* [1995–].

———. *Annual Report* (various titles), 1953–1999.

———. *The Facts About Women As Users of SBA Services: Fiscal Years 1974, 1975, 1976*. Washington, D.C.: SBA, 1976.

———. *Financing Entrepreneurial Business: An Agenda for Action*. Washington, D.C.: SBA, 1992.

———. *The Future of SBA*. Washington, D.C.: SBA, 1986.

———. *Report of the Size Policy Board on Size Standards Guidelines* (unpublished report, 1985).

———. Office of Advocacy. *Small Business in the American Economy*. Washington, D.C.: GPO, 1988.

———. Office of Advocacy. *The Study of Small Business: Conducted and Prepared Pursuant to PL 94–305*. 3 vols. Washington, D.C.: SBA, 1977.

U.S. White House Committee on Small Business. *Small Business in the American Economy*. Washington, D.C.: GPO, 1962.

U.S. White House Conference on Small Business and Small Business Administration. *The White House Conference on Small Business: The Event, the Results, the Continuing Process*. Washington, D.C.: SBA, 1980.

Vatter, Harold G. "The Position of Small Business in the Structure of American Manufacturing, 1870–1970." *Small Business in American Life*, ed. Stuart W. Bruchey, 142–68. New York: Columbia University Press, 1980.

Vatter, Harold G. and John F. Walker. *The Inevitability of Government Growth*. New York: Columbia University Press, 1990.

Vaughn, Donald Earl. "Development of the Small Business Investment Company Program." Ph.D. diss., University of Texas at Austin, 1961.

"Vesco, Robert L(ee)." *Political Profiles: The Nixon/Ford Years*, ed. Eleanora W. Schoenebaum. New York: Facts on File, 1979.

Vinyard, C. Dale. "Congressional Committees on Small Business." Ph.D. diss., University of Wisconsin, 1964.

Vogel, David. *Fluctuating Fortunes: The Political Power of Business in America*. New York: Basic Books, 1988.

———. "Why Businessmen Distrust Their State: The Political Consciousness of American Corporate Executives." *British Journal of Political Science* 8, no. 1 (January 1978).

Walker, John F. and Harold G. Vatter. *The Rise of Big Government in the United States*. Armonk, N.Y.: M.E. Sharpe, 1997.

Walker, Juliet E.K. *The History of Black Business in America: Capitalism, Race, and Entrepreneurship*. New York: Macmillan, 1998.

Wallsten, Scott. "Can Government-Industry R&D Programs Increase Private R&D? The Case of the Small Business Innovation Research Program." Formerly at http://www.Stanford.Edu/~Wallsten/Govindrd.Pdf (November 1997):1–31. Copy in author's possession.

———. "Rethinking the Small Business Innovation Research Program." In *Investing in Innovation: Creating a Research and Innovation Policy That Works*, ed. Lewis M. Branscomb and James H. Keller, chap. 8. Cambridge: MIT Press, 1998.

Walstad, William B. *Entrepreneurship and Small Business in the United States: A Gallup Survey Report on the Views of High School Students, the General Public, and Small Business Owners and Managers*. Princeton, N.J.: Gallup Organization, 1994.

Washington, Booker T. *The Negro in Business*. Chicago: Afro-Am Press, 1969.

———. *Up from Slavery*. Garden City, N.Y.: Doubleday, 1901.

Weatherford, M. Stephen. "The Interplay of Ideology and Advice in Economic Policymaking: the Case of Political Business Cycles." *Journal of Politics* 49, no. 4 (1987):925–52.

Weaver, A. Vernon. Interviewed by David E. Gumpert and Susan E. Maxwell. "Evaluating the SBA: Its Programs, Problems, and Future." *Harvard Business Review* 57, no. 2 (March–April 1979):182–98.

Weidenbaum, Murray. "Government Regulation and Medium-Sized Business." *Society* (1998):60–63.

Weir, Margaret. *Politics and Jobs: The Boundaries of Employment Policy in the United States.* Princeton, N.J.: Princeton University Press, 1992.

Wharton, William Boyd. "The Small Business Investment Company Program Promulgated by the Small Business Investment Act of 1958: Development, Operation, and Evaluation." S.J.D. thesis, The George Washington University, 1979.

Whitaker, John C. "Nixon's Domestic Policy: Both Liberal and Bold in Retrospect." *Presidential Studies Quarterly* 26, no. 1 (winter 1996):131–53.

White, Theodore H. *America in Search of Itself: The Making of the President, 1956–1980.* New York: Harper & Row, 1982.

Will, George F. *Restoration: Congress, Term Limits, and the Recovery of Deliberative Democracy.* New York: Free Press, 1992.

Willing, Pearl Rushfield. "A History of the Management Assistance and Educational Programs of the Small Business Administration From 1953 to 1978." Ph.D. diss., New York University, 1982.

Wilson, James Q. *Bureaucracy: What Government Agencies Do and Why They Do It.* New York: Basic Books, 1989.

———. *Political Organizations.* New York: Basic Books, 1973.

Workman, Andrew A. "Manufacturing Power: The Organizational Revival of the National Association of Manufacturers, 1941–1945." *Business History Review* 72, no. 2 (summer 1998):279–317.

Yancy, Robert J. *Federal Government Policy and Black Business Enterprise.* Cambridge, Mass.: Ballinger, 1974.

Zeigler, Harmon. *The Politics of Small Business.* Washington, D.C.: Public Affairs Press, 1961.

Zelnick, Bob. *Backfire: A Reporter's Look at Affirmative Action.* Washington, D.C.: Regnery, 1996.

Zimmer, Basil G. *Rebuilding Cities: the Effects of Displacement and Relocation on Small Business.* Chicago: Quadrangle Books, 1964.

Zimmerman, Joseph. *Curbing Unethical Behavior in Government.* Westport, Conn.: Greenwood Press, 1994.

Zweig, Michael. "The Dialectics of Black Capitalism." *Review of Black Political Economy* 2 (spring 1972):25–37.

INDEX

Higgs, Robert, 68, 133–34
Hill, William, 9
Hodges, Luther H., 23, 32–33, 45
Hofstadter, Richard, 136
Hoover Commission, 8, 14
Horne, John E.: black enterprise, 46; de-
centralization efforts, 23, 38; on discrimination against small business, 28;
on Federal Home Loan Bank Board,
35–36; in Kennedy defense, 31–32,
33; press conferences, 154 n 50; as SBA
administrator, 22–23; *Small Business in
the American Economy,* 33–34; as White
House Committee on Small Business
chair, 26–27
Horowitz, David, 109
Hughes, Jonathan, 136
Hullin, Tod R., 75–76
Humphrey, George M., 9
Humphrey, Hubert H.: Civil Rights Act
support, 41; and Foley, 35–36, 37–38;
minority loans, 43; presidential bid, 64;
on SBA, 23; War on Poverty, 47
Hurricane Agnes, 85

inflation, 76, 95
inner-city crime, 164 n 62
inner-city violence, 59–60
insurance, subsidized, 85
Interagency Task Force on Small Business
Finance, 111
Interagency Task Force on Women Business
Owners, 99
interest-group representation, 3, 128–31
interest rate subsidies, 54–55
iron triangle, 124

Jackson, Jesse, 62, 115
Jacoby, Neil, 18
Javits, Jacob K., 40, 47
Jeffries, LeRoy W., 45
Jenkins, James, 116
Johnson, Einar, 76
Johnson, Lyndon B.: on civil unrest, 60; and
Foley, 50; inattention to SBA, 131;
Loan Policy Board abolition, 23; poli-
tics of overpromise, 51; on racial
equality, 41; SBA administrator ap-

pointments, 55, 64; Small Business
Investment Companies legislation, 18;
small business politics, 34; succession
to presidency, 36, 37; War on Poverty,
47; and Watts riots, 50

Kefauver, Estes, 15
Kelley, Richard, 56
Kennedy, John F.: affirmative action, 39–
40; assassination, 36, 37; big business
politics, 31–34; economic policies, 32,
33, 34–35; election, 20; New Frontier
declaration, 21; set-asides, 26, 27; on
Small Business Investment Companies
industry, 24; small business politics,
21–23, 131
Kennedy, Robert, 33
Kerner, Otto, 62
Kerner Commission, 62
kickbacks, 87–88
King, Martin Luther, Jr., 2, 35, 40–41
Kleppe, Thomas S.: accusations against, 88;
denied requests, 96; and minority enter-
prise, 90–91; replacement by Kobelinski,
96; restructuring efforts, 82–85; as SBA
administrator, 82; scandal handling, 88,
89; strong administration of, 134; and
Thurmond placements, 171 n 14
Kobelinski, Mitchell, 96–97
Koch, Ed, 89
Kreps, Juanita, 97
Kriger, Charles, 63, 73, 76
Kristol, Irving, 106

Labor Department, 159 n 3
labor reform, 106, 107, 178 n 45
labor-surplus regions, 22–23
labor unions: black capitalism denunciation,
63; and Kennedy, 32
Laham, Nicholas, 114, 118
laissez-faire ideology, 109, 110, 119
Lamm, Richard, 106
Lance, Bert, 97
LaNoue, George R., 103
Laun, Louis, 87, 89
Lender Certification Program, 111
Levitt, Arthur, Jr., 107
loan guarantee programs, 22, 59, 65, 77, 121